BEHIND
GLASS
DOORS

Robert Crawford

Associate Professor Robert Crawford teaches advertising and history in the School of Communication at the University of Technology Sydney. His publications include *But Wait, There's More ... A History of Australia's Advertising Industry, 1900–2000* (2008), *Consumer Australia: Historical Perspectives* (2010), and *Bye the Beloved Country: South Africans in the UK, 1994–2009* (2011).

Jackie Dickenson

Before completing a PhD in History at the University of Melbourne, Jackie Dickenson worked in advertising in Britain and Australia. She is the author of three monographs: *Renegades and Rats: Betrayal and the Remaking of Radical Organisations in Britain and Australia* (2006); *Trust Me: Australians and Their Politicians* (2013) and *Australian Women in Advertising in the Twentieth Century* (2015).

Robert Crawford and Jackie Dickenson

BEHIND GLASS DOORS

The World of Australian
Advertising Agencies
1959-1989

UWAP

First published in 2016 by
UWA Publishing
Crawley, Western Australia 6009
www.uwap.uwa.edu.au

THE UNIVERSITY OF
WESTERN
AUSTRALIA

UWAP is an imprint of UWA Publishing
a division of The University of Western Australia

National Library of Australia Cataloguing-in-Publication entry

Creator: Crawford, Robert, author.

Title: Behind glass doors : the world of Australian advertising agencies, 1959–1989 / Robert Crawford, Jackie Dickenson.

ISBN: 9781742586670 (paperback)

Notes: Includes bibliographical references and index.

Subjects: Advertising agencies—Australia—History.
Advertising personnel—Australia—Interviews.
Advertising—Professions—Australia—History.

Other Creators/Contributors:
Dickenson, Jackie, author.

Dewey Number: 659.1125

Typeset by J & M Typesetting
Cover design by Upside Creative
Printed by McPherson's Printing Group

uwapublishing

CONTENTS

ACKNOWLEDGEMENTS

Behind Glass Doors has had a long gestation and there are many people to thank.

The University of Melbourne provided two small grants in 2007 and 2008 that were used to seed the project. Thanks to the latter of these grants, we were able to fund a workshop attended by twenty current and former advertising practitioners in May 2009, at which we tested the feasibility of an oral history of the Australian industry. We thank everyone who came that day for their generous participation, but we are especially grateful to Mike Reed and Rosem'ry Bertel, whose enthusiasm for the project contributed greatly to its progress.

Two scholars deserve special thanks for their efforts at this stage of the project. First, we are ever grateful to Professor Susan Smulyan of Brown University who wowed the industry workshop with her knowledge of American advertising and helped them to grasp the value of an oral history of their industry. Second, our thanks go to Professor Liz McFall of the Open University, whose work provided the intellectual framework for the project and who, in 2010, though prevented by volcano ash from travelling to Melbourne as the guest speaker at a symposium on advertising histories, kindly made the trip later in the year and inspired our post-graduate students with her incisive analysis.

The Australian Research Council funded our project through its Discovery scheme and we are grateful to all of the team members who worked so hard to secure that funding: the Chief Investigators Professor John Sinclair of the University of Melbourne and Professor Linda Brennan of RMIT University, and the Partner Investigators Professor Sean Nixon of Essex University and the aforementioned Professor Smulyan. Professors Nixon and Smulyan both spent time in Australia collaborating with the team here, contributing to workshops in Melbourne and Sydney, and, in Professor Smulyan's case, advising UTS post-graduates. Professor Smulyan was also an exceptionally generous host to the Australian team in her home city, and helped complete interviews and conduct research in the US.

Our team also included three outstanding Australian research scholars: Phillip Mills in Sydney who provided valuable contextual research in the early stages of the project, and, in Melbourne, Dr Rosemary Francis and Dr Wendy Dick. Dr Francis brought her considerable oral history skills and experience to the task of interviewing the Melbourne practitioners and Dr Dick transcribed those interviews, as well as organising archival material and generally helping to keep the project on track.

We are especially grateful to Rod Blakeney who allowed us to archive records and advertising material from his agency, Barry Banks Blakeney, which closed in 2014 after forty years, and to Toni Lawler, Luella Copeland-Smith, and Adelle Webster who gave us valuable documents relating to their advertising careers. Some of this material has been used to produce this book. We are also grateful to Jeremy Light for providing access to past copies of *AdNews*, to Ash Farr at McCann for providing access to the agency's scrapbook from the early 1960s, and to

Acknowledgements

John Gutteridge at J. Walter Thompson for putting us in contact with the agency's alumni network.

Robert would like to thank the School of Communication in the Faculty of Arts and Social Sciences at UTS for providing him with the time and resources to complete the project. He would also like to express an enormous thanks to his wife, Rebecca, who has provided unwavering support for the project from the beginning all the way to the end.

And finally, our sincerest thanks go to the 120 former advertising professionals in Sydney, Melbourne, Adelaide, Brisbane, Perth, and New York who answered our questions with generosity and unwavering enthusiasm. Without their support, this history would never have been written.

PREFACE

John Sinclair

The advertising agency business has played a pivotal role in the emergence of a consumer society in contemporary Australia, and its integration with the global order. *Behind Glass Doors* lets us see the history of how this process developed over a decisive period in the latter twentieth century, culminating in what is rightly identified here as the industry's 'golden age'.

Robert Crawford and Jackie Dickenson are leading scholars in the history and historiography of the advertising industry in Australia. Their approach is rigorously academic, but it also demonstrates a sound knowledge of the structure and workings of the industry, including the actual practices of advertising. Accordingly, this book will appeal to people involved in the advertising business, at the same time as it is welcomed by scholars as a uniquely informed contribution to the nation's economic and cultural history.

Indeed, it is the extensive interviews with actual advertising agency personnel of the era which forms the prime information source throughout the book. The list of interviewees reminds us of how many distinguished Australians began their creative careers in advertising – Peter Carey and Ken Done, for instance – but it also includes some of the foremost entrepreneurs and managers who built and maintained the leading agencies of the period. The authors are able to draw on their respondents' recollections in a way which is rich in colour and evocative of their times and milieu, but woven into a valid historical narrative which moves over the crucial decades, never bogged down in mere anecdote.

They begin with the influx of the US and UK advertising agencies from 1959, and the consequent impact of this internationalisation on the professional orientation of advertising personnel. The advertising industry in Australia thus came to be positioned between the influences of both these countries, notably in its experience of the 'creative revolution,' and subsequently also as a stepping-stone to South East Asia. Pursuing their central theme of the impact of globalisation upon professionalisation, Crawford and Dickenson cover recruitment and training; relations with clients; support staff; and agency principals. They trace the shifting tensions between creativity and financial management inherent in advertising, and provide comparative insights across agencies with regard to how they adapted their practices in response to global trends. The coverage takes us through the golden age up to 1989, after which new challenges have arisen to confront the industry, both nationally and globally, in the digital era.

Behind Glass Doors is the major output from Australian Research Council Discovery grant DP120100777 Globalising the magic system: a history of advertising industry practices in Australia 1959-1989, funded 2012-2014, with myself and Robert Crawford as Chief Investigators. Jackie Dickenson was the Senior Research Associate on the project, while Partner

Investigators were Susan Smulyan of Brown University (USA); Sean Nixon of the University of Essex (UK) and Linda Brennan of RMIT University.

John Sinclair
Honorary Professorial Fellow
School of Historical and
Philosophical Studies
The University of Melbourne

INTERVIEWEES*

ALDRICH, Keith. Creative. Worked London and Melbourne from 1970s.
Agencies: Masius, J. Walter Thompson (JWT), Mattingly.

ALWILL, Ian. Account Management. Worked Sydney, Philippines, and
Japan from 1960s. Agencies: Clemenger, JWT, SSCB:Lintas, Leo
Burnett, Mojo, McCann-Erickson.

ANDERSON, Michael. Account Management. Worked Sydney,
Melbourne and Asia-Pacific from 1950s. Agencies: Canny Paramor
& Canny, Briggs, Canny, James & Paramor (BCJ&P), USP Benson,
Fortune, Monaghan Dayman Adams (MDA).

ANDREW, Carl. Creative. Worked Melbourne in 1960s. Agency:
Thompson Ansell Blunden (TAB).

BALL, Michael. Agency Management. Worked Melbourne, New York,
Toronto, London, and Asia-Pacific from 1950s. Agencies: JWT,
Ogilvy & Mather (O&M), Ball Partnership.

BASSETT, Lloyd. Creative. Worked Perth from 1950s. Agencies: A.J.
Williams, Warnock Sandford Williams, Marketforce.

BEGG, Austin. Agency Management. Worked Melbourne from 1960s.
Agencies: Young and Rubicam (Y&R), Begg Dow Priday (BDP).

BENNETT, Rod. Creative. Worked Adelaide, Sydney, and Melbourne
from 1960s. Agencies: Fortune, Berry Currie, Clemenger, Kutt
Skinner Bennett (KSB), Y&R, Badjar.

BERTEL, Rosem'ry. Creative. Worked Melbourne from 1960s. Agencies:
USP Benson, MDA, Lintas, George Patterson, Rees Bertel Maddocks
and Reaordan (RBM&R), Dutton Bertel Hickox Stewart and
Luscombe (DBHS&L).

BEVINS, John. Creative. Worked Sydney from 1960s. Key agencies:
Hansen Rubenoshn-McCann Erickson, O&M, John Bevins

BLACK, Ray. Creative. Worked Sydney from 1960s. Key agencies: Pope
Kiernan Black (PKB), John Bevins.

BLAKENEY, Rod. Creative. Worked Sydney, London, and Melbourne from 1950s. Agencies: David Jones, USP Benson, S.H. Benson, USP Needham, Barry Banks Blakeney (BBB).

BLUNDEN, Andy, interviewed for Betty Blunden. Creative. Worked Melbourne from 1950s. Agencies: Ralph Blunden/TAB, Masius.

BORLAND, Stephanie. Creative. Worked Spain, London, Melbourne, and Asia-Pacific from 1960s. Agencies: USP Needham, JWT, Mattingly, George Patterson.

BOSTON, Margaret. Researcher/Planner. Worked London from 1950s. Agency: O&M.

BOX, John. Creative. Worked Melbourne from 1960s. Agency: Box Archer Emery.

BRIERLEY NEWTON, De. Creative. Worked Sydney, Hong Kong, and Auckland from 1970s. Agencies: JWT, Leo Burnett, Fortune, Schofield Sherbon Baker (SSB), Doyle Dane Bernbach (DDB).

BRYSON, Reg. Planner. Worked Sydney and London from 1960s. Agencies: Compton, Masius, USP Needham, The Campaign Palace.

CAREY, Peter. Creative. Worked Melbourne, London, and Sydney from 1960s. Agencies: TAB, Masius, McSpedden Carey, Grey Worldwide.

CARO, Jane. Creative. Worked Sydney from 1980s. Agencies: Fortune, USP Needham, The Campaign Palace, Forbes McPhee Hansen.

CATANZARITI, Eugene. Planner. Worked Melbourne in 1980s. Agencies: Leo Burnett, Lintas.

CHARLTON, Peter. Agency Management. Worked Melbourne, London, and Sydney from 1960s. Agencies: Lintas, McCann-Erickson.

CHRISTOPHERSON, Leonie. Creative. Worked Sydney and Adelaide from 1950s. Agency: David Jones Advertising Department.

CLEMENGER, Peter. Agency Management. Worked Melbourne from 1950s. Agency: Clemenger Batten, Barton, Durstine & Osborn (BBDO).

CLEREHAN, Esther. Traffic. Worked Melbourne from 1970s. Agencies: O&M, MDA, Mattingly.

COPELAND-SMITH, Luella. Account Management. Worked Sydney from 1970s. Key agencies: Y&R, O&M, FCB Direct.

COUSINS, Geoff. Agency Management. Worked Sydney and Asia-Pacific from 1960s to 1990s. Agency: George Patterson.

COWPER, John. Account Management. Worked Sydney from 1960s. Agencies: Hansen Rubensohn-McCann Erickson, Fortune, Murray Evans, JWT.

COX, Graham. Account Management. Worked Sydney from 1960s. Agencies: Best & Swift, George Patterson.

CUNNACK, Renny. Agency Management. Worked London, New Zealand, and Melbourne from 1960s. Agencies: Pritchard Wood, O&M.

DANIEL, Greg. Agency Management. Worked Brisbane and Sydney from 1960s. Agencies: Le Grand, USP Benson, DDB Needham, The Campaign Palace, Clemenger.

DAVIS, Faie. Copywriter. Worked Singapore, Melbourne, and Sydney from 1960s. Agencies: Jackson Wain, Batey Ads, O&M, SSCB:Lintas and, DDI Adworks/Filmworks.

DAWSON, Ian. Account Management. Worked Sydney from 1970s. Agency: JWT and, MDA, Mojo MDA.

DELBRIDGE, Noel. Creative. Worked Melbourne from 1950s. Agency: Masius.

DONE, Ken. Creative. Worked London and Sydney from 1960s. Agency: JWT.

ELLIS, Mike. Print Production. Worked Melbourne from 1980s. Agency: McCann-Erickson.

FAHEY, Warren. Creative. Worked Sydney from 1960s. Agencies: Jackson Wain, Hansen Rubensohn-McCann Erickson.

FARRELLY, Tania. Planner. Worked Melbourne from 1980s. Agency: O&M.

FEARNLEY, Trevor. Account Management. Worked London and Sydney from 1960s. Agencies: JWT, SSCB:Lintas, Hansen Rubensohn-McCann Erickson, Ad Partners.

FOX, Mo. Account Management. Worked Sydney and London from 1980s. Agency: JWT.

FRASER, Colin. Creative. Worked Melbourne from 1960s. Agency: George Patterson.

FULTON, Margaret. Account Manager. Worked Sydney from 1950s. Agency: JWT.

GASKIN, Paul. Research. Worked Melbourne from 1960s. Agency: JWT.

GOSLING, Max. Agency Management. Worked Sydney from 1970s. Agency: SSC&B:Lintas and, McCann-Erickson.

GRAHAM, Greg. Media. Worked Sydney from 1970s. Agencies: McCann-Erickson, USP Needham, DDB, JWT.

GRAY, Steve. Account Management, Agency Management. Worked Sydney and Melbourne from 1970s. Agencies: Leo Burnett, Mojo.

HALL, Robyn. Administration. Worked New Zealand, Sydney, and London from 1960s. Agencies: Dormer-Beck, JWT.

HAMILL, Alex. Agency Management. Worked Sydney and Singapore from 1950s. Agency: Jackson Wain, George Patterson.

HAMILTON, Peter. Agency Management. Worked Sydney, New York, and London from 1960s. Agency: McCann-Erickson.

HANSEN, Derek. Creative. Worked London, Melbourne, and Sydney from 1960s. Agencies: JWT, Collett Dickenson Pearce (CDP), Foote Cone & Belding (FCB), Forbes McPhee Hansen.

HARRINGTON, Lee. Administration. Worked Melbourne from 1980s. Agency: Mattingly.

HARRIS, Bruce. Agency Management. Worked Sydney from 1950s. Agencies: Lintas, George Patterson, SSC&B:Lintas.

HARTLEY, Allan. Creative. Worked Brisbane from 1960s. Agencies: Le Grand, McCann-Erickson, Pemberton, DDB Needham, Garnsey Clemenger.

HENSCHKE, Laura. Account Management. Worked Lima, and Sydney from 1970s. Agencies: JWT, FCB.

HORNIDGE, Richard. Account Management. Worked Melbourne from 1960s. Agencies: John Clemenger, S.H. Benson, USP Benson, Jackson Wain, Lintas, Fortune, Advertising Associates, Barry Banks Blakeney, McCann-Erickson.

HUNT, Lionel. Creative. Worked Melbourne from 1960s. Agencies: Masius, The Campaign Palace.

JACKSON, Marie. Account Management. Worked Melbourne from 1970s. Agency: O&M.

JARRETT, Bruce. Creative Director. Worked Sydney from 1950s. Agency: George Patterson.

JOBBINS, Joy. Account Management. Worked Sydney and Melbourne from 1950s. Agencies: Richardson Cox, Carden Advertising, TAB.

KILLEY, Andrew. Copywriter. Worked Adelaide from 1980s. Key Agencies: Agencies: NAS Macnamara, George Patterson, Martin Kinnear Clemenger, KWP, Y&R.

KINGSTON, Wayne. Agency Management. Worked Melbourne, Singapore, New York, San Francisco, London, and Sydney from 1970s. Agencies: Mojo MDA, O&M, DDB Needham.

KINSELLA, Graeme. Account Management. Worked New Zealand, Sydney, and Kuala Lumpur from 1960s. Agencies: Dobbs-Wiggins McCann-Erickson, Hertz Walpole, Leo Burnett, George Patterson, SSB/Fortune Communications, FCB.

LAUCHLAN, Bruce. Creative. Worked Melbourne from 1970s. Freelance illustrator.

LAWLER, Toni. Account Management. Worked Melbourne from 1980s.
Agencies: MDA, Mattingly, O&M, Leonardi & Curtis.

LAWRENCE, Neil. Creative. Worked Melbourne, Singapore, Adelaide,
and Sydney from 1980s. Agencies: NAS Coventry Vaney, Burrows
Lawrence Dobell, SSB, Chandler Hambleton, O&M, Leo Burnett,
Y&R.

LIGHT, Jeremy. Journalist. Worked Sydney from 1970s. Company:
AdNews.

LUSCOMBE, Kevin. Agency Management. Worked Melbourne from
1960s. Agency: Luscombe & Partners.

MACKAY, Hugh. Researcher. Worked Sydney from 1960s. Agency:
JWT.

MARA, Jane. Media. Worked Sydney from 1970s. Agencies: Coudrey-
Campbell-Ewald, Murray Evans, O&M, MDA, FCB.

MARTIN, Julian. Account Management. Worked Sydney from 1980s.
Agency: Mojo.

MARTIN MURPHY, Chris. Planner. Worked London, Sydney, Adelaide,
and Melbourne from 1960s. Agencies: Garland Compton, Y&R, The
Campaign Palace, Magnus Nankervis & Curl, Mojo MDA, O&M.

MATHER, Ron. Creative. Worked London and Melbourne from 1960s
to 1990s. Agencies: Saatchi & Saatchi, Masius, The Campaign Palace,
Gough Waterhouse.

MATTINGLY, David. Agency Management. Worked Melbourne from
1960s. Agencies: MDA, Mojo MDA, Mattingly & Partners.

McBRIDE, Janice. Creative. Worked Melbourne from 1950s. Agency:
Paton Advertising.

McCALLUM, June. Account Management. Worked Melbourne from
1960s. Agencies: Fortune, TAB.

McDONALD, Ian. Media. Worked Sydney from 1960s. Agencies: Hansen
Rubensohn-McCann Erickson, SSB, John Bevins.

McFARLANE, Tom. Creative. Worked Melbourne, London, and Sydney
from 1970s. Agencies: Handbury, Thomson White, Masius, Mullins
Clarke Ralph, JWT, DDB.

McINTYRE, Greg. Production. Worked Melbourne from 1980s. Agency:
Scali McCabe Sloves (SMS).

McLAY, Russell. Agency Management. Worked Sydney from 1960s.
Agency: George Patterson.

MERCHANT, Dennis. Media. Worked Sydney from 1950s. Agencies:
Canny Paramor & Canny (CPC), Jackson Wain, Hansen Rubensohn-
McCann Erickson, Y&R.

MERCHANT, Gay. Administration. Worked Sydney in 1960s. Agency: Jackson Wain.

MERCIER, Simone. Account Management. Worked Sydney from 1980s. Agency: George Patterson.

MILES, Anne. Production. Worked Melbourne from 1980s. Agencies: McCann-Erickson, JWT, Grey Worldwide, Y&R.

MURPHY, Gabrielle. Account Management. Worked Melbourne in 1980s. Agency: McCann-Erickson.

NEWTON, John. Creative. Worked Sydney from 1970s. Agencies: JWT, Leo Burnett.

NICOL, Helene. Production. Worked Melbourne and Sydney from 1970s. Agencies: Carden Advertising, Masius, SSB.

NILSSON, Claire. Art Director. Worked Melbourne from 1960s. Agencies: TAB, Masius.

NUNN, Graham. Copywriter. Worked Adelaide, London, Melbourne, and Sydney from 1970s. Agencies: Martin Kinnear Clemenger, Y&R, BDP, Foster Nunn Loveder.

O'BRIEN, Simon. Worked Adelaide and Melbourne from 1960s. Agencies: JWT, O&M, O'Brien McGrath.

OTTEN, Suzie. Account Management. Worked Sydney, Melbourne, and New York from 1970s. Agencies: USP Needham, MDA, O&M.

OTTON, Ric. Agency Management. Worked Brisbane, and Melbourne from 1960s. Agencies: Masius, Mojo MDA.

PALMER, Rob. Account Management. Worked Sydney from 1960s. Agency: JWT, USP Needham, Leo Burnett, Clemenger, Mojo.

PRIDAY, Paul. Creative. Worked London, Melbourne, and Sydney from 1960s. Agencies: JWT, Masius, Singleton Palmer Strauss McAllan (SPASM), BDP.

RANKIN, Peter. Agency Management. Worked Melbourne from 1950s. Agency: Clemenger.

REED, Mike. Post-Production. Worked Melbourne from 1970s. Company: Mike Reed & Partners Post Production (MRPPP).

RIGBY, Roger. Production. Worked Sydney from 1950s. Agency: Clemenger.

RITCHIE, Michael. Production. Worked Sydney from 1980s. Agencies: George Patterson, O&M.

ROBERTSON, Alan. Media. Worked Sydney and London from 1970s. Agencies: Lintas, Hansen Rubensohn-McCann Erickson, JWT.

ROOM, Jack. Creative. Worked London and Melbourne from 1960s. Agencies: JWT, KSB, Y&R, Badjar.

RUTHERFORD, Fysh. Creative. Worked Melbourne and Hong

Kong from 1970s. Agencies: MDA, Clemenger, Leo Burnett, KSB,
Connaghan & May, Masius, George Patterson.

SATTERTHWAITE, Mike. Finance. Worked Sydney in 1980s. Agency:
Saatchi & Saatchi.

SCHALK, Willi. Agency Management. Worked New York from 1970s.
Agency: BBDO.

SCHIRMANN, Kaye. Creative. Worked Melbourne, Singapore, and
Sydney from 1980s. Agencies: O&M, Mattingly, Masius, Leonardi &
Curtis, John Bevins.

SHANNON, Bill. Agency Management. Worked Melbourne from 1970s.
Agencies: Carlton Caruthers Du Chateau, O&M, SMS.

SMALLACOMBE, Patrea, for Betty Quin. Creative. Worked London and
Adelaide from 1950s, and 1960s. Agency: NAS MacNamara.

SPENCER, Hugh. Creative. Worked Wellington, Sydney, Launceston,
Bangkok, New York, Tokyo, and Melbourne from 1960s.
Agency: Carlton Caruthers Du Chateau, Jackson Wain, JWT,
McCarthy Watson.

SPRY, Malcolm. Account Management. Worked Melbourne and Sydney
from 1960s. Agencies: USP Benson, MDA, Mojo.

STEEDMAN, John. Media. Worked Sydney and Adelaide from 1970s.
Agencies: McCann-Erickson, JWT.

STEWART, Robin. Creative. Worked Toronto and Melbourne from
1960s. Agency: Masius.

STITT, Alex. Production. Worked Melbourne from 1960s. Company:
Weatherhead & Stitt.

STITT, Paddy. Creative. Worked Melbourne from 1950s. Agencies: JWT,
Paton Advertising, Ralph Blunden/TAB.

STOLLZNOW, Max. Research. Worked Sydney from 1970s. Agency:
Hansen Rubensohn-McCann Erickson.

STRACHAN, Ian. Training. Worked London, Melbourne, and Asia-
Pacific from 1960s. Agency: O&M.

STRAUSS, Mike. Creative. Worked South Africa, Sydney, Melbourne
and London from 1950s. Agencies: Van Zyl & Van Zyl, McCann-
Erickson, JWT, Walker Robertson Maguire, Grey, SPASM, FCB,
D'Arcy Masius Benton & Bowles (DMB&B).

VON ADLERSTEIN, Marion. Creative. Worked Sydney, London, New
York, and Melbourne from 1950s. Agencies: London Press Exchange
(LPE), JWT, USP Benson.

WATSON, Doug. Creative. Worked Sydney, Melbourne, and Perth from
1960s. Agencies: FCB, Hertz Walpole, O&M, Campbell-Ewald,
McCarthy Watson, Mojo MDA.

WEBSTER, Adelle. Media. Worked Sydney from 1940s. Agency:
Goldberg Advertising.

WILD, Geoff. Account Management. Worked Sydney, Melbourne, and
Asia-Pacific from 1950s. Agency: Clemenger.

WISHART, Valwyn. Copywriter. Worked Melbourne from 1940s.
Agencies: Richardson Cox, Carden Advertising.

WRIGHT, John. Account Management. Worked Adelaide, London,
and Sydney from 1960s. Agencies: Clem Taylor O'Brien, George
Patterson, JWT, Y&R, Mojo MDA.

* Agencies recorded up to 1989.

INTRODUCTION

As a fresh-faced Michael Ball passed through the glass doors at the Melbourne office of the J. Walter Thompson in 1958, he had little knowledge of the world he was entering. After a short interview with the creative director, Ball landed a job as a junior copywriter. His first question did not concern salary or benefits; it was simply 'what is a copywriter?' The former University of Melbourne student knew more about theology and New Testament Greek than he did about the art of writing and producing advertisements.[1]

His unfamiliarity with the advertising industry was something shared by the majority of those who entered the agency industry at this time. Ball would have no formal training scheme to help him adjust. Like so many others, he learnt on the job – writing in the office in the mornings, drinking with other creatives in the afternoons, and sometimes writing again in the evenings. Ball was a quick learner, and he soon developed a sophisticated understanding of advertising and the advertising industry.

Three years after joining JWT, Ball relocated to New York with his wife, where he worked as account executive on the Shell account. When the account moved to Ogilvy & Mather, Ball moved across with it. Over the next three decades, Ball rose through the ranks of the multi-national agency, improving its everyday operations and leading its entry into Australia and the Asia-Pacific region. At one stage, he was touted as the successor to David Ogilvy, the founder of O&M and one of the giants of twentieth-century advertising. In many ways, Ball's rise reflects the story of Australia's advertising agencies during the period spanning the 1960s through to the end of the 1980s. Over this time, these agencies progressively adopted a more professional and global outlook.

The industry that Ball joined in the 1950s was different from the industry that he left some three decades later. Australia's advertising agencies in the 1950s were operating in a small market at the outer reaches of the British Empire. After the enforced austerity of the Depression and war years, Australians were finally in a position to consume, and the advertising industry was ready to help out. At this time, advertising agencies were not the only firms creating advertisements. Department stores such as Myer and David Jones also ran their own advertising departments that surpassed many agencies in terms of size and creative output. Radio stations similarly employed their own copywriters and production teams to create spots and announce-ments for clients.

The agencies themselves were still a cottage industry. Aside from JWT, Lintas, and a handful of local firms, the standard Australian agency was a relatively small operation. As they were dealing with local newspapers and radio stations, the vast majority of agencies were single-city operations. Most bore the name of their entrepreneurial founder, who had started the agency working as an account executive and copywriter. The founders' ability to attract business had enabled them to employ further staff and, subsequently, establish specialised departments covering account service, advertisement production and agency administration. Of these, it was the account service department that held sway.

Over the 1960s advertising agencies in Australia began to change. The momentum did not come from within. It was the agencies' clients, the advertisers, who drove it. In the context of the global post-war economic boom, Australia was fast becoming an affluent consumer market.[2] With international firms eager to enter this lucrative arena, competition for the consumer's attention was intensifying. In this climate advertising became an indispensable tool. Competition and television-commercial costs prompted clients to invest more in their advertising and marketing strategies. Advertising expenditure continued to climb throughout the 1970s and the 1980s, and agencies were the key beneficiaries. They were able to indulge themselves in the production of large campaigns and were rewarded with enormous salaries and enviable work conditions. Advertising had become a glamour industry. Dazzled by the agencies' stylish offices and generous lunches, many advertisers were happy to give their agencies free rein in the hope that the ensuing campaigns would have the nation singing their brand name.

Bigger budgets came with bigger expectations. International advertisers were particularly keen to see a replication of the support offered by their American or British agencies. With the newly arrived branches of multi-national agencies happily obliging, local agencies were forced to follow suit. The professionalisation of the advertising agency affected various aspects of its operations and structure as well as its creative output. Education and training would be an integral part of this process. When Ball joined JWT, few in the industry had matriculated from high school. By the time he departed, a significant proportion of new staff had a degree. This up-skilling also revealed itself in the attention paid to marketing. Agencies similarly paid greater attention to their own training schemes, ensuring that employees were inculcated with their specific approach. Although agencies hoped that the more disciplined approach would also enhance their creative output, the reality was that the creative department marched to a different beat. It had long been and still remained a random mixture of personalities and backgrounds. However, the creative department's position in the agency hierarchy went from being peripheral to central. While clients enjoyed long lunches with their account service executives, their primary reason for hiring an agency was its capacity to create ads that worked. They wanted the magic and they were willing to pay for it.

As agencies realised that their reputation was only as good as the reels they showed to prospective clients, they were prepared to expend more effort and significantly more money on keeping their creative stars happy. This emphasis on creativity not only affected the structure and operations of the advertising agencies, it would also have a direct impact on the type of campaigns they created. The professionalisation of the agencies was also being driven by the globalisation of the advertising industry. Multi-national agencies directly and indirectly exposed Australian advertising professionals to the latest practices and ideas being implemented abroad. Changes in technology further facilitated this access. As the advertising agencies came to be seen as more professional and worldly in their outlook and practices, they were able to satisfy the advertisers' expectations. Ultimately, the agency's successful repositioning of themselves as glamorous partners rather than mere service-providers to their clients created a 'golden age' for Australian advertising agencies and, in particular, the managers and the creatives.

It was not, of course, a 'golden age' for everyone. The changes affecting agency operations meant that employees in certain departments were becoming vulnerable. Account service staff saw their status slowly erode as clients and agency management placed a new emphasis on creative work, while support staff, such as tea ladies and lift operators, fell victim to the agencies' drive for greater profitability. Others struggled with the prevailing agency culture. Australian advertising's hyper-masculine environment meant that the agency could be a challenging and difficult workplace for women. Few rose through the ranks, fewer still found their way into senior positions within the agency hierarchy.

Advertising's glory days were fleeting. The forces that enabled advertising to grow from a cottage industry to a global enterprise would also consume it. As agencies adopted a more professional approach to their work, so too did their clients. Advertisers were also training staff. The appointment of marketing managers and, later, brand managers to oversee their marketing strategy would have a significant impact on their relationship with the agency. As the managing directors focused on running their businesses, they left it to their marketing experts to deal with the agency.

For the advertising CEO David Mattingly, the denial of access to key figures in the client's firm 'was a major revolution in the advertising world, it changed everything'. Agency frustrations with their perceived demotion were compounded by the marketing team's attitude towards advertising. They considered advertising to be just one part of a broader marketing strategy, and demanded that the agency follow their directives. As the agency–client relationship was relegated to junior marketing executives, clients reduced their advertising budgets yet still demanded the same level of service that they had previously enjoyed.

With less money and influence, advertising's glamour began to fade. Globalisation similarly eroded the status of Australian advertising agencies. While technology had facilitated greater connectivity, Australia's size and distance nevertheless remained an issue. Individual Australian advertising agents certainly fared well on the global stage, but Australian agencies did not enjoy the same opportunities. They were subject to the decisions made elsewhere by clients (concerning budgets or strategy) and agency head offices (client selection or office operations). The decline of the Australian advertising agency in the 1990s underscores the degree to which the period spanning the 1960s, 1970s, and 1980s was a high point for the industry.

Studies of the globalisation of advertising have generally focused on the decisions and actions of the largest multi-national agencies and, to a lesser extent, those responsible for leading them.[3] Such accounts have identified the key turning points and the defining characteristics of the industry's globalisation, but their focus on the activities occurring at the macro scale has overlooked the ways in which local agencies and staff engaged in these processes.

While more recent accounts have begun to redress this imbalance, they nevertheless tend to focus on the actions of key agencies or prioritise the voices of leading figures.[4] Such emphases reflect the nature of the sources at hand. As few agencies have maintained their archives, those that are accessible (such as the J. Walter Thompson material held at Duke University's Hartmann Center) have understandably had a significant impact on scholarship concerning the historical development of the advertising agency business.[5] The decisions to keep certain materials and to dispose of others have also skewed scholarship towards the actions of key agency figures. A similar emphasis can be discerned in the industry press, where the journalists' sense of newsworthiness sees them following the big moves in the industry and speaking only to major industry figures. Of course, the agencies have been equally engaged in this process, circulating media releases, offering interviews with key figures and dishing the dirt on competitors. While we value and use these same sources, we feel that they function much as the ubiquitous glass doors fitted throughout the agencies – providing a glimpse of the agency at work but restricting access to it.

In *Advertising: A Cultural Economy*, Liz McFall contends that academics have devoted too much time to the analysis of advertisements as texts and too little time examining how those texts are produced. Her warning against '[d]isregarding the practices and institutions of advertising' is relevant to our study.[6] We believe that advertising cannot be fully understood without reference to those who are responsible for creating and selling it. Of course, we do not claim to be pioneers in this field. In his sociological study of British advertising agencies in the 1990s, Sean Nixon observes that scholars examining contemporary advertising practices have paid 'some attention … to the formal practices, institutional arrangements and types of expertise prevalent within this sector'.[7] Nixon's study would dig deeper to examine the social make-up of the British advertising industry, its informal cultures and the subjective identities of key practitioners. Building on the foundations set by McFall and Nixon, we seek to explore questions within the Australian context, albeit from a historical perspective.

This study also expands on the work undertaken on Australian advertising history. In 1984, John Spierings observed that the advertising industry cared little for its past and that any attempts 'at writing advertising history are hindered by the paucity of original primary source material'.[8] Since then, a growing body of work has managed to overcome these challenges. Although John Sinclair's *Images Incorporated* focuses on advertising as an international institution, its Australian references nevertheless situate Australia's advertising industry within a broader context.[9] Robert Crawford's *But Wait There's More...* provides a more national perspective, outlining the development of Australia's advertising industry over the twentieth century and the degree to which it was informed by an abiding desire for legitimacy.[10] More recently, Jackie Dickenson's *Australian Women in Advertising in the Twentieth Century* uses the experiences of individual women to illustrate the 'ambiguous role of women in the advertising industry' in Australia and, indeed, abroad.[11] *Behind Glass Doors* sits somewhere between these studies. By connecting the local, the national, and the global over an extended period, we seek to develop a more comprehensive account of advertising agencies, their everyday operations, and the people responsible for them, as well as the different ways that they have connected with the world around them.

Our study uses oral history testimony to give voice to the people who worked in the industry. Patrick Fridenson's contribution to *The Oxford Handbook of Business History* claimed that 'Oral history has become a standard practice in business history for the study of the 20th and 21st centuries to an extent that is still unrivalled in most other parts of the historical profession'.[12] Rob Perks, however, suggests such claims may be exaggerated. While various American business historians have readily taken up the call to use oral history, Perks observes that 'oral evidence has been absent or subsidiary' in British business history, adding that 'virtually nothing about the use of oral sources in business and corporate history, or about commissioned oral history, has been published in *Oral History* during its forty-year history'.[13] Perks suggests that this reflects 'the political origins of the British oral history movement, which emerged ... as a radical alternative to the traditional historical study of male elites'.[14] The situation in Australia appears similar. A survey of the catalogue of the *Oral History Australia Journal* reveals some forty-eight articles on 'work', which is defined as 'articles about paid and unpaid work, unemployment, the 1930s Depression, and the labour movement and labour history'. The journal has published twenty-four articles under the 'Industry, Business and Commerce' heading, which covers 'banks and banking, organisations and associations, and public sector services as well as industrial and company histories'.[15]

For their part, Australia's business historians appear to have been, arguably, even more reluctant to engage with oral history. Since 1997, only three articles in the *Australian Economic History Review* have cited oral history as a keyword or a major methodological approach.[16] By interviewing the leaders, the creatives and the unsung workers, we hope to help bridge the divide between Australia's oral historians and business historians.

This study of the advertising agency in Australia is based on the insights and reflections revealed during our interviews with 120 men and women who either worked in or with Australian advertising agencies over the period spanning 1959 to 1989. Some enjoyed long and illustrious careers in the advertising industry, others worked only briefly before pursuing a different course. A handful is still employed in the industry. As Part II reveals, our interviewees worked across all departments in the advertising agency – management, creative, account service, media, production and administrative support. The vast majority spent time working in the industry's key agencies, namely McCann-Erickson, J. Walter Thompson, George Patterson, Clemenger BBDO, Ogilvy & Mather, Monahan Dayman Adams, Mojo and The Campaign Palace. Each semi-structured interview followed the respondents' professional career in advertising and invited them to reflect on their experiences of life at the advertising agency. Face-to-face interviews were conducted in Sydney, Melbourne, Brisbane, Adelaide and New York. Other interviews were conducted over the phone and via email. Our interviewees were universally generous with their time, with interviews generally running for one to three hours. Over the course of these interviews, the participants offered detailed and often candid insights into the professional, technical, political, cultural and social aspects of agency life. In revealing themselves to be clever, articulate and insightful individuals, our interviewees exemplified the reasons why the advertising agency business had prospered during the period under study.

The interaction between globalisation and professionalisation that underpinned the advertising industry's best years forms the structure of this book. We have therefore divided the study into two parts. Part One follows the globalisation of the advertising industry and reveals the ways that Australian agencies and advertising professionals were involved in this process. Part Two focuses on the advertising agency and the professionalisation of its everyday operations. While the two sections are distinct, their stories are fundamentally intertwined. There would be no professionalisation without globalisation and no globalisation without professionalisation.

Part One demonstrates that Australians were actively engaged in the globalisation of the advertising agency industry.

Chapter 1 opens with the arrival of McCann-Erickson in Australia from New York in 1959 and follows the actions of McCann-Erickson and the other multi-national agencies as they commenced operations in Australia in the 1960s. Ensuring that their new operations had the right outlook, the right approach, and the right staff would be an abiding concern for each new arrival. Such efforts not only laid the foundations for their own operations, they also affected local agencies that had no international connections.

In Chapter 2, we examine the multi-national agencies' efforts to train staff in their Australian offices. By sending Australians to work in New York, London and other major offices, these agencies were establishing consistent approaches and outlooks across their networks. The multi-national agencies were not the only ones to benefit from the experiences gained during these travels. As the travellers subsequently moved to other agencies, the skills and insights they gained from their time abroad were transferred across the industry.

Such experiences are explored further in Chapter 3, which focuses on Australia's relationship with South East Asia. The region not only offered further opportunities for Australians to gain international experience, it also enabled Australian agencies to revisit their place within the international agency networks. Building on historical networks and Australia's proximity to the region, Australian agencies played a leading role in integrating the region into the global agency networks. In the process, Australia also emerges as an active proponent of globalisation.

Chapter 4 brings the focus back to Australia and explores the so-called Creative Revolution in Australia in the 1970s. Tired of the formulaic work and regimented practices at the

multi-national agencies, a new generation of Australian creatives opted to open their own boutique agencies that embraced
creative work. As clients made it clear that they wanted a creative campaign, the multi-national agencies began to follow the
boutiques' lead and increasingly invested in enhancing their
own creative credentials. The emergence of independent media
agencies to service the boutiques' media needs was another
result of the Creative Revolution, and one that would have
significant long-term impact on all agencies and their operations.

Covering the 1980s, Chapter 5 begins with an industry
brimming with confidence. Billings were at an all-time high and
agencies excitedly eyed the new opportunities in an increasingly
globalised marketplace. Some responded to these opportunities
methodically, others were positively bullish in their approach.
As the realities of dealing with global advertisers and global
agency networks revealed themselves, however, this self-assured
outlook gradually dissipated. And, by the end of the decade, it
was clear that the golden age was drawing to an end.

Part Two ventures beyond the glass doors at reception
and into the agencies' plush offices to uncover the degree to
which the professionalisation brought by globalisation affected
the everyday practices of all departments. In Chapter 6 we
trace the ways in which young people entered the advertising
business, as well as the training they received, finding a gradual
professionalisation of qualifications linked to the expansion of
university education, especially from the late 1960s. A decade
later the industry underwent another shift, as more women than
ever before took up advertising work, claiming the lower-level
jobs now eschewed by tertiary-educated men.

Behind this rise in education and professional standards were
the agencies' clients, who were themselves taking advantage of

Australia's expanding university system. Chapter 7 explores this client-driven change in more depth, as it examines the shifting nature of agency–client relationships across the period. The 'hail-fellow-well-met' approach to keeping a client happy – an approach that had worked for most of the twentieth century – became less potent from the 1960s, as better-educated clients demanded more accountability from their agencies. The restructuring that grew out of the global financial challenges of the early 1970s and the end of the long boom would lead, eventually, to ever-more assertive clients in this respect, until, by the onset of the recession at the end of the 1980s, they were questioning the financial structures at the heart of the agency–client relationship.

Chapter 8 explores the shift in power from account management to the creative department – the copywriters and art directors – which began during the 1960s, as Australian advertising agencies responded first to the creative revolution that emanated from New York, then incorporated the British version of that revolution by employing hundreds of expatriate copywriters and art directors. As boutique agencies set a higher bar, creative standards rose and talented creatives became increasingly valuable. By the 1980s, creative directors had become the agencies' highest-paid executives, although their reign would be short-lived.

Chapter 9 turns to groups of advertising workers much less celebrated than those working in the creative department. These were the support staff – the researchers, media buyers, administration and finance staff, traffic managers, production managers, freelancers and suppliers – whose efforts were crucial to the smooth running of an advertising agency. The chapter explores the effects of technological change and professionalisation on these groups, finding that, in many respects, the everyday lives of these workers were more affected by change across this period than those working in the core areas of the agency, for example, account management and the creative department. This is especially true when their experience is compared to that of the subjects of the final chapter.

Agency principals – the CEOs and managing directors – are the subjects of Chapter 10. This chapter traces the shift from family-run agencies to the sophisticated, highly professional agencies of the late 1980s, examining the changes that drove that shift. It also explores the challenges principals faced in these years, including securing and keeping new business in an increasingly competitive market. Most agencies also struggled to hang on to good staff, and the chapter discusses the strategies the best agencies employed to address this problem. With the exception of increased expectations of their financial performance imposed by globalisation, this group was less affected by change in this period than others in the agency.

Looking back on the period spanning the 1960s to the 1980s, Alex Hamill observes that 'It was probably the great creative era' for Australian advertising agencies. Exciting, fun, and awash with money as they rode the back of the long boom, agencies were a glamorous workplace unlike any other in Australia. Such a climate attracted highly creative and intelligent individuals, as well as a fair share of eccentrics. Australian advertising certainly had its share of mad men and women, and it is hardly surprising that so many interviewees likened their agency experiences to the television series *Mad Men*. Stories of staff using motorcycles, guns, and chainsaws in offices have become the stuff of agency folklore. But by the end of the 1980s, such stories were already becoming a thing of the past. Some glamour remained, but the twin forces of globalisation and professionalisation that had underpinned the agency industry's development over the last three decades were fundamentally changing their operations as well as the type of person they were letting in. 'In 1990 I wouldn't have been hired, full stop', muses Hamill, who headed Australia's largest agency in 1990 having entered the industry as a 15-year-old despatch boy. His progress is that of the industry writ large. As we listen to the insights and experiences of those who worked in Australian agencies during these three decades, we hear the story of an industry whose form and function helped usher Australia into the global age.

CHAPTER ONE

ARRIVING IN AUSTRALIA

Rumours circulate quickly in the advertising industry. So when the senior vice-president and general manager of McCann-Erickson's international operations landed in Sydney in May 1959, the chatter soon began. Was McCann-Erickson setting up an Australian branch? If so, when? How would they do it? Interviewed by the trade journal *Broadcasting and Television (B&T)* shortly after arriving, Arthur (Art) L. Grimes was still light on the details. 'We don't know how we're going about it yet, whether we'll open up our own office, or whether we'll do it in co-operation with another agency', the New York native explained. He therefore wanted to meet the locals and to ascertain whether or not an Australian operation was worth the cost. However, Grimes was certain about one thing: 'I am here to make a decision on it, after which I may need to return to gain financial committee approval.'[1] Within six months, McCann-Erickson announced its decision. The *Sydney Morning Herald* covered the announcement with headline: 'Aust., U.S. Agencies in Merger', while the *New York Times*' headline offered a more revealing interpretation of the move: 'McCann is invading Australia'.[2] Over the next decade, the steady flow of overseas agencies setting up operations in Australia suggested that the *New York Times* had, in fact, been right.

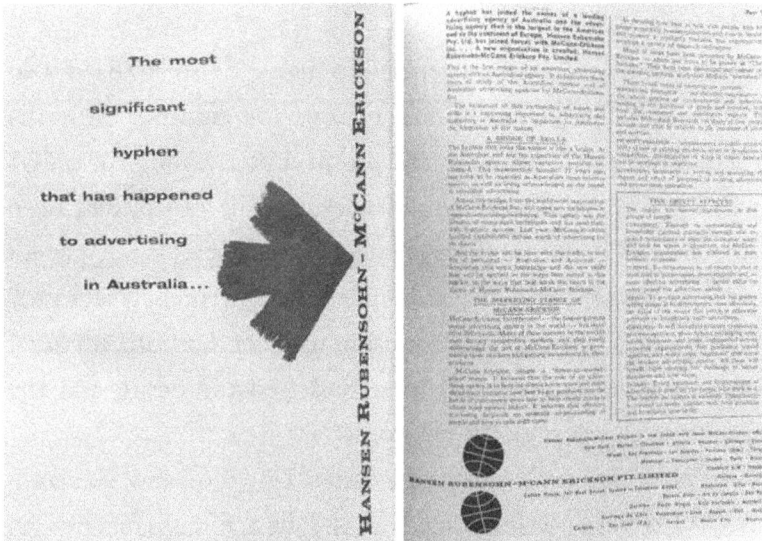

Figure 1.1 McCann Erickson finally announces its entry into the Australian market. B&T, 8 October 1959, pp. 12–13. (Courtesy of B&T)

McCann-Erickson's arrival in Australia in 1959 signalled a new era for Australia's advertising industry. While overseas agencies had been operating in Australia since the 1920s, their impact on the local advertising industry was restricted by their lack of numbers. When Grimes first visited Australia, there were only two agencies operating as local offices of a multinational corporation. By 1970, eleven of the top fifteen billing agencies in Australia had international owners. The sheer number of agencies moving into Australia over the course of the 1960s meant that they had a more profound impact on the local advertising industry. This chapter will explore this influence by examining the multinational agencies' differing strategies for entering Australia, their efforts to establish a functional branch office, and their active importation of ideas and skills. Such practices demonstrate the agencies' efforts to implement a systematised approach to establishing global networks.

Old Networks

The first foreign-owned agencies to arrive in Australia did so in the interwar period. Their reasons for entering Australia varied. Some were drawn by the prospect of accessing Australia's small but expanding consumer market while others had been compelled to do so by their clients. The agencies' strategies for entering Australia also differed – from the entrepreneurial to the methodical. Their common decision to enter Australia revealed, however, that agencies had long possessed the desire and the capacity to develop global networks.

Establishing its Sydney office in 1924, the New Zealand–based Goldberg Advertising was the first foreign agency to commence operations in Australia. The office quickly built up business and, within three years, the agency's proprietor Frank Goldberg relocated the agency's head office from Wellington to Sydney. The agency continued to operate until 1968, when it was bought out by the British agency Masius, Wynne-Williams.

In 1925 the British Samson Clark agency opened an office in Melbourne. Noting that 'it was decided to make the attempt & to run it for a year unless the prospects seemed very doubtful, in which case it would be closed earlier', the agency's directors revealed a rather phlegmatic approach to expanding their operations abroad.[3] Three staff members were despatched to establish the office, including one of the agency's directors. The agency quickly found its footing and the *Samson Clark Gazette* was soon reporting that the 'regular Australian mails reveal fresh progress every week'. Significantly, the agency sought to capitalise on its networks. While its British clients had been using Australian firms to place advertising in the local press, the Australian branch would take over this role '[as] these contracts expire', ensuring that 'all the incomings from these accounts in our own hands'.[4]

The Depression saw the agency merge with Price-Berry in 1930 to form 'the largest advertising firm in Australia'.[5] The merger collapsed during World War II, leading Hugh Berry to establish Hugh Berry Advertising (renamed Berry Currie in 1960).[6]

Campbell-Ewald's entry into Australia was short-lived. In 1929 the *Sunday Times* reported the formation of 'the new Australian-Canadian form of advertising service agents, Campbell-Ewald'.[7] Seeing the global expansion of the General Motors corporation, the Canadian office of the Detroit-based agency was hoping to take advantage of its American and Empire connections. Rather than setting up from scratch, the agency opted to buy into a local firm. With little knowledge of Australia, the Canadians asked prominent businessman Sir Mark Sheldon for advice. A board member of Tooheys, Sheldon recommended the Fox Advertising Service, which handled the brewery's account. Unfortunately for Campbell-Ewald, Fox was unprofessional at best and ill-suited to being a subsidiary of a large firm. In addition to new levels of administration, the Canadians would send through leads and recommendations. Incompetence ensured that little eventuated. Consequently, former staffer Roger Welch was required to write 'long reports to Toronto inventing excuses for our non-success. This was a big strain on the imagination.'[8] As losses continued to mount, Campbell-Ewald withdrew from Australia. However, the Campbell-Ewald name did not entirely disappear from Australian advertising – it would reappear in Australia in the 1960s.

The J. Walter Thompson (JWT) agency would realise Campbell-Ewald's dream when it landed the General Motors (GM) international account. As part of the deal, JWT agreed to establish an office wherever GM had an office. With GM plants operating in Melbourne and Adelaide, JWT prepared to enter Australia. Discussing the agency's takeover of the GM account, James Webb Young, the head of JWT's international operations, noted that 'it is entirely possible that a plan similar to that contemplated in Canada might be worked out as there are a number of agencies in Australia about the same type as the Canadian agencies'. Australia, he added, 'presents no language difficulty [and] should be one of the easiest for us to tackle'.[9]

In 1930 JWT entered Australia, opening offices in Melbourne and Sydney. Like others in the JWT network, it was expected that the Australian offices would be self-sufficient within a year and that the profits for the following year would be used to pay off the company's investment.[10] The Depression and the loss of the GM account forced the Melbourne office to close. Timely account acquisitions narrowly averted a similar story in Sydney. However, as the economy improved, so too did the fortunes of JWT Sydney. The office deftly leveraged its connections with New York and London to enhance its operations. Research had been identified as a unique service from the very outset and Australian staff received 'a great deal of useful literature from JWT in New York'.[11]

Although other agencies such as Weston claimed to operate market research departments, JWT identified its market research operations as part of the JWT brand.[12] Its commitment to research went beyond publicity, JWT's research department would prove to be a fertile training ground for pioneering market researchers William McNair and Sylvia Ashby.[13] The growing popularity of radio in the late 1930s provided another opportunity for JWT to tap into American expertise. In 1939 the agency brought out Phil Mygatt from the US via Canada to produce a local variation of 'Lux Radio Theatre'.[14] Producing other popular programmes such as 'Dad and Dave' (modelled on the American 'Amos 'n' Andy') for Wrigley's chewing gum and 'Mrs 'Obbs' for Bonnington's Irish Moss cough mixture, JWT emerged as one of Australia's largest agencies within a decade of its arrival.

The fifth multi-national agency to establish an office in Australia was Lintas, which commenced operations rather unobtrusively in Sydney in 1931. Unlike the other arrivals, Lintas was established as an in-house agency for the Anglo-Dutch soap manufacturer Unilever (its title being an acronym of Lever International Advertising Service). Like JWT, Lintas's entry into Australia was driven by its major client, although it also sought other accounts. It wasted little time in tapping into the Lintas global networks, importing cases of posters and advertisements from Britain and Europe within months of arrival.[15] Ted Moore, who had worked at Lintas from 1936 to 1939, recalled that the majority of artwork undertaken for Unilever accounts involved adaptations of American material. Two-tone shoes, for example, 'were painted out'.[16] However, the flow of information was not necessarily one way, as reprints of local campaigns were also being shipped to London.[17]

By the 1960s, Goldberg Advertising, JWT, and Lintas had all been operating in Australia for some three decades and had become adopted locals. Registering itself as an Australian company in 1935, JWT had taken the title J. Walter Thompson Australia.[18] Twenty-five years later, JWT Australia's head, Tom Carruthers, revealed the agency's dual identity, explaining that 'although JWT is a completely Australian agency, we regard ourselves primarily as part of an international team'.[19] The arrival of a new wave of multinational agencies would nevertheless shake things up – for locals and adopted locals alike.

Moving In

With a Kelvinator refrigerator in the kitchen, a Bush Simpson television in the lounge room, and a Holden in the garage, Australians living in the late 1950s were enjoying a higher standard of living than ever before. Australia was in the midst of an economic boom. As part of its 'World Market Series' booklets for clients, JWT published *The Australian Market* in 1959. In it, Australia was described as 'one of the world's principal market areas; its future expansion will be firmly based on increasing population and growing investment'.[20] As technology overcame the tyranny of distance, Australia presented an increasingly enticing prospect for major firms with international ambitions. Such conditions would also catch the attention of advertising agencies harbouring similar aspirations. Following in McCann-Erickson's wake, a steady stream of multi-national agencies entered the Australian market by way of outright buyouts, new start-ups, and minority shareholdings.

The formation of Hansen Rubensohn-McCann Erickson (HRMcCE) in October 1959 marked the beginning of a new era in Australian advertising. Unlike the previous generation of foreign-owned agencies that had successfully commenced operations in Australia, McCann-Erickson opted to buy out an established local agency. Hansen-Rubensohn opened its doors in Sydney in 1928. The agency's co-founder Sim Rubensohn had previously worked in real estate and at Goldberg Advertising. Something of a wheeler-dealer, Rubensohn had built up his agency on the back of a strong network of business and political associates. However, the schmoozing was reserved for clients only. Within the office, Rubensohn was an autocrat. Bryce Courtenay thus described him as an 'utter bastard' towards his staff.[21] Despatch boys such as Ian McDonald were

ordered to perform a range of tasks for the boss that had little
to do with the agency's operations – from working till dark
in Rubensohn's garden out in Dural to carrying his racetrack
winnings from the bookies to the bank. By 1959 Rubensohn
headed Australia's third-largest agency: for the six months spanning June–December, the agency's 140-strong staff helped it
amass a profit of £14,304.[22]

Selling out to McCann-Erickson at the height of the agency's success would provide the 55-year-old Rubensohn with a
healthy nest egg for his retirement. McCann-Erickson's decision
to enter Australia was no less straightforward. The industry
press thus reported that the '[m]ajor reason for the Australian
affiliation is McCann's need to supply advertising, marketing
and merchandising services to its many clients which have set
up local operations'.[23] While the major soft drink manufacturer
Coca-Cola was not mentioned, it was integral to the move.
McCann-Erickson had secured the account in 1955, promising to facilitate Coke's strategy of integrating its American
and international campaigns. Realising this aim meant that
Australia was important for McCann-Erickson and Coca-Cola
alike. Australia's geographical position also played in its favour,
as it offered McCann-Erickson a convenient springboard for
entering into South East Asian markets.

Less than a year later, another Australian agency announced
that it had formally joined forces with an international agency.
United Service Publicity, better known as USP, was formed in
1945 by ex-servicemen in Melbourne. Over the next fifteen years
the agency attracted a steady stream of new clients, including
GMH, Heinz and Shell. Success enabled it to create an in-
house research office as well as a marketing department.[24] It also
attracted the attention of the British agency S.H. Benson, which

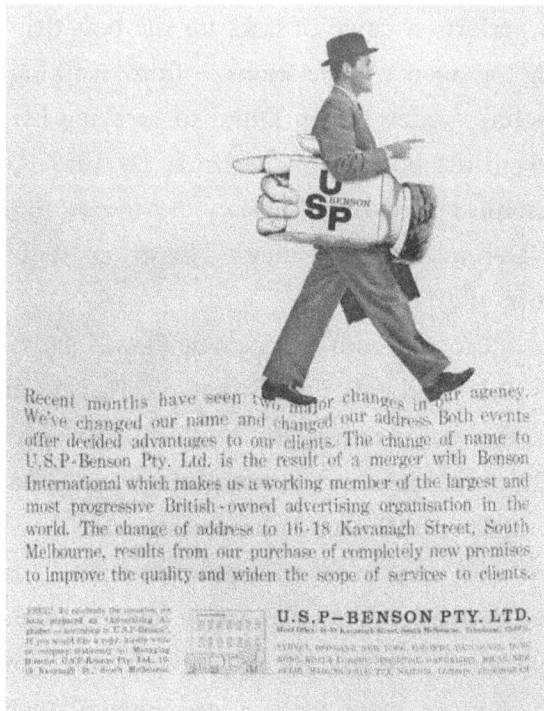

Figure 1.2 British agency S.H. Benson enters Australia.
B&T, *18 May 1961, p. 18 (Courtesy of B&T)*

held the Shell account and was in the process of restructuring its international network of offices. USP presented a logical partner and in August 1960 it announced that it would be selling a 25 per cent share to the British agency. Announcing the deal, USP's chairman denied that his agency had sold out to overseas interests: 'Although the company's new name – USP-Benson – suggested an equal partnership in Australia, the British company had a minority interest, and the Australian management group continued to operate precisely as in the past'.[25] This minority interest increased in 1967 when both S.H. Benson and its new American partner Needham, Harper & Steers bought into the agency. Further international deals saw the agency move away from its British partners to become USP Needham in 1971.

Where McCann-Erickson's entry into Australia came as a welcome surprise, Ted Bates's arrival was a jolt. In March 1964, Australia's largest agency, George Patterson (known as Patts), announced that it would be selling an 80 per cent stake to the American agency. Speaking to the industry press, Patts's chairman, L.W. 'Bill' Farnsworth, explained that the deal was 'the inevitable result of over 20 years' close association, mutual clients and friendship between the principals of both companies'.[26] George Patterson's presence in South East Asia was a key part of the deal, providing Ted Bates with an instant network in the region (see Chapter 3).

On the Patterson side, the deal also addressed a problem concerning the cost of the agency's shares – its size and profitability meant that few Australians could afford to invest in the agency.[27] Despite being the subject of a takeover, George Patterson's name remained in place. Farnsworth also declared that Patts would 'continue to operate in exactly the same manner as it has over the past 30 years' and that it would 'be completely independent from the New York Company'.[28]

For the trade journal *B&T*, such promises could not detract from the fact that the largest agency in Australia had sold out so quickly. While it recognised that such deals 'represent a fact of life and the increasing internationalisation of business', *B&T* looked ahead with trepidation, asking whether there would 'be any large Australian agencies left in a few years when the Americans have stopped picking the field over, and what is this going to mean to Australian advertisers and media?'[29]

The flow of multi-national agencies entering Australia did not abate. Within months of Patts's takeover, rumours were circulating about Foote Cone & Belding's (FCB) entry into Australia. Having recently become a public company, FCB was in the midst of developing a worldwide presence. By November 1964, it was official. FCB bought out Briggs, Canny, James, and Paramor, which had been a merger of two smaller Sydney and Melbourne agencies that had sought a national presence five years earlier. Maintaining its wary outlook, *B&T* observed that '[t]here are misgivings and headshakings at the loss of independence of a fine Australian agency – but no anti-American sentiments'.[30] Over the next few years, the flow continued. Campbell-Ewald returned in 1966 when it merged with Coudrey-Gotham to become Coudrey-Campbell-Ewald. Grey merged twice with local shops, first with Browne & Bruce in 1965 and then with a larger local agency, Thompson Ansell Blunden, in 1967. The British agency Masius, Wynne-Williams acquired Australia's first international agency (Goldberg Advertising) and Melbourne's oldest agency (Paton-Hughes) in 1968. The regularity of such mergers attracted less media coverage and the trade press's cursory accounts of these mergers in the second half the decade revealed that mergers had ceased to be front-page news.

Leo Burnett's acquisition of Jackson Wain in 1970 generated greater comment. Over the 1960s, Jackson Wain had established its own network of offices across Australia, the UK, and South East Asia. By 1970 it boasted the third-largest billings. Already in the mid-60s, commentators were predicting that it would need an international partner to maintain its dominance in South East Asia.[31] As Australianness had become a part of the Jackson Wain brand, its decision to sell out to its long-time partner, Leo Burnett, in 1970 was all the more surprising. Ever the salesman, Jackson Wain's director, Frank Grace, looked ahead not backwards. He presented the takeover 'as a logical flow-on to the Australian agency's establishment of an overseas network' that would 'more readily identify the agency as a member of the world-wide group'.[32]

Of course, buying out an agency was not the only strategy. A small but significant number of multi-national agencies opted to enter Australia by establishing their own branches from scratch. While the start-up costs and the lack of local accounts meant that this was a more vulnerable option, it nevertheless facilitated greater consistency across the multi-national agency's networks. In 1962 the British agency Pritchard Wood commenced operations in Sydney. The agency was owned by the Interpublic holding company, which also included McCann-Erickson and HRMcCE. Former general manager of HRMcCE John Bristow would head the new operation. As the expanding HRMcCE was struggling with conflicting accounts, Pritchard Wood offered an alternative that ensured that the profits remained in the same company. Vic Nicholson recalled that the Pritchard Wood title was deliberately chosen to 'contrast with American influence. It would give rationalisation to the British international company and to the Anglophile Australian that there was an alternative in international agencies'.[33] Conceding that Pritchard Wood was treated as little more than a sideline, Nicholson revealed that the agency's primary function in the Australian market was a strategic one.

Ogilvy & Mather's entry into Australia was less opportunistic than that of Pritchard Wood. In 1964 the British-based Crowther & Mather and the US-based Ogilvy, Benson & Mather merged to form Ogilvy & Mather International (O&M). Headed by the quintessential adman David Ogilvy, the new agency quickly consolidated its operations in Europe and North America before considering its options in the Southern Hemisphere. Michael

Ball, an Australian working in the agency's Toronto office who had been involved in the merger, was selected by Ogilvy to tour Australia and the Asia-Pacific region and to develop a plan for the agency. In 1965 the 29-year-old spent several months travelling across the region to ascertain whether O&M should enter the region and how. Ball advised O&M to enter Australia but not to buy into an agency, as the good ones were unavailable. Moreover, he felt that O&M's research-led approach to advertising offered something unique to the Australian market: 'I thought that if we go and offer something quite different in Australia, then we will stand out, and I can go back as an Australian with credibility and start from scratch.'[34] The Australian office would then be used as a base for entering New Zealand and Asia.

The arrival of Young and Rubicam (Y&R) in 1969 was equally planned. Rumours of Y&R setting up in Australia had been circulating since 1964. It was the recruitment of Arthur Holland to work in the agency's New York offices in 1967, however, that signalled Y&R's intent to set up an Australian branch. Described 'as a leading figure in creative advertising in Australia' who could work as an art director, a copywriter, and a manager, Holland had been the principal of Rodgers Holland Everingham, one of the first agencies in Australia to prioritise the creative side of advertising over the account-service side.[35] He was to spend a year or two as a senior creative at Y&R before returning to Australia to establish a Y&R office. The appointment of someone with creative and management experience to train in the agency's headquarters hinted at the type of operation that Y&R hoped to establish in Australia. Y&R's Sydney office opened its doors in May 1969.

Y&R was given three years to cover its start-up costs – much longer than JWT had in 1930. But without any accounts to its name, the new operation would need all the time it could get. The fate of Y&R in Australia lay in the hands of its staff. Where some agencies had a reputation for sending out average or poor performing staff – known as 'dead wood' – to their Australian offices, Y&R sent out award winners.[36] Holland returned as creative director, but it was Joseph 'Joe' DeDeo who led Y&R's Australian push. The Princeton-educated DeDeo was admired by colleagues and competitors alike. Dennis Merchant, who had been the agency's first local recruit, considers him 'the best boss I ever had' and one of the best 'all round' advertising men who 'had a great understanding of the creative process, [was a] very astute judge of creative work … [and] came from a research background'.[37] DeDeo later recalled that Y&R had considered mergers, but he was of the view that 'If we had anything to contribute, we should be able to make it on our own. I felt this so strongly that I said it was the only basis on which I'd take the assignment.'[38]

By the end of the decade, Australia's advertising agency industry had undergone a radical transformation. Through strategic acquisitions, mergers, and start-ups, the multinational agencies had come to dominate the scene. While some were perturbed by this development, the vast majority of Australian advertising professionals considered it part and parcel of con- temporary advertising – particularly those who hoped to attract the next overseas suitor. Entering the Australian market was but the first step for these agencies. The next step, the establishment of a successful office, would prove to be a much harder and longer task.

Establishing the Right Ideas
'Every Thompson office derives its particular character from its

setting', explained the in-house journal *J. Walter Thompson News* in 1959. 'Sydney, basking in a Southern California climate, is best described as a shirt-sleeve office … In structure, it is Thompson-New York in microcosm'.[39] After thirty years in Australia, JWT had struck a balance between the local and the international. For those agencies that had just landed in Australia, the immediate task was to shift the balance towards the international. Having spent so much on their Australian ventures, these multi-national agencies were determined to ensure that their latest acquisitions conformed to the ideologies, strategies, and practices that had helped elevate them into global corporations.

In 1960, Sylvester 'Pat' Weaver, chairman of McCann-Erickson International, landed in Australia. His task was to introduce local staff to McCann-Erickson. From a New York viewpoint, Hansen-Rubensohn's 32-year history counted for little; HRMcCE was little more than twelve months old. Weaver had arrived to open a day-long seminar entitled 'This is McCann'. Nine speakers addressed the audience, using films, tapes, and some '700 colour slides' to 'familiarise Australian executives with the McCann-Erickson techniques and concepts'. Clients and media were also invited to listen to the speakers talk about 'communications research and McCann's contribution to this progress'.[40] As research and marketing had been the cornerstone of McCann-Erickson's success in the US, it was no surprise that HRMcCE would be expected to adopt a more research-oriented approach. Such an emphasis further affected an impact on the agency's internal operations, which became highly systematised.[41] The agency also established a reputation for being American in terms of its outlook on advertising as well as its cutthroat internal politics – such impressions would deepen in the 1970s as Rubensohn withdrew from the agency's operations.[42]

If HR McCE projected the image of being the big American firm, O&M considered itself 'the most international of international agencies … we called ourselves "one agency indivisible"'.[43] To establish consistency across the network, O&M distributed 'magic lanterns'. Based on David Ogilvy's writings, these slides told 'the story of how to make an ad … how to sell automotive, how to sell fashion' and were used to inculcate staff and clients alike with the Ogilvy way.[44] Attendance to these slideshows was often mandatory and staff would grumble about having to go to 'another one of those things again', especially when it delayed them from getting to the pub.[45] O&M's indoctrination efforts did not end with the slideshows. Julian Martin, who moved to O&M from Masius, was impressed by the highly structured approach to other parts of agency practice: 'There was a book for everything … There was a book on how to write a letter.' While Martin had written letters before, it initially took him weeks to get his supervisor's approval for his first letter for O&M: 'She wouldn't let this letter go out until it was done exactly the Ogilvy way – purpose of letter, background section, key recommendations, discussion, summary.'[46]

With their red carpets, black doors, and bare white walls, O&M's offices in Australia were little different to any other O&M office in the world. The subsequent office alterations that saw 'David Ogilvy's mantra written all over the walls' further tightened the connection between the agency's outposts and its charismatic leader.[47] Former staffers such as Doug Watson recall the agency rules and the expectation that staff would strictly adhere to them: 'there was no individual respect, it was like an army'.[48] Agency rules and Ogilvy's homilies not only governed the office decor and creative output, at the agency's upper echelons, the wives and partners of senior staff were vetted. These women were also given advice about the appropriate ways of entertaining client partners.[49] Michael Ball outlines the rationale for this approach: 'companies need to have a culture and a set of beliefs. By establishing a clear template for operations in Australia and worldwide, O&M sought to facilitate the management of this network whilst creating a recognisable brand for clients.'[50]

Others adopted different ways of inculcating staff with the agency doctrine. At Leo Burnett offices in Australia and across the globe, a bowl of green apples at the reception desk served as a daily reminder of the agency's founder and its New York roots.[51] Y&R often used gifts to staff to build up goodwill within its network. While some were of a personal nature, others sought to foster greater unity across the ranks. Unable to export the profits from its Italian operation, Y&R bought a huge slab of Italian marble. It was then cut down into blocks which were distributed to each staff member across the globe. Inscribed on each block were the agency's mottoes 'Understand through Discipline' and 'Compel with Imagination'.[52]

Maintaining a global network required more than instructions and inspirational gifts. As experts in the field of communication, multi-national agencies understood that they also needed to maintain strong and clear lines of communication within their own networks. In 1960 McCann-Erickson vice-president Robert E. Healy explained that 'When I visited Australia two years ago … I said we would bring advertising know-how and techniques to Australia.' Recent visits from senior McCann figures were therefore 'in keeping with our policy of sending top officials throughout the world, so that they should thoroughly acquaint themselves with clients and staffs'.[53]

The advent of the jetliner meant that Australia was becoming more accessible than ever before. Keeping 'an eye on the natives' through increasingly regular visits became a normal part of agency life. By 1978, Geoff Lindley of O&M Sydney joked that 'we like to think the head office is a Boeing over Los Angeles or somewhere'.[54] The impact of such arrivals depended on the visitor's place in the agency hierarchy. Senior international figures inevitably warranted significant attention both within the office and the industry press. At Y&R, Luella Copeland-Smith recollects that there was 'an absolute furore' in the agency in the week leading up to the arrival of a key visitor from the head office.[55] For David Ogilvy's 1979 visit, a local public relations consultant was hired to handle the guru's media appearances.[56]

In between visits the agency's head office was kept abreast of developments in Australia through regular reports. The most important of these was the financial report, which was used by head office to measure the success of its Australian investment. Reporting procedures appeared to become more stringent as time wore on. In the 1970s HRMcCE sent through quarterly reports to New York, while Y&R filed monthly reports.[57] By the 1980s the UK agency Saatchi & Saatchi was receiving daily reports.[58] Technology in the form of telexes and faxes facilitated this increased flow of information moving both ways.

Of course, some agencies enjoyed greater autonomy than others. As the largest and most profitable agency in Australia, George Patterson was in a position to keep its overseas owners at bay – and senior staff knew it. A popular anecdote recounted by ex-Patts staffers concerned the chairman Farnsworth and his rule of refusing to meet uninvited visitors. When Ted Bates sent through a message informing Farnsworth that one of their accountants would be visiting over the next week, Farnsworth instructed the agency's lift driver to deny the American permission to enter the building. After three days of waiting in the hotel, the visitor returned home, whereupon Farnsworth announced he was ready to receive him.[59] An Australian flag was also visible whenever senior American dignitaries visited, a none-too-subtle reminder that the most profitable part of the Ted Bates network did not consider itself subservient to its overseas owners.[60]

Developing the Right Approach

'Getting your hands on information in 1970 was a very time-consuming and quite often expensive process', notes Ian Dawson.[61] Larger agencies such as JWT, therefore, operated their own libraries which subscribed to advertising and market-ing periodicals published locally and overseas. *Printer's Ink*, *Ad Age*, and *Campaign* were commonly read by staff along with the advertisements contained in such publications as *Vogue*. In addi-tion to providing background information on campaigns, these publications exposed readers to new ideas and approaches being used overseas. Creative staff encountered similar difficulties. 'We were interested in what the rest of the world was doing', observes the television producer Helene Nicol, adding that 'it wasn't as easy to see it [overseas work] then as it is now'.[62] Show reels of award-winning television commercials (TVCs) from overseas were therefore screened at cinemas, while individual agencies used their international connections to gain access to the creative work being undertaken on pertinent accounts. For television post-production experts such as Mike Reed, overseas show reels were inspirational: 'you saw 52 fresh ideas in the space of five minutes, sometimes you would have to spend four or five days reading a book to maybe get an idea ... it was instantaneous like a drug ... you got that hit'.[63]

At HRMcCE, the new approach was to be the implementa-tion of McCann-Erickson's marketing and research methods.

From the announcement of the merger it was anticipated that 'many new marketing techniques will be introduced in Australia, which deviate from the established pattern, but have proved extremely successful overseas'. Specifically, HRMcCE would have access to 'a special formula for pre-testing advertising, which to date has been a close kept secret of McCann's. It takes note of 169 elements which influence the effectiveness of an advertisement, and has been employed with marked accuracy.'[64] With the weight of the McCann research machine behind it, HRMcCE needed to spruik its new approach to prospective clients. General manager John Bristow conceded that research did not come cheaply before adding that 'relative to the cost of failure arising from lack of intimate knowledge of the market, research appropriations seem almost minute'.[65]

International connections also provided Australians with new frameworks for creating and testing advertising campaigns in a more strategic way. Each agency adopted its own approach. In the late 1950s staff at JWT were using the T-Square tool.[66] Used across the JWT network since 1919, the T-Square required staff to consider five questions: what are we selling; to whom are we selling; where are we selling; when are we selling; and how are we selling.[67]

At Lintas, advertisements followed the highly prescriptive UPGA (Unilever Plan for Good Advertising) guideline. By the late 1960s, Stephen King in London's JWT office challenged these marketing-focused tools. Calling for tools that firstly identified the desired response from consumers and secondly helped generate advertising that would stimulate the desired response, King and Jeremy Bullmore devised the T-Plan.[68] The T-Plan asked five questions: where are we; why are we there; where could we be; how could we get there; and are we getting there.

By 1970, the T-Plan was being used at JWT in Sydney. Having received little such direction at his previous agencies HRMcCE and Lintas, Alan Robertson considered this 'much more disciplined way of approaching' advertising to be a revelation.[69]

Other agencies similarly devised tools that helped systematise their marketing and creative approaches. John Clemenger, which sold out a 35 per cent share to Batten, Barton, Durstine & Osborn (BBDO) in 1972, readily utilised the BBDO four-point process: '1. Know your prime prospect. 2. Know your prime prospect's problem. 3. Know your product and how it can solve your prospect's problems. 4. And break the boredom barrier.'[70] Y&R's Strategy Selection Outline and SCORE (Simple, Credible, Original, Relevant, Empathetic) creative briefing format were both imported directly from the head office and were warmly received by local staff – some of whom would continue to use these principles long after they had moved on from the agency.[71]

A simpler way of ensuring the right approach was to copy a TVC produced overseas. As Australian regulations required all TVCs to contain at least 80 per cent Australian content, advertisers could not simply import commercials. Coca-Cola's desire for a single image across the globe meant that HRMcCE was initially re-filming American TVCs in Australia. Its first original TVC for Coca-Cola appeared in January 1961.[72] Re-shooting overseas commercials frame for frame would continue to be common practice through to the 1980s.[73] Another way of circumventing Australian regulations and ensuring that the campaign adopted the right approach was the practice of 'ghost-crewing'. This practice saw Australian crews being sent abroad to produce a TVC but the actual work was entirely done by overseas production teams.[74] While it was an expensive strategy, it nevertheless ensured that the campaign would follow the right approach.

Importing the Right People

In 1958, Lloyd Ring (Deke) Coleman stepped down as the managing director of JWT in Australia. For the last seventeen years he had led the agency's Australian office, having previously directed the JWT's continental European operations from Paris. Described as a 'world citizen', Coleman was born in Brockport, New York, and studied at Rochester University and Columbia University.[75] His replacement, the straight-talking John Sharman, had joined the Sydney office's despatch department in 1941. Sharman was also the first local to head JWT's Australian operations and would go on to become an executive vice-president responsible for Asia–Pacific, South and Central America, and Canada. While Sharman demonstrated that Australians were as capable as their American or British counterparts, various agencies nevertheless felt that their Australian investments would benefit from an increase in international experience.

The first individuals despatched by head office to Australia would take up management positions. At HRMcCE, David Hopkins was moved from the Los Angeles office to Sydney in 1962 to take over from John Bristow as general manager. Peter Clemenger described him as 'an innate politician'. Writing on Australian conditions for the American trade journal *Advertising Age*, Hopkins revealed a diplomatic pragmatism. While Australians were described as being 'very receptive to new ideas', he also cautioned readers against applying American marketing techniques in a doctrinaire manner.[76] In the battle for the Nabisco account, Clemenger remembered Hopkins's less diplomatic side: 'We were the local boys with a bit of flair, but the McCann international strength finally crushed us. They moved in the "heavies" from New York, and that was that.'[77] Another senior American, Vincent Tutching, was brought out to open HRMcCE's Melbourne branch. Local staff claimed that the appointment of a vice-president of McCann-Erickson International to this post was a vote of confidence, which 'demonstrates the importance McCann attaches to the growing market in Australia and the South West Pacific'.[78]

As O&M and Y&R were both opening entirely new branches, the new management was directly selected by head office. However, the recently arrived managers at both agencies wasted little time in bringing on board local staff. Ball explained that O&M's 'staff will be Australian and we will be looking for Australians with international advertising experience ... But there will be with us generally a senior copywriter from an over-seas branch in rotation.'[79] Visiting his three-month old offices in Australia, Ed Ney, head of Y&R's international operations, boasted that his agency was similarly trying not to be heavy-handed in its appointments: 'We have 1500 people employed worldwide outside the USA and of these only a handful – 25 to 30 – are Americans.'[80]

As the management issues abated, the Australian offices of multi-national agencies looked to import staff with specific new skills or expertise. In 1960 HRMcCE brought out Mike Larbalestier from the Marplan research agency in London to direct its new research department. As Clemenger's anecdote about Hopkins reveals, expert copywriters would be flown in when agencies were pitching for new accounts. Graham Nunn, who worked on Y&R's pitch for the Chrysler account that famously included a surprise visit from legendary racing driver Stirling Moss, highlights the important role played by overseas experts: 'It was the Sydney office of Y&R that basically put the pitch together. They came down to Adelaide for the pitch but they had gotten in … Al Hagar, who was a car specialist from Y&R Detroit … they also had the Americans from Sydney and they were all ex-New York Americans.'[81] Y&R would land the client, and Hagar would later become head of Y&R in Australia.

A more common import was the English copywriter. While reports in the trade press in the early 1960s reveal that English agencies lacked the research orientation of their American counterparts, Australian offices displayed a growing admiration for English creativity and were eager to emulate the clever advertising coming out of London. Moreover, importing saved them the time and costs of training someone.[82] In 1968 Lionel Hunt noticed a copywriter opening at Masius in Melbourne. Hunt had previously worked as an account executive in agencies across Australia before returning to Britain for two years. The interview was conducted at the agency's London office with Hunt as the 'lunch companion' of Jack Wynne-Williams.[83] Having secured Wynne-Williams's approval, Hunt could take up his position at the agency's Melbourne office.

A decade later, agencies would adopt a more proactive approach to recruiting creative talent. Outlining Grey's recruitment procedure, creative director Peter Carey explained that '[t]here are only two other countries where you'd find really good art directors and we ruled out the US because of the high salaries. We started going through the UK agency art book – *Design and Art Direction* – to see who was doing good work there.'[84] Recruitment agencies also set up London offices creatives and account service staff alike to Australia.[85] Many also arrived of their own volition. Some were persuaded by an Australian spouse wanting to return home, others were lured by the promise of sun, sand, and surf. Frustrated by the hierarchy of JWT in London, where the senior account service positions were reserved for Oxbridge graduates, Trevor Fearnley arrived in Sydney as a '£10 Pom' in 1972. He had nothing lined up: JWT had no vacancies nor did HRMcCE. His experience at JWT London, however, persuaded HRMcCE to speak to him. Despite arriving 30 minutes late for the interview, Fearnley walked out with a job at the multi-national agency.

———————

When McCann-Erickson announced its intention to enter Australia, *Broadcasting and Television* exclaimed 'Let 'em come!' predicting that the '[e]xtension of the McCann-Erickson agency to Australia will, we bet, heighten the interest in Down Under along Madison Avenue'.[86] It certainly did. By the early 1970s, the vast majority of major multi-national agencies boasted offices in Australia. While the arrival of agencies from overseas had been nothing new, the speed and number of agencies setting up in Australia certainly was. Their reasons varied. Most were led by clients, but many were also motivated by entrepreneurial ambition. Each had brought a new perspective on advertising and agency practice, which was reflected in the different ways they went about establishing successful branches in Australia. Of course, the task of setting up the agency's Australian operations was also part of the broader project – the establishment and maintenance of a global network. The next step would be to send Australian staff out into the world to broaden their experiences and sharpen their understanding of contemporary global advertising.

CHAPTER TWO

STUDYING ABROAD

At 3.35pm on 29 July 1959, a gleaming new Qantas 707 screamed down the runway at Sydney's Kingsford Smith airport before swiftly soaring into the winter skies. It was the inaugural flight in the first jet service linking Sydney to San Francisco via Fiji and Hawaii. Headed 'today ... the world becomes smaller', an advertisement for the flight predicted a new era of travel: 'There are no words to describe fully the incomparable comfort, convenience and pleasure of pure jet travel ... You must experience them for yourself.'[1] It would be some time before those responsible for such copy would find themselves jetting off overseas. Overseeing the finances at George Patterson, Russell McLay recalls that travel was expensive: 'You didn't say "get on a plane and go up there for a week". You'd be talking about an equivalent today of $20,000 maybe. You don't do that lightly.'[2] However, as the costs fell, a growing number of Australian advertising men (and in the main they were men) were able to experience the 'pleasure of pure jet travel', as they flew out to the agency's offices in the US, Canada, and the UK.

The benefits of travel were discussed in *Broadcasting and Television* in 1960.[3] Bill Lockley, the general manager at HRMcCE, identified three key reasons why advertising executives should travel abroad. The first was to broaden the traveller's awareness – 'an indefinable "something" is acquired that comes only from rubbing shoulders with different people in different countries, in different situations and of different circumstances.' Secondly, travel was educational. It not only enabled travellers to see 'people and places which previously he has only read about', they could also draw on this knowledge when speaking 'to clients – often very widely travelled people themselves – on their own terms'. Thirdly, Lockley considered travel to be inspirational: 'Personal acquaintance with so many new ideas, principles and techniques in other parts of the world can't help but fire the travelling executive with enthusiasm … It is certainly inspirational to see a really big New York agency in action and to talk to and work with some of the key figures in the advertising world today.' Agencies large and small increasingly saw the benefits of such travel and were willing to send staff to gain firsthand experience of the latest developments overseas. The acceleration in the number of Australian advertising professionals travelling to the major advertising centres from the 1960s both reflected a changing world and contributed to it. As travel became a part of staff training, it would also become more formalised. The multi-national agencies that sent their employees abroad were not only expecting the returns outlined by Lockley, they were also hoping to capitalise on their global networks.

Informal Travel

In 1913 George Patterson made an important decision: 'Quite suddenly, despite slender finances, I decided to go overseas to try to get some real advertising experience.'[4] He travelled to London, but finding that 'English advertising practices did not offer the type of experience I was seeking', Patterson travelled on to New York.[5] International travel was not new to advertising professionals. In the interwar period, the entrepreneurial Frank

Goldberg was a regular visitor to the UK, the US, and, of course, New Zealand.[6] Until the influx of multi-national agencies into Australia in the 1960s, Australian advertising professionals had largely funded their own travels abroad. For Australian agencies, sending a staff member to London or New York was both costly and time-consuming. Moreover, few had any formal connections with overseas offices. Needing 'a change of scene' and 'to see generally what was going in the world at large', W.A. 'Bill' McNair from JWT's research department was able to arrange six months' leave in 1938 to visit the agency's London and New York offices – albeit at his own expense.[7] Such self-funded trips would continue into the post-war period. As access to the US became restricted with the introduction of the 'green card' shortly after World War II, Australian advertising professionals travelling abroad usually ended up in London.

The decision to travel 'home' was not necessarily motivated by a desire to enhance one's advertising acumen. Marion von Adlerstein had long wanted to travel to Britain and Europe. In 1956 she accompanied her then-husband to London. After working in a department store and spending the summer travelling Europe, von Adlerstein applied for a position at the London Press Exchange (LPE). 'Australians', she notes 'were very suspect over there because they … got a job earned a little bit of money and said … hooroo we're off to the Continent'. As a former colleague from Sydney had been with LPE for five years, the agency was prepared to appoint von Adlerstein as a copywriter. She would remain with LPE for five years. After seven years in the UK, she returned to Australia – for 'a working holiday'.[8]

Of course, many were more career-minded when they set out on their overseas adventure. In 1963, a 19-year-old Derek

Hansen had spent a couple of years in New Zealand's advertising industry and knew that his career lay in copywriting. However, he was already underwhelmed with what he was seeing around him: 'the copywriting they were doing ... was so prosaic, it was so proper ... I just simply couldn't do this ... I thought bugger this. Full of ego and confidence in my own ability, I got on a boat and went to England.'[9] In the early 1950s, Bruce Jarrett worked as a copywriter and an art director, a feat that few in the industry could manage. Correctly predicting that television would have an enormous impact on the creative side of an agency's work, he looked abroad. Britain did not yet have commercial television while the US restricted immigration. Jarrett, therefore, opted to hone his television skills in Canada.[10]

As Graeme Cox discovered, travelling abroad did not guarantee international advertising experience. Having scrimped and saved so that he and his wife could travel to England, the account executive arrived in 1962 and duly contacted London's largest agencies for work. He received a lukewarm response. When interviewed, he discovered that the problem lay with him being an account executive. Interviewers thus explained: 'You are new to this country ... You don't know anything about English markets, ... English marketing, ... English media. ... You might be able to talk up a storm at a face to face with your client. But you don't know what advice to give. ... If you were a writer, [that's] a different ... maybe there might be a position for you.' Cox subsequently took up a job in sales and adopted the view that he was on a working holiday.[11]

The flow of informal travellers seeking professional experience abroad would of course continue throughout the 1960s, 1970s, and 1980s, and remains a rite of passage for many young Australians. However, the arrival of the multi-national agencies, coupled with the advent of quicker and cheaper flights, offered an easier way for Australians to gain access to such experiences.

Newsmakers

The flow of advertising professionals arriving in Australia and departing Australia for overseas was regularly reported in the industry press. In addition to feature stories on eminent arrivals, *B&T* also documented the arrival and departure of the less noteworthy in its 'Newsmakers' column. The information on the flow of staff overseas was provided by agencies and many used the column to engage in low-level public relations while others simply ignored it. Offering a snapshot of the flow of advertising professionals rather than a definitive record, the 'Newsmakers' column nevertheless provides a unique insight into the increasing links between Australia and the global advertising industry.

In 1960, the 'Newsmakers' column contained details on movement of some eighty individuals. Many were moving between numerous destinations. Almost half of the trips involved the UK (47 per cent) and a fifth concerned the US (21 per cent). Canada (11 per cent) and Europe (9 per cent) were the other major destinations. In 1970, the overall number of individuals involved in overseas travel had climbed to 126. Although the actual number of individuals moving between Australia and these four regions remained relatively consistent, the overall proportion of trips fell from 86 per cent to 67 per cent. Travel between Australia and the US (23 per cent) and Europe (11 per cent) had marginally increased, while the movement to and from Canada had marginally decreased (8 per cent). The most significant changes occurred in the flow between Australia and the UK, which had fallen significantly to 26 per cent. At the same time, travel within the Asia-Pacific region grew almost three-fold, from 10 per cent to 29 per cent. This growth reveals a broader shift in the way that Australia's advertising agencies were connecting with the international advertising industry (see also Chapter 3).

Illustrating the growing importance of global networks, multi-national agencies were the most diligent in reporting their movements in the 'Newsmakers' column during the 1960s. HRMcCE was the most active with ninety reports detailing their movements. Lintas (forty) and FCB (thirty-seven) were also active in this field. While O&M had only arrived in 1967, its twenty announcements were only fractionally fewer than the twenty-one listed by the long-standing JWT offices. As Australian-owned agencies with international networks, both Fortune (twenty-seven) and Jackson Wain (nineteen) also featured prominently. In contrast, very few movements were recorded at Australia's largest agency. While George Patterson proudly claimed to operate autonomously from Ted Bates, its absence from 'Newsmakers' reflected a reluctance to reveal too much to competitors rather than any actual reluctance to engage with its international networks.

Formal Networks

'[S]ometimes I wonder if we aren't a travel agency as well as an advertising agency', mused USP's general manager, Harper Wilson, in 1960, 'but that is part of the price we and most other leading Australian agencies pay willingly to keep ourselves on top'.[12] As agencies such as USP sold out to overseas interests, travel assumed an even greater importance. Circulating valued staff through the agency's global networks not only exposed the individual to the latest developments overseas, it helped build greater cohesion across the network as travellers eagerly applied their skills upon returning home.

Senior management were the first to be flown abroad at the agency's expense. Six months after helping negotiate the HRMcCE merger, John Bristow was sent on a two-and-a-half-month tour of McCann-Erickson's operations in New York and London. Upon his return to Australia, Bristow announced the agency's plan to send more staff to visit McCann-Erickson's offices in the US and the UK.[13] Lockley, the general manager of the Sydney office, and Bill Diamond, a senior group head, were the first to be sent abroad.[14] They would join counter-parts from McCann-Erickson's Mexican, Brazilian, Argentine, Colombian, and German offices to attend the agency's inaugural International Workshop in New York. Lockley and Diamond were not the only Australians in attendance. Three others who had recently been recruited from Canadian agencies by Bristow also participated before returning home to Australia.

The Workshop was to be the first of a semi-annual series that outlined the agency's approach to account service, creativity, marketing, public relations, sales promotion, and research. A few months later, Tony Clark, a group director, and Charles Scruby, the head of the television and radio department, were despatched to New York.[15] In 1963 Lockley was sent to Harvard University, where he was enrolled in the thirteen-week advanced management programme together with managers from the agency's New York and Cologne offices. For Lockley, the course was intensive and eye-opening: 'I feel I now have a wider appreciation of the environmental and other factors that affect commercial and industrial undertakings.'[16] By the late 1960s, the agency was sending out the next level of agency leaders. In 1967 a senior copywriter, Peter May, spent six months in a 'combined working and training programme in Interpublic offices in London, New York and Puerto Rico'. May claimed the experience gained abroad was more comprehensive than the 'usual three-week "quicky" tour'.[17]

At George Patterson, the connection with the head office in the United States was more muted than that at HRMcCE. Patts's managing director Bill Farnsworth outlined the formal training scheme that had developed in the five years since selling out to Ted Bates:

> I would say the biggest contribution would be in the training of our staff in New York and London and the visits three times a year of a Bates creative director to Australia. All the technology used in our research is very largely based on Bates techniques, but again it is an interchange and they have benefitted from some of the work we've done. There is constant interchange of staff, although there is no training of Bates staff here. We usually have two people in New York all the time.[18]

Geoff Cousins was in the process of vacating his role as managing director of Cathay in Hong Kong to take on the role of managing the Sydney office when he was informed that he would be heading to New York for a year. The move to the US was initiated by senior managers at Ted Bates, who had been concerned that they knew little about the man who was next in line to head the George Patterson operation. With a young family and already running parts of the Sydney business, Cousins was reluctant to go to New York: 'What the hell was I going to do for a year? I clearly couldn't run a business or anything even vaguely like it. I got over there, and they didn't really know what to do with me either.' He rejected an offer to work in Bates's international division, telling them: 'If I'm here, I've got to be here for a year, I will do something useful – I'll write ads.' After giving the New York office enough time to meet him, Cousins returned to take over Patts's Sydney office. At the junior level, Patts set up intra-agency competitions where young staff members could win a placement in New York – a scheme that was also replicated at John Clemenger.[19]

Figure 2.1 Scholarships provided George Patterson's junior staff an opportunity to gain international experience.
Advertising News, *4 August 1978, p. 6 (Courtesy of AdNews)*

As Australian operations of both Y&R and O&M had started from scratch, management in both agencies understood the importance of using overseas travel to train local staff to follow the standard protocols. In 1972 Graham Nunn, a young copywriter, was selected from Y&R's Adelaide office to attend a month-long programme with other young creatives at the agency's New York office. Nunn noted that they were 'taught or indoctrinated into the Y&R way'. He recalls that 'they had just developed this thing called the Work Plan, which was their strategy document' and that it 'was going to be their next big thing'. As such, he and fellow attendees were 'schooled in the thing every day, and they had different heavies from different departments'. Nunn was then expected to return to Adelaide and 'really make that thing work'. O&M had 'a policy of bringing in talent from its overseas offices and affording Australian executives the chance to work abroad and travel'.[20] Its overseas training programmes were as much about inculcating staff with the agency's ethos as they were about acquiring new skills. Michael Ball explains that this was a very conscious emphasis: 'It's easier to take people from scratch and train them in those beliefs than to get people who are so cemented in their views … To change those views is harder than to train them from scratch.' His aim was to train them up to become 'disciples of Ogilvy and Mather'. Faie Davis, who joined the agency in the 1970s, remembers attending international creative meetings where David Ogilvy himself would address participants. Davis feels that such seminars were 'very entrepreneurial' and helped foster loyalty and camaraderie within the agency ranks. Over the 1980s, O&M's Australian offices would become an increasingly important base for training O&M staff in the Asia-Pacific region.[21]

Formal networks provided staff with firsthand experience of the latest overseas practices and developments. By encouraging staff to bring these approaches and insights home and to apply them locally, multi-national agencies not only benefited from their global reach, they also helped reinforce their global networks. Moreover, their time in the United States, Canada, and Britain also provided staff with a more comprehensive understanding of Australian advertising and where it sat in the global context.

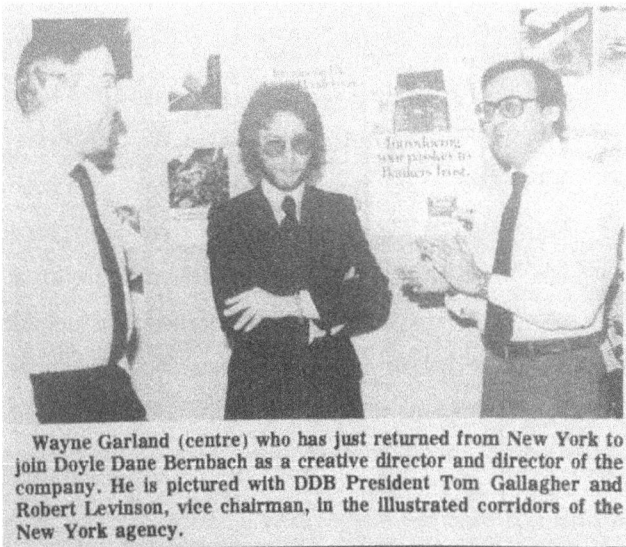

Wayne Garland (centre) who has just returned from New York to join Doyle Dane Bernbach as a creative director and director of the company. He is pictured with DDB President Tom Gallagher and Robert Levinson, vice chairman, in the illustrated corridors of the New York agency.

Figure 2.2 Being feted by Madison Avenue was still noteworthy in the late 1970s. Advertising News, *20 January 1978, p. 2 (Courtesy of AdNews)*

On Madison Avenue

Returning from a visit to the US in 1959, John Cumming observed that at a glance American agencies seemed superior to their Australian counterparts 'in most respects. But not in all ... the reasons why we fall short give us no cause for shame. You can put the basic differences down to population and the size of the American market.' In terms of the agency operation, Cumming identified research as a key difference: 'Creatively, we are as good as they. Take out the research, and their copy is on par with ours.'[22] Cumming's comments on size and approach would be echoed by other Australian advertising professionals visiting the US.

'The first thing that hit you was that New York advertising was a corporate business', recalls Julian Martin. By comparison,

Australian advertising was 'a cottage industry'. Like the sky-scrapers that dominated the city streets, the sheer size and scale of the agencies impressed Australian visitors to Madison Avenue, the home of American advertising. Even the very largest of Australian agencies was dwarfed in comparison. When Geoff Wild returned home from his 1965 trip to the Advertising Congress in Paris that also included stops in the US, the UK, and Hong Kong, the trade press reported that his main impression of the US 'was that far more personnel work on an account overseas than do in Australia'.[23] Over the coming decades, the numbers working in these American agencies continued to expand. As such, they possessed a level of specialisation within their ranks that was simply unavailable in Australia. Australians working in Madison Avenue also recalled that the size of the American talent pool meant working with and learning from extremely bright and talented individuals.

As the excitement of being on Madison Avenue faded, Australians working in New York began to see that size was not everything. 'New York agencies … were very hard-working, very strict, very disciplined. They weren't the creative hotpots that we imagined Madison Avenue to be. They were much more factories … of hard-driven, research-driven advertising', recalls Wayne Kingston, who arrived in New York with his then-partner Suzie Otten in the late 1970s. Being accustomed to working in smaller agencies, Australians arrived in the US with a somewhat broader outlook on the advertising process. 'The creative department found me very refreshing over there because I loved the creative process and I wasn't the typical account person', notes Kingston.[24] For Otten, the strict division of labour at O&M's New York operation seemed to inhibit coherence within a campaign:

There were people in these offices who would never see anyone in the media department. ... They used to fill out ... these media schedules and then they would put them in a little out tray ... After they had done those plans, they had no idea where they went. They were all living in little isolated work environments. It was such a shock to me because I used to walk around and talk to people.[25]

Agency structures posed another challenge. Layers of management were employed to oversee each decision. As a copywriter at Ted Bates, Cousins experienced a 'very bureaucratic' operation whereby 'a dozen people would write an ad' which would then be tested.[26] Writers received a 'small salary and they got a bonus for every commercial that got through' the test. The sense of being a small cog in a huge machine eventually got to Hugh Spencer, who had been working as an account executive at JWT's New York office: 'I came to the ultimate realisation that if I went up to the client ... and stood on his desk and dropped my trousers and pissed all over him, I would be shot. But nothing else would change. The relationship between J. Walter Thompson and Listerine antiseptic wouldn't change a bit!'[27] Such comments also reflect Australian conditions – with fewer staff and smaller hierarchies, Australian advertising professionals felt that they could make a larger contribution to the agency fortunes.

Up the Road from Madison Avenue
With its established commercial media and close links with American agencies, a small but significant number of Australians seeking international experience considered Canada as a viable

alternative. Blane Hogue was working as an account executive at Lintas in 1965 when he decided that he wanted to get out of Australia. His colleagues were somewhat confused by his decision to head to Canada. While Lintas could have organised a place for him in London, Hogue was determined to try his luck in the Deep North:

> Professionally I thought that North America was likely better than England to learn about advertising techniques for the future. I thought advertising was most advanced in America, almost an American invention in its modern form, but likely would be pretty closely followed by Canada. For immigration reasons it was not possible to go for any length of time to, say, New York, but also I thought the Canadian model would be closer to but more advanced than what was happening in Australia.[28]

As Hogue intimates, Canada also offered the prospect of providing entry into the US via the backdoor. Working in Montreal, Hogue encountered few Australians. The majority seemed to be in Toronto and, to a lesser extent, Vancouver.

Canada nevertheless proved to be an important training ground for Australians. Working at a Toronto art studio, Robin Stewart found that 'I was learning so much about how to really do it and do it fast'.[29] Both O&M and HRMcCE drew heavily on Canadian-trained expatriates when commencing their Australian operations. However, Australian access to Canada would become more restricted in the 1970s as the government clamped down on immigration.[30] With access being restricted,

Canada's importance diminished in Australian eyes. Moreover, Australians were no longer viewing North American advertising as being at the cutting edge.

The Creative Capital

After a year of visiting and working for agencies across North America, Europe and the Middle-East, Keith Naughton, joint managing director of Nichols-Cumming in Sydney, identified a key difference between American and British advertising practices. 'Americans', he claimed, regard 'advertising as a business, whereas the British regard it as a profession'.[31] By the late 1960s and early 1970s, this difference between the American focus on process and British emphasis on outputs was being summed up in a single word – creativity. While Bill Bernbach's pioneering combination of art directors and copywriters had inspired the Creative Revolution along Madison Avenue in the late 1950s and early 1960s, it would be the creative work coming out of London in the late 1960s and early 1970s by agencies such as Collett Dickenson Pearce that really caught the attention of Australian creatives.[32] Eager to be a part of Swinging London, many joined the throng of creative young Australians heading off to London's 'Kangaroo Valley' around Earl's Court.

As with New York, Australians were impressed by the size and scale of operations. Returning to Sydney after two years at Erwin Wasey Ruthrauff & Ryan, Bill Currie similarly identified the London agency's large teams of specialised staff as a key difference from Australia.[33] JWT's London offices at 40 Berkeley Square also employed an army of specialists. Although it was the oldest and largest international office in the agency's network, it was the agency's Britishness that impressed ex-staffers. As Sean

Nixon observes, the agency's success in the post-war decades had seen it 'go native' with the office developing its own approach to advertising as well as its own style of advertisements.[34]

For new arrivals in London, JWT certainly conformed to the image of being an establishment agency. Having commenced work at JWT's Wellington office, the secretary Robbie Hall arrived at JWT London via a short stint with JWT Sydney. 'It was very different from anything I'd ever known', she observes. 'It was an extremely sophisticated company. The executives that worked there ... had been educated at Eton and Harrow. They'd been to Oxford and Cambridge.' (O&M also embarked on the active recruitment of Oxbridge graduates – see Chapter 6.) Hall adds that women at JWT shared a similar pedigree: 'A lot of the girls were "Sloanies" ... they had just finished school in Switzerland or Paris, and they had come back and they wanted an amusing job until they met the right man.'[35] Starting out as despatch boys at JWT London, Paul Priday and Trevor Fearnley recall the hierarchical nature of the office.[36] Fearnley likens the agency to 'an English boarding school ... the prefects, for us, were the account executives, the housemasters were the account directors'.[37] Without a degree, Fearnley would be unable to progress to a senior account position.

Such class divisions were also evident in other agencies. Working briefly at Allardyce Palmer in Soho in the early 1970s, John Newton recalls the account directors 'were private school boys ... thick as duckshit' and the creatives were cockneys.[38] At Lintas, Peter Charlton headed the agency's African, Middle East, and West Indies operations. He had been instrumental in attaining international accounts from Rowntree. However, when the head of Lintas Worldwide lunched with the head of Rowntree and he did not invite the lower-ranked director, a 'pissed off' Charlton decided that he had enough of London's class divisions.[39] As a junior in the late 1980s, Mo Fox found that 'sexism in the UK was coupled with class … it was insidious and foul'. As a 'colonial' and a female, she had to be 'three times as good' to be accepted by her peers.[40]

Arriving at JWT London in 1965 via the United States, art director Ken Done found advertising agencies in Swinging London to be much more progressive than the conservative, business-focused agencies in New York. Within the creative department at least, the British agencies were less interested in background than creative ability. At LPE in the late 1950s, von Adlerstein worked alongside 'real poets and writers because it was felt they added quality. They could write. English advertising was often … literary. It played on words … it had class.'[41] While the number of creative writers finding work in Australian agencies hints at a degree of cultural cringe in this observation, it nevertheless highlights the British agencies' veneration of the creative side of advertising.[42]

Von Adlerstein also observed that British agencies were more interested in recognising and fostering creative talent than their Australian counterparts. Over the 1960s, the agencies' quest for creativity would see them open their doors further. Done remembers JWT making use of the famed 'cockney photographers' David Bailey and Terence Donovan.[43] Done's own creative work would undergo a significant change at JWT when he was teamed up with copywriter Llewellyn Thomas, son of poet Dylan Thomas. Although the art director–copywriter team combination had been initiated by Bernbach and was already being used in some Australian agencies as early as 1959, this collaborative approach was new to Done, whose work had largely been restricted to 'solving visual problems'.[44]

By the mid-1970s, JWT's collaborative approach began to include the media department. Rather than being an afterthought, media directors such as Alan Robertson were being engaged in the planning processes. Robertson was excited by this 'more academic approach' and he 'could see that the product that came from that collaboration was much better than the isolated efforts at the other agencies'.[45] For Reg Bryson, inspiration came from having access to better resources. Unable to land a position at one of the creative agencies, Bryson took up an account executive position at the more businesslike Masius, Wynne-Williams. Bryson found that the agency's in-house researchers were not number crunchers in 'corduroy suits' but rather 'innovative and creative-type thinkers' who could offer new approaches to solving a client's problem.[46] Seeing the work being done by strategic planners at agencies such as Boase Massimi Pollitt and JWT, Bryson was able to transition into the role of a strategic planner. As we will see in Part II, Done, Robertson, and Bryson were able to apply their lessons and insights to local agencies when they returned home.

———————

'How many arguments have I lost on the subject of sending creative men to overseas seminars and film festivals etc.? God knows!' grumbled Ross Hazelton, group creative director at SSC&B:Lintas. Claiming that 'I have often heard it described as a "nice little trip on the company" … coupled with a sly smile', Hazelton argued that travel was vital to creative and dynamic advertising.[47] While many agencies were unable or unwilling to send staff abroad, a significant number appreciated Hazelton's stance. Whether it was undertaken informally or formally, travelling abroad was an important experience for Australian advertising practitioners. Travel not only enhanced their skillset, it also helped foster a more cosmopolitan attitude. Moreover, it increased the worldliness of Australian advertising agencies and served to complement the multi-national agencies' efforts to instil an international perspective into their practices. To this end, travel helped legitimise claims that Australian advertising lay somewhere between the American and British approaches. Pointing out that 'We have an art director who has just returned from working in America for a year, a London-trained typographer, and a London-trained copy chief', the managing director of USP Benson NSW claimed that his agency was contributing to the development of an Australian style of advertising, which combined 'the noisier, louder (and more blatant) approach of America with the more subtle and often more verbose attitudes of England'.[48]

Of course, it was not always possible to apply the lessons gleaned abroad to Australian conditions. Australian agencies simply did not have the wherewithal to replicate the size of the operations in New York and London. Clients were also a challenge. When Derek Hansen arrived in Australia in 1968, he struggled to convince the locals to see the merits of the kind of creative work that was currently being done in London: 'I could go into meetings, we'd have really great stuff, and you'd just watch eyes glaze over because they wanted pretty pictures and a jingle. They wanted what George Patterson did and what USP Benson's did and what J. Walter Thompson did.' Others returned to discover that Australia was not necessarily a sleepy backwater, and that the best Australian advertising work and advertising professionals generally stood up well against the work being conducted overseas.[49] 'I was never screamingly successful overseas and I certainly never made a fortune. But I rarely felt outclassed', explained former director of Grant Advertising International Gareth Phelong, who had just returned to Australia in 1969 after almost two decades abroad.[50] Unencumbered by layers of bureaucracy, Australians found that they were in a position to implement innovative strategies in all aspects of advertising practice. As we will see in the next chapter, such lessons and experiences would prove invaluable for those Australian agencies that were weighing up the prospect of spreading their own operations into South East Asia.

CHAPTER THREE

ENTERING ASIA

Flipping through *B&T* in March 1972, many readers would have paused at the half-page advertisement calling for account executives and creative writers to take up positions in South East Asia. The announcement sought to pique the interest of ambitious and adventuring admen:

> The positions available offer opportunities for young men under 30 to take up senior appointments and achieve a level of responsibility that will later fit them for top advertising positions when they return to Australia. The salaries and conditions offered are sufficient to enjoy the best the East has to offer and should make international travel possible at the end of the contract period. There are currently 20 Australians working the various Cathay offices, out of a total staff of 270.[1]

Inserted by George Patterson on behalf of its regional subsidiary, the advertisement revealed the relationship between Australia's advertising agencies and their counterparts operating in South East Asia. Like the other Australian 'fortune hunters' identified by Agnieszka Sobocinksa, the enterprising admen that responded to such advertisements saw in Asia unique opportunities that were not available in New York or London.[2]

Figure 3.1 Only the young, adventurous, and ambitious need apply.
B&T, *25 March 1971, p. 27 (Courtesy of B&T)*

Although Australian advertising professionals had been plying business in Asia since the interwar period, the number of Australians moving into the region from the 1960s onwards dramatically increased. Already in 1963, *B&T* predicted 'the ever-strengthening links between Australian agencies and those in South East Asia, since there is the clearest understanding here now that our economic destiny is leading us more to Asia than our traditional markets in Europe'.[3] Airlines brought Australians into closer contact with the region – whether it was their destination or, indeed, a stopover on the way to Europe. Confronted with the realities of their geographic location within the Asia-Pacific region, Australians began to see the opportunities that lay before them as well as their ability to act on them. From the 1960s to the end of the 1980s, Australian agencies (both locally owned and multi-national offices) played an active and important role in the region, establishing offices, training staff, and servicing accounts. In the process of formalising their connections with the Asia-Pacific, Australian agencies managed to strengthen their own position within global advertising networks.

Early Adventurers

In the interwar period, Australians travelling to Asia for business purposes became more commonplace.[4] As Australian advertising agencies were still developing national networks, few entertained the idea of formally entering key markets in South East Asia. However, individual Australians travelling to the region discovered that they could make a living from advertising, particularly in the British colonies. While some would join the agencies already operating in the region, others would venture out on their own. Their efforts would be disrupted by the Japanese occupation during World War II. Re-establishing their agency operations in the post-war period, these pioneers would play a key role in connecting Australia with the region.

Ernest Mozar was just eighteen when he first travelled abroad. Born in Balranald, NSW, the young clerk had enlisted to serve in the Australian Imperial Force in October 1914. Mozar went on to serve in Gallipoli and the Western Front before being wounded and captured in April 1917. After bouts of ill-health, he returned to Australia in 1919.[5] By 1927, it seems that Mozar had itchy feet. Moving to Singapore, he found work at the Progressive Publicity Co. before establishing his own agency,

Masters. Ruling on a case brought against Mozar by his former employer, the judge commented that advertising agencies had been 'comparatively new in this part of the world'.[6] The agency prospered, aided in no small part by securing the local accounts of large multi-national advertisers such as Cadbury. However, the Japanese invasion forced the agency to shut its doors and Mozar would again find himself behind bars as a prisoner of war, this time in the infamous Changi prison.[7]

Another pioneering Australian who spent World War II in a Japanese prison was Elma Kelly. '[B]rave, entrepreneurial and single-minded', Kelly was responsible for creating Cathay Advertising, one of the largest advertising agency networks in Asia.[8] Upon completing a science degree at the University of Melbourne in 1918, she started her working career as a chemical analyst. Kelly was also active in various feminist groups, where she picked up the rudiments of publishing from a journalist friend who published in *Women's World*.[9] Such skills would play a crucial role in Kelly's career transformation, when in 1931 she adventurously followed her lover to Shanghai. When the prospect of running a magazine came up, Kelly claimed that she had experience for the job. The publisher, Frank Millington, also ran an advertising agency, Millington Ltd. Kelly proved herself an adept advertising executive and by 1934 she had left Shanghai to run Millington's struggling Hong Kong office. Despite the large expatriate British community in Hong Kong, her staff largely consisted of Russians and Chinese as well as an Australian aide. Under Kelly, the office broke even in the first year and would continue to make an annual profit until the Japanese invasion, when the agency shut its doors and Kelly was imprisoned in the Stanley prison camp. However, as the Japanese were entering the colony, the astute manager took the precaution of instructing her accountant to draw up lists of the agency's debtors – such foresight would pay off after the war ended.

Moving in

As with other parts of the globe, the relationship between Australia and Asia in the 1940s and 1950s was still generally based on informal links. This would change in the 1960s, when advertising agencies began to realise that they could not claim to be global if they did not have a presence in Asia. The region's strategic importance was not lost on Australian agencies. Moving to capitalise on their geographic location, Australian advertising agencies increasingly formalised their connections within the region. Some established a formal presence by opening a local office while others acquired local agencies either independently or via global deals made by the head office. In each case, Australia strengthened its place in the region. By 1978, seven of the fourteen major multi-national agencies operating in Indonesia, Malaysia, and Singapore had their regional headquarters in Sydney.[10] Such a presence also helped reinforce the importance of these agencies' Australian operations.

When Ken Landell-Jones was demobilised in 1945, the former officer looked to start his own manufacturing business. Facing a shortage of raw materials, Landell-Jones opted for a career in advertising and founded his own agency, Fortune.[11] The agency would grow solidly over the 1950s before getting its big break in 1960 when it landed the Cathay Pacific airlines account. Australian directness ultimately secured the deal for Fortune when Landell-Jones bluntly told Cathay Pacific's management that he could not say anything positive about the airline or its advertising.[12] An office in Hong Kong was duly established and it would spend its first twelve months exclusively working on the Cathay Pacific account. The office was initially run by the former manager of Fortune's Melbourne office, who was expected to 'travel consistently to Tokyo, Free China, Singapore, Saigon, Malaya, Karachi, Calcutta, the Philippines, and other smaller markets'.[13] Over the coming decade, Fortune opened branches in Singapore, Kuala Lumpur, Manila, Bangkok, and Jakarta, but Hong Kong played a key role in 'planning and placing advertising in sixteen Asian countries, overcoming the problems of translating copy into local vernacular, accurately selecting media ... and maintaining contact with importers and manufacturers' agents'.[14] The Cathay account remained integral to the network. With a strong background in Australian airlines, Michael Anderson was appointed managing director of Fortune Far East in 1965 (before being poached to head the Hong Kong office of the American agency Wells Rich Greene). Of course, the Sydney head office kept a close eye on things. In the first five years of the Fortune's Asian venture, Landell-Jones had travelled abroad no less than twenty-one times.[15]

By 1971, Fortune's successful Asian network had given it enough confidence to look further afield. Rather than selling out, it bought into the DDI consortium (Dancer Fitzgerald Sample in the US, Dorland in Germany and Dorland in the UK) to form Dancer Dorland Fortune (DDF).[16] Landell-Jones would become chairman of the new agency. However, towards the end of the 1970s, Fortune was coming under pressure. At the international level, Dancer Fitzgerald Sample agency was buying out DDF shares. It was the loss of Cathay Pacific and Woolworths's accounts in 1982, however, that ultimately led to the demise of Fortune. A merger with Advertising Business Holdings would form Fortune Communication Holdings while its offices and clients were taken over by Sherbon Schofield

Baker, which had steadily grown in size and stature since its creation in 1976.[17]

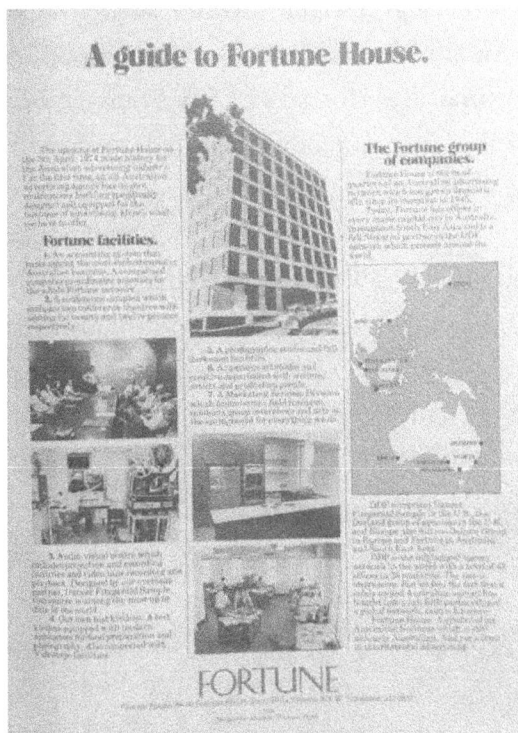

Figure 3.2 Fortune was one of the first Australian agencies to establish
a network across South East Asia.
Advertising News, 26 April 1974, p. 25 (Courtesy of AdNews)

Qantas airlines led Jackson Wain into the international market. In 1963 the agency took 'the first step in a programme of overseas expansion' by sending a director, Hedley Cousins, to London. While the new Park Lane office sought to provide its Australian clients with 'on-the-spot advertising and mer-chandising advice and service in Britain and ... a closer link with Europe', its primary task was to oversee the 'placing in Britain of advertising for ... QANTAS, under the direction of Jackson Wain's headquarters in Sydney'.[18] By 1966, the agency had secured another major airline, Malaysia-Singapore Airlines, and it was now operating offices in Hong Kong, Singapore, Bangkok, and Kuala Lumpur. Jackson Wain was billing over $2 million in the region and employing around 100 staff.[19] As with Fortune, the size of Jackson Wain's network in the region as well as its profitability attracted attention from multi-national agencies looking to enter the region. Upon negotiating a deal to sell out to Leo Burnett in 1970, Frank Grace (formerly chairman at Jackson Wain and now chairman at Leo Burnett) explained that contemporary advertising trends left the agency with little choice: 'We are convinced that the global agency structure is the only intelligent answer to agency profitability and client needs in the 1970s and beyond.'[20] Ironically, it would lose the Malaysia-Singapore Airlines, shortly after the merger to McCann-Erickson, which still had a limited presence in the region.[21]

Cathay Advertising was formed by Elma Kelly and the remnants of the Millington staff after the war.[22] Kelly funded the venture using payments received from Millington's pre-war debtors, friends and a deceased estate.[23] The agency quickly established its presence in Hong Kong, before opening offices in Singapore, Bangkok, and Kuala Lumpur over the course of the 1950s. As Cathay Advertising was an Asian network without formal Australian links, George Patterson moved to form a connection with Kelly's operation. The Australian agency was motivated by its client, Colgate-Palmolive. Having opened a plant near Kuala Lumpur, Colgate-Palmolive requested that its closest agency, George Patterson, handle its advertising for the region. Without a presence outside Australia, Patts sought to establish formal connections with Cathay Advertising, and in 1963 it bought a minority interest in Kelly's network. 'They feel there is to be a big influx of Australian business up in the Far East', wrote Kelly to a friend. 'They don't interfere in any way but will send us up staff as wanted – a great relief.'[24] Although the final comment reveals that Kelly was highly receptive to receiving staff and expertise from Australia, the assumption that the new shareholders would be content to leave things reveals the persuasiveness of George Patterson's negotiators.

George Patterson's link with Cathay would be integral to its own global ambitions. With large global accounts, Australia's largest agency was coming under pressure to sell out or to merge with a multi-national agency. As Ted Bates held the Colgate-Palmolive account in the US and lacked an international presence, it was the logical partner for Patts. During the course of the discussion, Bill Farnsworth boldly claimed that Patts owned offices throughout the region. In what would become a part of the agency's folklore, Farnsworth needed to make good on his claim as quickly as possible. Alex Hamill takes up this story:

> Undaunted, Farnsworth flew to Hong Kong and made Elma Kelly … an offer she could not refuse. She had no idea her company … was the only one that could give Bill what he had already promised to provide to Bates. Elma, who built her reputation as one of Asia's toughest negotiators, realised after she had signed the sale documents and never forgave him.[25]

Ted Bates's buyout of Patts (and Cathay with it) was formally announced in March 1964. However, the Cathay network's technical owner remained George Patterson International and it would continue to report to Sydney.[26] Significantly, the agency continued to operate as Cathay Advertising. Geoff Cousins, who was despatched to run the Hong Kong office in the early 1970s, recalls that the agency's identity would change in relation to the audience – for local accounts Cathay Advertising was a local agency; for large international accounts it was part of the Bates network. The offices would be rebranded Ted Bates in the mid-1970s. Announcing the Singapore office's new title, an advertisement for the agency explained that 'progress and streamlined communications are the order of the day and the time has come when we must assume the group image and identity'.[27]

After his release from Changi, Mozar re-established the Masters agency. The agency was soon back on its feet, and by the time it celebrated its twenty-first birthday in 1949, Masters boasted that it was handling 'English, American, Australian, Canadian and South African accounts' and that it also had 'associates through the English-speaking world'.[28] While the recruitment of Australian expatriates ensured that the agency maintained a connection with Australia, its acquisition of the British Overseas Airways Corporation account shifted it further into the British orbit. The airline's primary agency, S. H. Benson, established a formal connection with Masters in 1959. Two years later Masters sold out entirely to S. H. Benson, which was consolidating its international interests (that also included the buyout of USP in Australia).[29] It was anticipated that Australia would play a key role in managing the agency and training local staff.[30] A decade later, the office was acquired by O&M when it bought out S. H. Benson. As the Australians abandoned the new O&M office to return home to what had become USP-Needham, Michael Ball (who was now the general manager of O&M London as well as the chairman of O&M Australia

& New Zealand) was charged with the task of repairing the network's Asian acquisitions. Needing an immediate influx of senior talent, he looked to the US and Canada. Such a shift revealed that the region was no longer a British colonial enclave.

The agency that had hoped to use Australia as a springboard into Asia wasted little time in extending its operations into the region. McCann-Erickson arrived in Japan in 1961 when it created a new agency with local agency Hakuhodo. Within five years it was also running offices in Bangkok, Kuala Lumpur, Singapore, Hong Kong, and Manila. 'The establishment of the new Far Eastern offices fills a gap in our international network', observed HRMcCE director, David Hopkins.[31] While HRMcCE would have dealt with the offices in South East Asia, Japan remained a separate entity. In contrast to McCann-Erickson's speedy entry into the region, its global rival took its time. JWT's first foray into South East Asia had in fact occurred in 1930 when an office was briefly opened in Batavia in the Dutch East Indies. After World War II, it returned to the region when it established offices in Tokyo and Manila in 1956. Associate agencies were used in other parts of the region with the creative work being done in Australia.[32] JWT only moved to create a more formal presence in South East Asia in the 1970s. With JWT regional headquarters based in Sydney, the chief executive officer of Australian operations echoed sentiments of competing agencies when he announced that Australia 'will be used to guide and develop our growth in SE Asia'.[33]

By the time Batten, Barton, Durstine & Osborn (BBDO) looked at entering Asia in 1974, its executive vice-president explained that Australia offered more than a convenient base: 'We can't manage from New York ... If we enter these markets we would do so, not necessarily with financial assistance from the

Australian company, but we would lean heavily on local management ability.'[34] Clemenger's successful entry into Asia helped elevate Peter Clemenger to BBDO's board. The promotion prompted some introspection from Clemenger, who candidly commented that 'we're a bit more important to them than I realised'.[35] As BBDO's actions reveal, the strategic role played by Australian-based advertising agencies in leading the push into Asia and subsequently maintaining these networks served to enhance Australia's position both regionally and globally.

Having the Right Background and Outlook

In his 2010 novel *Fortune Cookie*, Bryce Courtenay offered a vivid description of Singapore's advertising scene in the early 1960s:

> There were very few advertising agencies, in any meaningful sense of the term, in Singapore at the time. Most were simply a couple of scruffy back rooms along dirty corridors in old buildings. ... Then there were the mostly Chinese-owned ad agencies in narrow rat-infested, garbage-choked lanes, up dank, dirty stairs in old buildings that smelled of bad toilets. These looked after the Chinese businesses, producing small print ads for the newspapers and magazines in languages other than English.[36]

He also mentions the 'legendary' Elma Kelly and the 'recent entry Jackson Wain' as the key agencies operating in Singapore, but provides little description of their operations. Drawing on his own memories of visiting McCann-Erickson offices in the region some forty years earlier, Courtenay's impression conforms to the 'Far East' stereotype.[37] Others associated the region with cheap booze and sex. Such images were circulating in Neil Lawrence's mind when he was offered a position as the creative director at O&M in Singapore in the mid-1980s. Lawrence wasn't exactly impressed by the invitation: 'My first thought was "Has my reputation slipped that much that they think I want to go and do that?" And the second thing was "Now, where is Singapore?"' Looking back, he concedes that 'I'm not proud of those two thoughts at all, but that's what I honestly thought.'[38] While Lawrence's initial dismissiveness reveals that the stereotype of the 'Far East' as a mysterious, exotic, and somewhat backward place was still alive and well in advertising circles, his subsequent outlook nevertheless reveals that this perception was not fixed. Despite the unique challenges encountered in Asia, these agencies and their Australian staff discovered that the region also offered significant opportunities that would help strengthen Australia's position within the global advertising networks.

The sense that an invitation to work in Asia was a demotion had some substance – certainly in British and, to a lesser extent, American circles. Rather than sack underperforming or problematic senior staffers, British agencies found it more convenient to despatch them 'to the colonies' in South East Asia.[39] For those who had problems with alcohol, the combination of tropical heat and comfortable clubs did little to curb their proclivities. Australians also recall being unimpressed with the quality of some of the Americans they encountered in the region in the 1960s and 1970s.[40] Of course, Australians also contributed to this negative stereotype. Jean-Francois Lacour, SSC&B:Lintas's Asia-Pacific regional manager, warned that the 'second-rate Australians had a very bad image' in Bangkok and Malaysia.[41] In the 1990s it was said that many Asian agencies contained Australians who had been unable to make it in London.[42]

Underpinning the negative impression of Asia were deeply entrenched colonial attitudes. Arriving at the British-run Young agency in Singapore in the mid-1950s, Shakib Gunn recalled the 'inappropriate respect expatriates received' and the ways in which the agency upheld colonial divisions. In addition to occupying senior positions, expatriates physically differentiated themselves from the locals by wearing 'white linen or sharkskin suits and ... bow ties. The rest of the male staff dressed uniformly in white slacks and shirts'.[43] A 1962 photograph of the Cathay staff in Hong Kong indicates a continuing difference between the Caucasian managers, who all are seated, and the locals, standing behind them.[44]

Colonial attitudes were not restricted to local staff. Senior O&M people in the head office dismissed the region as 'Mickey Mouse countries'.[45] Various Australians who travelled to the region were troubled by such colonial attitudes as well as the racism underpinning it. John Newton was working temporarily in Singapore before being offered a more permanent position at Batey Ads: 'We were the Raj and it wasn't much different in the agency'.[46] Increasingly uncomfortable with the division between the expatriates and the locals, Newton rejected the offer and moved on to Europe.

At Cathay's Hong Kong office, Geoff Cousins dealt with more overt racism. When a senior Chinese account executive informed Cousins that he had been kicked by the American CEO of the agency's largest client, Cousins was initially incredulous. He approached the client about the story, who confirmed that it was true, explaining: 'It's a good lesson for you. You gotta kick those people or you'll never get anything out of them'.[47] Well aware that he might lose the account, Cousins responded that he would not stand for such behaviour and that the agency would immediately drop the client if it happened again. Word of Cousins's stance spread through the Chinese community and Cathay became an employer of choice for locals.

As Australian offices took direct responsibility for over-seeing Asian networks, they adopted the conventional colonial outlook as to who should be given the task of running the local offices. They needed people they could trust – having the right background was therefore essential. Such emphasis was hardly novel. Expatriates had long been considered an integral part of running a successful agency in Asia. Throughout the 1950s Masters had sourced management, account service, creative and reproduction staff from the UK and Australia.[48] Kelly's relief that the deal with George Patterson would see expatriates moving through Cathay revealed their continuing importance in the 1960s. Following the well-established practice, Australian-based networks starting out in the region despatched their own to take on the senior positions. Recounting Fortune's first days in Hong Kong, Landell-Jones explained: 'When we started we had one Australian and two Chinese. The creative work was done in Australia.'[49]

Expatriates were not only drawn from Australia. Of the 179-strong staff at Jackson Wain's overseas offices in 1970, '107 are Asian, 31 English, 21 New Zealanders, 18 Australian and two American'.[50] Multi-national agencies also recognised the important contribution that Australians were making to the region. In 1973 Don Johnston, JWT International's executive vice-president, believed his Australian offices would provide 'the dynamic creative professional assistance and leadership in the growth of advertising throughout Asia and the Southwest Pacific ... JWT Australia already is exporting good advertising.

We prepare work here for our offices and associate companies in Asia. The trend will grow and expand in future.'[51]

Looking back on BBDO's entry into the Asia–Pacific region, the president of the agency's international operations, Willi Schalk, recalls that his Australian colleagues at Clemenger played an integral role in the agency's expansion – particularly in the acquisition of a Japanese agency, a notoriously difficult task that few others had succeeded in doing. Schalk feels that the Australians he worked with had a greater respect for the region and its cultures, as well as a more flexible approach to problem-solving than their American counterparts.[52]

The relative size of Australian offices compared to New York or London also worked to the Australians' advantage. 'We were familiar with smaller scale businesses. And everything in Asia in 1974 was small scale compared to Western countries', observes Ian Dawson, who had been selected to launch JWT's Kuala Lumpur office.[53] George Patterson's senior management deliberately selected account directors who 'had what we considered to be reasonable business nous. … [they] needed to get on with the local government people, local landlords, local tax authorities … The managing director had to do these things himself.'[54]

They would also need to be flexible within the office. Upon returning from a visit to McCann-Erickson's Asian operations, Arthur Chipper, the creative director at HRMcCE in Sydney, noted that Australians in smaller offices 'usually had to handle two agency jobs – creative men taking on account service duties and clients' while 'contact men' would lend 'a hand with copy-writing assignments'. As a creative, he also noted their 'enviable autonomy and creative freedom'.[55]

Of course, the task of parachuting expatriates into key positions was not always straightforward. As with any position, some were simply unsuited for the job they were sent out to do. Others struggled to adapt to the local conditions and cultures. Local laws could also prove challenging. Malaysia's affirmative-action *bumiputra* policies that sought to enhance the position of Malays by restricting the influence of Chinese and Indians posed a significant but not insurmountable challenge. Graeme Kinsella recalls that Leo Burnett's Kuala Lumpur office in the 1970s struggled with the local staff's lack of experience: 'in order to get high level creative work ... we used to import creative people from the Sydney office on a regular basis for about a month to two months at a time to do all the work and send them back out again. They were allowed to be in there for that time on their visas.'[56]

The 'Far East' stereotype had a bearing on the type of person who took up a position in an Asian office. In 1953 Masters advertised for a junior account executive in the *Sydney Morning Herald*. The applicant was to be 'between 23-25 years of age – preferably single'. Appealing to the ambitious youngster, the agency sought to assuage any concerns about its own status by describing itself as an 'old established European Advertising Agency'.[57] Such statements seemed to reinforce an image of Asia as the domain of the intrepid adventurer. To this end, Australians felt that they had an innate advantage over their British and American counterparts, as they considered themselves to be more flexible and more capable of working in challenging conditions.[58]

As the Masters advertisement revealed, age was also important. The preference for youthful applicants not only reflected their lower wages, it also showed a desire for the dynamism and the ambition that came with good young applicants. When

Alex Hamill arrived in Singapore in 1968, his age informed his outlook: 'I wasn't thirty and bored with my life, I was twenty-five and hungry. I was young enough to think, "Shit, I can do OK here."'[59] Of course, the flip side to Hamill's account was the boozy excesses of expatriate lifestyle – which many Australians, irrespective of age, happily embraced. While agencies remained interested in youthful applicants, their attitude to an employee's marital status was changing. In 1971, JWT selected Ian Alwill ahead of another colleague to lead the agency's Manila operations. While his marketing degree was a key point of difference, being married was also a factor as the agency felt a posting in Asia 'had potential dangers for someone unmarried'.[60]

Gender was an important consideration. While Australia's advertising agencies were notoriously blokey workplaces, many felt that the sexism in South East Asian advertising circles was worse. In her brief time working at Fortune's Hong Kong office, De Brierley-Newton struggled with the cultural attitudes towards gender: 'I was in a position of authority there, as far as the agency was concerned. But they would socialise, and it would be men socialising.' Women did attend these boozy nights, but only in the capacity of helping the drunks home. Not surprisingly, Brierley-Newton struggled: 'I didn't fit that.'[61]

Such attitudes were not restricted to clients – sexism also thrived across the agency networks. Faie Davis arrived in Singapore as the wife of an adman but soon found work as a creative director. The position was with Batey Ads, a local creative agency founded by Ian Batey, a British-born, Australian-trained adman. She recalls that the agency's affiliated partners overseas were often 'put out' at having to deal with a female creative director.[62] However, it was Suzanne Mercier's experience at George Patterson that was more common for women: 'Every once in a while a talented individual would be sent up to run Asia. When it came to be my turn, they said "Oh, women don't do well in Asia". So, I actually didn't get the option to go up there. … I didn't even think twice about it, that was the land-scape.'[63] George Patterson, it seems, had conveniently forgotten that its profitable Asian network had been created by a woman.

Local staff working in the Asian offices also had expectations about the staff arriving from abroad to take on senior positions in their office. While Sydney offices were not inclined to invest the funds and time to send candidates out to see whether they gelled with the locals, they did need to consider whether the individual had the personality and skills to operate effectively in a foreign setting. As Mike Holbech, managing director of Leo Burnett in Hong Kong, explained, expatriates needed to take note of the locals, and increasingly so: 'the stronger the Chinese executives and creative people become in an agency, the more demanding they are of absolute excellence in their expatriate people'.[64] A decade later, a television director based in Kuala Lumpur noted that there was an 'an active dislike by local staff of foreign Creative Directors' on account of their large sala-ries and their inability to appreciate, let alone understand, the local market.[65] Sending out the wrong person with the wrong attitude not only threatened to alienate local staff, it could also endanger the agency's relationship with clients – current and future.

Profitable Exchanges

'To succeed in Asia', asserted Michael Ball in 1982, 'agencies must make a serious commitment in time, money, and talent. You have to send your *best* people to work in Asia, not those who can't make it to the top in Australia.' However, Ball believed that this flow was not one way: 'You have to train nationals year in, year out, both in the market and by bringing them to work for extended periods in Australia or other developed markets.' This two-way flow of skills and ideas not only built up the agency's regional capabilities, it also established a 'body of belief to help unify staff in Asian countries because they will have little else in common'.[66] While this strategy had taken O&M to the top in the region, it was by no means the only agency to use its network as broad training apparatus for staff in Australia and across the Asia-Pacific region.

After several years of running the Brisbane office of George Patterson, Geoff Cousins was 'tapped on the shoulder' for a new challenge. 'At Patterson's we did have a very good system of moving senior people through South East Asia, much more than we did within Australia actually', explains Cousins. 'If you did well, then the expectation was when you came back to Sydney or Melbourne, you would get a better job than the one you had when you left … and I benefitted from that.'[67] As a stint abroad in the agency's international networks was regarded as a sign of the agency's faith in one's progress, most accepted the offer. Graham Cox was offered the role of managing director in Kuala Lumpur but declined. Looking back on the decision, he concedes that 'I probably set myself back, permanently, because I declined it. It was … considered to be something of a plum.'[68] Geoff Wild headed Clemenger BBDO's entry into the Asia-Pacific region. Wild confesses that he been 'very envious' of the way that George Patterson and other multi-national agencies used their regional networks to train promising staff.[69] When Clemenger established its Asian network in the 1980s, Wild consciously emulated Patts by using these offices as means of promoting staff and broadening their experiences.

Contact between the Asian branches and their Australian head offices was initially infrequent. In the late 1960s, phone calls and air travel were very expensive and the managing director of George Patterson, for example, only visited once every eight months.[70] Contact would increase, however. At Leo Burnett in the 1970s, Australian chairman Frank Grace would be on the phone almost every day with his Asian network.[71] Movement between the offices similarly increased over time. As Patts's senior financial officer Russell McLay recalled, travelling through the Cathay network in the 1970s and 1980s every six months, and more regularly if there were any major issues.[72] Patts also regularly despatched account executives and creative staff to ensure that accounts were being handled appropriately and to address any problems that the office was experiencing.

For many offices, the global networks beyond Australia did not amount to much. At JWT's Kuala Lumpur office, Dawson recalls that Australia was much 'more amenable to offering up resources' than either New York or London.[73] Calling on the Australian office for help did not always mean sending out staff. When JWT's Manila office was pitching for the Ford Fiera account, the office decided that it lacked the expertise. 'They came to Sydney', remembers Ken Done. 'They gave me the responsibility of it. I took about five people. We worked for an entire weekend, night and day'.[74] Inter-office collaboration within the region only occurred where offices shared a common account.[75]

For the young men being despatched to head the Asian offices, their primary task was simple: keep the existing clients happy and grow the business. Management working at the coalface understood that they needed to pay closer attention to local conditions. Wild was shocked to discover that

Clemenger BBDO's joint venture in Jakarta was running three sets of accounts – one for the Indonesian government, one for Clemenger BBDO, and one for the accountant. As networks expanded, it became increasingly difficult to maintain a close focus on each office. O&M's Ball thus warned his colleagues against adopting a complacent attitude towards their Asian offices: 'For one man to attempt to run a large Australian agency and an Asian network demonstrates foolhardiness or lack of understanding of the complexities of Asia.'[76] Dawson's initial experience with JWT in Malaysia had revealed to him the strategic importance of Kuala Lumpur as well as the limitations of JWT going it alone there. His strategy for the agency called for the development of a joint venture with locals that operated on a hub and spokes model. John Sharman, JWT regional director, took the new plan on board and sent Dawson back to Kuala Lumpur with Sharman's blunt challenge ringing in his ears: 'OK, smartarse, it was your idea, make it work.'[77] While other agencies were reluctant to go into partnership with locals, there was nevertheless a growing realisation that expatriates did not necessarily have all the answers. At HRMcCE, Hopkins was troubled by the lack of local input in advertising campaigns: 'there is only one formula that I know for failure. That is, advertising created by expatriate copywriters and approved by expatriate marketing men without analysis by the very best local people you can find.'[78] When Cousins took over Cathay in Hong Kong in the early 1970s, he, too, was concerned by the agency's setup:

> A lot of the big international advertising agencies up there relied … far too heavily on *gweilos*, foreign devils, to not only run the business … but … to staff all the

senior positions. I thought that was crazy. We had a bit of that ... in most of those offices, to varying degrees and I thought too much of it in Hong Kong. ... So if you looked at the executive team, there was certainly more foreigners than there were locals. I didn't think that was a good idea and set out to change. And we did change, very quickly.[79]

Cousins's confrontation with the violent American client had earned him respect from local staff. Many now wanted to work for Cathay. Attracting the best and brightest local talent enabled it to land new accounts. Such was Cathay's success in the region that it 'had to stop pitching'.[80]

Writing in response to Hopkins's criticisms of excessive dependence on expatriates, the director of London Press Exchange in Singapore countered that: 'There is no earthly use paying homage to the local expert unless he understands contemporary marketing techniques. ... The very best local people are sometimes not capable of providing the know-how that's required.'[81] This point was not lost on the multi-national agencies operating in Asia. Many understood that if they were to see more local staff entering senior positions, they would need to pay greater attention to training them for these roles. Already in 1967, JWT Australia was laying claim to being 'a post-graduate training centre for senior executives from the company's near-north offices'.[82] George Patterson had long been running an informal training scheme for its Asian network. Offices would nominate candidates to work in Sydney or Melbourne for periods of three months up to two years. As the networks expanded, the number of nominations exceeded the positions on offer. Staff members were selected by senior management in Sydney who had encountered the applicants on their tours of the Asian network. Although the positions were open to all departments, they were generally given to account directors (who worked in Australia as account executives), particularly those who were working on Colgate in their home country. The scheme was not formalised but McLay notes that George Patterson invested significant amounts into the exchange: 'We had to put them up in an apartment ... you've got to pay them Australian wages, which was far more than they were earning in those days ... plus their airfares, communication, et cetera. So it was a positive thing for those staff.'[83] The agency also sought to protect its investment – anyone moving to another agency within a set period of returning home would be obliged to repay the costs of the trip to Australia. Overall, the opportunity to train in Australia and to return home to take on a more senior role meant that few left the Patterson network.

O&M's use of Australia as a training ground for staff in its network accelerated in the 1980s. In February 1983 Luella Copeland-Smith from O&M's Sydney office attended the 'Senior Account Management Programme' in Melbourne.[84] Participants came from offices across the Asia-Pacific region as well as India, South Africa, and East Africa. The two-week programme required attendees to take part in a question and answer session with Michael Ball, listen to presentations by senior O&M staff, present on their office's operations, and participate in numerous exercises and tasks aimed at enhancing their presentation skills, their client-management skills, and their contribution to creative work. Such programmes were overseen by Ian Strachan in the Melbourne office.

Initially employed as O&M's finance director, Strachan moved into training in the 1980s. Reflecting the growing importance that O&M attributed to training, Strachan went from hosting programmes at the Melbourne office to staging events at the offices in New Zealand and Asia. By the end of the 1980s, he found that he was spending more time in Asia than Australia and in 1991 he moved to Hong Kong to become O&M's regional training and developmental director for the next twelve years. From his new base, Strachan had the task of training leaders in each country. Such a shift signalled a change in the way that Australian-based advertising agencies were connecting with the neighbouring region. While Australians were still having an impact on advertising in Asia, it seems that the region's centre had moved on from Australia.

When the executive president of JWT International visited Australia in 1973, he predicted that the young Australians work-ing abroad would be of immense benefit to Australia: 'These young men, with broadened experience, are returning home with higher standards and higher goals. This interchange of people, ideas, talent, technique and plain, ordinary goodwill makes for better advertising, and better opportunity for advertis-ing men and women.'[85] The movement of agency staff between Australia and South East Asia confirms this claim. Travellers moving in both directions often returned home with more than enhanced skills; their time abroad had provided them with an opportunity to see the bigger picture. Hugh Spencer's time at JWT Bangkok, for example, enabled him to experience the strategic side of advertising and the connections between advertising and marketing. Others returned home with a better understanding of communication principles, client needs, strategic thinking, or agency management. As a former creative director of McCann–Erickson and Leo Burnett in Hong Kong observed: 'the fanciful picture of idle afternoons spent sipping ever-lasting pink gins under punka wallahs has faded with the wind.'[86]

Australians had also played a key role in assisting the entry of multi-national advertising agencies into South East Asia. While their appropriation of key roles was consistent with the practices that had been pioneered by Americans and British (when entering Australia and other parts of the globe), their role in educating and promoting local staff revealed that they were heeding a warning voiced by the regional director of SSC&B:Lintas: 'You have to be very careful, when it comes to Asia, not to replace one former colonialist with another, not to replace the bloody English or the bloody French with bloody Australians.'[87] Significantly, the role played by Australian offices in the region did not go unnoticed at the global level. The experience and insights that Australians like Cousins, Hamill, Ball, and Wild acquired in the development, organisation, and management of Asian operations led their respective agencies to invite them to join the global board. Australians were not simply profiting from advertising's globalisation, they were playing an active role in directing it. As the next chapter reveals, Australia's active involvement in establishing these global networks would also feed back into advertising practices at the local level.

CHAPTER FOUR

EMBRACING CREATIVITY

'The world is going creative', observed Brisbane-based creative director Paul Jones in 1967. And it was the young
who were leading this shift. Jones felt that this generation's
interest in music was leading many into other creative fields
such aesthetics and writing. 'I think the advertising industry,
among others, is going to benefit by this over the next few
years', he predicted.[1] Jones certainly had a keen sense of the
Zeitgeist; his 'It's Time' campaign for the ALP a few years later
famously encapsulated the excitement and hope surrounding
Gough Whitlam's ascent to power. In 1979 Jones would again
be at the forefront of Australian creative work when he chaired
the inaugural Australian Writers and Art Directors Association
(AWARD) awards celebrating creative excellence in advertising.

From the late 1960s, creativity was increasingly recognised
as the lifeblood of a good advertising agency. Creative directors
such as Arthur Holland were beginning to suggest that creativity
was to be found in all parts of the agency.[2] Looking back, Renny
Cunnack agrees. Cunnack believes that agencies were full of
people who were 'interested in … and attracted by creativity'.[3]
And they were not exclusively found in the creative department.
Managers, account executives, media planners, and receptionists
all enjoyed 'being around that kind of creative atmosphere'. It
was this energetic creativity that prompted so many agency

staffers to reminisce that life in the agencies as being fun, exciting, and a little glamorous – like *Mad Men*.

As a concept, creativity offered the agencies a way of reinventing themselves and their work in response to broader issues and developments at two levels. The first level concerned the consumer. In the US, advertisers were facing a backlash. The consumer movement of the 1960s was not only attacking advertisers and their promises, they were also questioning the very presence of advertising. Creative advertising was a response to this challenge. Dispensing with conventional promises and stereotypes, creative advertisements sought to offset cynicism by engaging the audience, often through wit and humour.[4] In Britain and, especially, Australia, the creative turn would also tap into broader nationalist sentiments.[5] At the second level, creativity provided Australian agencies with a convenient tool that would enable them to reinvent themselves in their clients' eyes. As this chapter will show, creativity enabled agencies to offer their clients something more than mere advertisements or marketing advice. Creativity similarly helped justify the agencies' practices and development, along with its excesses. Moreover, the agencies' embrace of creativity would also provide them with a means by which they could recast Australian advertising in the eyes of the world.

The Creative Revolution

Episode three, season one, of the hit series *Mad Men* opens with Don Draper on a train. He is scrutinising the famous print advertisement for Volkswagen with the headline 'Lemon'. At the office, the advertisement generates significant discussion. Draper's staff all recognise that the advertisement breaks the rules, but they are unsure about it. While some get the intended joke, others are confounded by the advertisement's unconventional approach, which seemed to criticise the very product it was meant to celebrate. Draper is not overly impressed, yet he recognises its impact: 'They must be getting results. They keep going back to the well.'[6] These scenes hint at the change that swept along Madison Avenue in the 1960s and reverberated in London and, later, Melbourne and Sydney. In 1962 the American trade journal *Printer's Ink* reported on an Australian advertising executive visiting the agency responsible for the Volkswagen advertisement. Referring to the 'Lemon' advertisement, his first question to the agency was: 'What brought this about?' His second was 'Have any of these campaigns ever misfired?'[7] This actual bemusement to the same campaign reveal that this new style of advertising and the so-called Creative Revolution did not immediately change advertising practices.

In his 1958 insight into the practices and operations of American advertising agencies, *Madison Avenue USA*, Martin Meyer observes that the standard practice of creating advertisements had the copywriter playing the primary creative role. However, Meyer observed that 'a few agencies' were adopting a different approach. One of them was Doyle Dane Bernbach (DDB), which stood out for working 'on the principle that the copywriter and artists are equal'.[8] Pioneered by copywriter Bill Bernbach, DDB's approach also gave rise to a distinctive style whereby copy and imagery were fully integrated. Devoid of puffery and 'advertisingese', the plain copy also used wry humour to connect with the audience.[9] It was DDB that had been responsible for the famous Volkswagen advertisements. As Thomas Frank notes, this type of advertising was revolutionary insofar as it 'broke decisively with the stilted, idealized, cliché-ridden style of the 1950s ... Humor, wit, and stylistic elegance returned from the advertising oblivion to which they had been exiled by the deadly-serious USP (unique selling proposition) scientism.'[10] Rather than patronising consumers, this new wave of advertisements sought to speak to them. Claims such as 'Avis is only No.2 … We try harder' thus struck a chord using honesty and avoiding hyperbole. Bernbach was not alone in challenging advertising's conventions. Over the 1950s and 1960s, David Ogilvy, Leo Burnett, and Mary Wells similarly broke the rules to produce their own brand of creative advertisements.

By the late 1960s, other external factors were contributing to advertising's creative push. The rise of the baby-boomer generation of consumers proved to be a serendipitous development for the agencies' creative revolutionaries. Questioning their parents' materialism as well as the capitalist system driving it, the baby-boomers posed an interesting challenge to the advertising industry. As Stephen Fox observes: 'The two had in common a lack of historical memory, a disdain for authority, a visual orientation, and a way of making rules *ad hoc*.'[11]

Creative advertising thus spoke to this new generation, while the more ambitious advertisers also hoped that their ads might speak for this generation. The emergence of the consumer movement provided a different impetus to creativity. As consumption levels increased, questions were being raised about the products being sold to consumers. Medical authorities were arguing that cigarettes were causing cancer, while Ralph Nader's *Unsafe at Any Speed* took on the safety record of the American automobile industry. Advertising's promotion of such dangerous products, as well as the overall increase in advertising, did little to enhance its reputation. In order to reach these cynical consumers, advertising needed to 'appear credible and honest'.[12] Creativity and wit provided a means by which agencies could assist their clients to sidestep this challenge by disarming consumer cynicism.

Across the pond, swinging London proved to be receptive to the Creative Revolution. Charting the arrival of these ideas into British advertising, Sean Nixon contends that the Creative Revolution 'was adapted, hybridised and indigenised in its importing to Britain. This was a process of reworking ... shaped by the sensibilities of practitioners working in this country, but also driven by recognition of the cultural differences between British and American consumers.'[13] New York agencies like DDB, he continues, functioned as 'a resource and stimulus' for British agencies to produce their own style of creative work. Stephan Schwarzkopf posits that this revolution also tapped into the European tradition of creativity 'as a visual–cognitive challenge for consumers'.[14]

The creative approach struck a chord. When studying at the London College of Printing in the early 1960s, John Hegarty recalled seeing Volkswagen advertisements for the first time: 'it was like having a light turned on in a darkened room. Suddenly I could see what I wanted to do.'[15] By the late 1960s, Collett Dickenson Pearce (CDP) was emerging as one of London's hottest creative agencies. Its advertisements emulated DDB's pattern: witty copy, sharp photography, and clean layouts. But CDP's style also drew on British sensibilities, often by way of understatement, puns, and wordplay. CDP's debt to DDB was also evident in the agency's operations. After a visit to DDB's head office, CDP had paired copywriters and art directors. It also placed the creative team at the very centre of the agency's operational structure and paid them the highest salaries.[16] In the

1970s, the creative work being done by agencies such as CDP and Boase Massimi Pollitt saw London eclipse New York as the epicentre of the creative advertising.

Looking on the developments in New York and London from afar, Australians wondered how the Creative Revolution would affect them. In 1967 *B&T* reported on the American trend:

> Never have we heard so much about creativity, originality, new thought and new themes in advertising as we are hearing today from the USA. ... Some of the more familiarly accepted creative standards are going out the door in America, to the horror of leading names, who are already crying out for a return to sanity. ... We're probably going to be shocked and astonished at what will come out of it, but we should have no illusions about it leaving the Australian advertising world untouched.[17]

Its prediction would prove correct – Australian advertising and the agencies responsible for it would be reinvented.

What Creative Revolution?

When McCann-Erickson took over Hansen-Rubensohn in 1959, creativity was something of an afterthought. The assumption was simple: good advertisements resulted from research and a scientific approach. Audiences and ideas alike were measured to discover what worked and what didn't. Imported advertisements from the US could be trusted as they had already undergone rigorous research. HRMcCE thus re-filmed many commercials in Australia. Its first original commercial for Coca-Cola, for example, only appeared in January 1961.[18] When the agency's Melbourne office began to lag in the mid-1970s, Peter Charlton worked hard to stabilise its teetering accounts and to win new clients. One of his biggest successes was to land the General Motors truck account against George Patterson: 'We won it on marketing and strategy, not creative … George Patterson said "oh well, it's a world account, of course they get it" but it wasn't.' McCann-Erickson's emphasis on research and its client-orientated approach provides an insight into the outlook of the large multi-national agencies. At McCann-Erickson and so many other agencies, creativity continued to run second to the business side of advertising.

The multi-national agencies' outlook was strongly informed by the nature of their clients. These firms expected their agencies to respect their achievements in the marketplace. While these clients expected value for their advertising expenditure and demanded excellent advertising, they were also risk adverse when it came to creativity. In 1965 *B&T* outlined the reasons for these clients' attitude:

> They are basically not experimenters in advertising because they don't want to be, nor could they be persuaded … Companies which have won dominance in their market have the task of staying there – and that makes them conservative. … They are cautious about their advertising, disinclined to change or alter ways of telling a story, more heedful of the tried and tested which has earned them their success, not influenced by any suggestions that their techniques may be old hat and out of date.[19]

There was little impetus to embrace the new wave of creativity if a solid campaign could keep the client happy. And if the client demanded a successful campaign from overseas be used locally, then the agency was left with little option but to re-shoot it, shot for shot. While Bill Farnsworth defended the re-shot commercials, claiming that they were 'thoroughly researched' and contained 'many local interpretations', the creative departments in these agencies were left underwhelmed when they were informed that they would be reshooting someone else's ideas.[20]

The sheer scale of operations at large multi-national agencies also affected the agency's creative capacities. In 1975 George Patterson's four offices employed 382 people. Leo Burnett (241) and HRMcCE (235) spread their staff across six offices while JWT's 204 staff members were confined to Sydney and Melbourne.[21] Such numbers reflected the growing size and complexities of campaigns as well as the agencies' need to adapt to changing client requirements. Ian Alwill owed his entry into advertising to this shift. In 1970 Alwill had just finished his commerce degree, majoring in the recently established marketing major at the University of New South Wales. He worked briefly as a product manager at Marrickville Holdings before moving to McCann-Erickson. It was an advertisement for JWT, however, that cemented his place in the agency structure. Alwill recalls that JWT was seeking 'people who don't have an advertising background but people who have a business background' – particularly individuals with marketing and business degrees as well as sales experience.[22]

The agency's senior management 'sensed there was a change coming, where the old school advertising people … the "Mad Men" era … was passing'. They were aware of the emerging-marketing concept and understood that JWT 'had to provide a wider spectrum of insights, with regards to products and how they could be sold, rather than the old world of "she'll be right, mate, leave it with us and we'll do the ads'". As Chapter 7 reveals, the agencies' actions were a direct response to the clients' enhanced understanding of marketing.

The expansion of staff and agency operations placed an increased importance on clear and structured internal processes. At HRMcCE, such processes were recalled by John Cowper as a defining feature: 'The one thing I learnt at McCann's was how be organised.' Outlining the way that HRMcCE produced its campaigns in 1964, general manager Bill Lockley revealed the assortment of boards and meetings involved with each job. The first task was to generate a creative brief. Produced by the account-service staff (and later planners), the creative brief set out the aims and direction of a campaign. By the time a plan (or brief) reached the HRMcCE creatives, it had already been through the agency's Product Group, Plans Review Board (PRB), and a meeting with the client. Once the creatives devised an idea in line with the plan, it would go back to the Product Group for a second meeting. From here, the next steps involved considerable discussion and review:

9. Product group meets to consider embryo creative work. The product can ... have a creative contribution coming from a research, a media person or an account executive. When the product group has blessed or disagreed with the creative direction we are moving in, it goes to a creative review board meeting.

10. Creative review board meets. This consists of myself or David Hopkins, two creative group

heads, and one AS [account service] director. The creative director attends if the campaign is sufficiently important. This meeting brings out much of the real planning material that is significant and will go to the client in the final plan. This meeting will also be reviewing the final or near-final written submission that will go to the client concerned.

11. Presentation of final plan and creative work. Copies go to the PRB four days in advance. If it is a really big do, we sometimes call for … a full dress rehearsal immediately before it goes to the client.[23]

As these large agencies further honed their standard procedures, they also developed more regulated formulas for the development of creative work. While these rules seemed to be the very antithesis of the creative process that had underpinned DDB's rise, they nevertheless functioned to ensure consistency for the advertisers and agencies operating across international markets. Reflecting that 'a process is good for getting it right, it's not good for getting it great', Ric Otton underscores the inherent conservatism of the large agencies, as well as the fundamental problem that the creatives in these agencies faced. For John Bevins, life at HRMcCE was akin to working in a 'factory' while O&M's rules and inward focus were 'stultifying'. It is hardly surprising that Bevins and numerous other creatives would rebel against the system and look for new ways to express their creativity. Rather than leave one large agency for another, a small but influential number looked to dispense with the formulaic processes by starting up agencies of their own.

Creative Hot Shops

It is a bold step to leave a well-paid position in a large and stable agency. Bolder still is the decision to open one's own agency. It is a high-stakes gamble that could pay off handsomely or cost one's savings and health. Deepening resentment with turgid agency processes and dull outputs, coupled with personal ambition and inspiration from abroad, meant that many entrepreneurial admen and adwomen were willing to take a gamble on their own abilities. The ensuing boutique agencies or creative 'hot shops' would form the vanguard for the Creative Revolution in Australia.

In January 1964 *Newspaper News* reported that the agency formerly known as William H. Rodgers & Associates would henceforth be known as Rodgers Holland Everingham (RHE) – 'no commas or hyphens'.[24] The absence of punctuation was a nod to Doyle Dane Bernbach's famous claim regarding the agency's title 'Nothing will ever come between us. Not even punctuation.'[25] William Rodgers's new partners were renowned creatives. Arthur Holland had run his own studio. Although he was best known for his art direction, he could also write copy. Denis Everingham was recognised as one of Australia's best copywriters. He arrived at RHE from JWT and had previously worked in Canada. Also known as 'The Bear', Everingham was the quintessential fast-talking, creative adman – full of ideas and always up for a scotch or any other distraction that came his way.[26] The new team made it clear that they were shaking things up and that RHE was avoiding the problems that impeded creativity in the large agencies. RHE's small size was therefore identified as an asset, with Rodgers explaining that it facilitated 'short lines of communication and quality control'.

Rodgers also claimed that RHE had eliminated another problem – the intrusive account executive who 'inhibits the creative team because he [sic] has the edge on them all the way … Time and again I've seen him misinform, misinterpret and misconstrue. Half the boring advertising … stem[s] from these factors.'[27] Challenging the view that creatives should only come in midway through a job, Rodgers stated that RHE had 'abandoned the account executive system and replaced it with account co-ordinating groups … This policy will allow the creative staff to be involved with the client at a campaign's birth instead of receiving instructions second-hand from an account executive.'[28]

Four years after RHE opened its doors, John 'Singo' Singleton decided that he too wanted his name on the agency's letterhead. Prior to his four-year stint at the mid-sized local agency Berry Currie, the feisty copywriter had previously worked for various multinational agencies – and had been dismissed from most of them. Together with Duncan McAllan, his art director at Berry Currie, the ambitious and headstrong Singleton set up his own agency.

Months earlier, two men in Melbourne had made similar steps. Copywriter Mike Strauss had followed account executive Rob Palmer out of the Melbourne office of Grey Advertising to form their own venture. For South African–born Strauss, the move was one partly borne of frustration and personal ambition. Arriving in Australia in 1961 via London, Strauss was shocked when his creative director at Noel Paton instructed him to copy competitors' advertisements. After a month he confronted his boss, telling him 'I'm here to create advertising of my own … I don't want to copy someone else's ideas, that's not what this is about.' A different director overheard the dispute and entered the fray, telling Strauss: 'You will never, ever make it in this industry.' The two fledgling agencies agreed to join forces to form a two-city operation – Singleton Palmer Strauss McAllan. (A report in the industry press using the principals' initials and a wayward ampersand saw the agency rechristened SPASM.)[29]

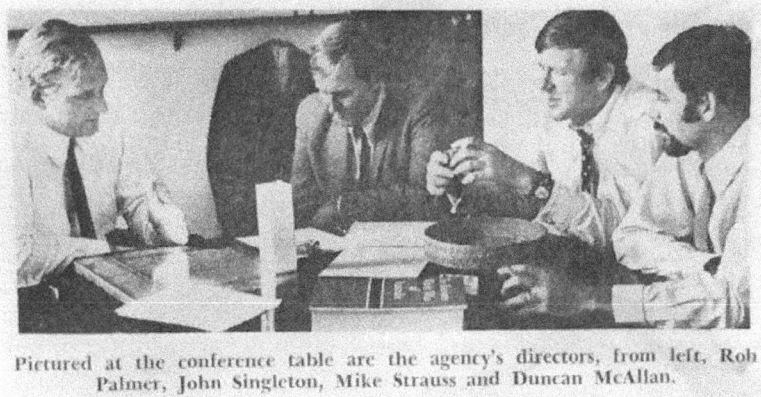

Pictured at the conference table are the agency's directors, from left, Rob Palmer, John Singleton, Mike Strauss and Duncan McAllan.

Figure 4.1 SPASM's directors crowd around the fledgling agency's conference table. B&T, *27 February 1969, p. 17. (Courtesy of B&T)*

With Singleton, Strauss, and McAllan all being creatives, it was no surprise that SPASM would embrace the creative creed. Echoing RHE, Singleton explained that his agency 'allows the client to deal direct with the originators of advertising and shortens lines of communication … It also allows the agency to trim "middle-man fat" and pay higher salaries to attract top creative and research talent.'[30] A more unique innovation was its decision to employ women in account-service positions. The agency's founders believed that women were 'much better than men at detail' and that they were also 'out to prove themselves in an industry like advertising, which has traditionally been male dominated'.[31] Singleton's reference to research talent reveals that the agency was not interested in creativity for the sake of creativity. In order to understand the consumer, SPASM made extensive use of the research services of Dr Peter Kenny, a former lecturer in psychology who had also headed the Australian Broadcasting Commission's Research and Statistics division.[32] Singleton had been impressed by his ability to gain insights into the consumer's mindset as well as his down-to-earth explanation of them.[33] A different initiative was the Communication Supermarket, a series of related companies operating across advertising, research, public relations, sales promotion and direct mail that serviced the client's marketing communication needs.[34] Far from challenging the old order, the Communication Supermarket concept consciously emulated Marion Harper's Interpublic network.[35]

Gordon Trembath and Lionel Hunt were working in the Melbourne office of Masius, Wynne-Williams in 1972 when they decided to venture out on their own. Despite its size and status as a local branch of a multi-national agency, Masius was recognised as one of Melbourne's hottest agencies. However, this did not diminish the two creatives' frustrations with the agency's operations. 'I remember having a couple of campaigns knocked back, and I was furious', explains copywriter Hunt.[36] One was a campaign for Toyota Crown, which featured the car on a revolving dais for sixty seconds with classical music in the background. At the end of the commercial, the tagline stated 'Toyota Crown – You either love it or hate it'. While Hunt and Trembath thought the idea 'was really clever', management stepped in and stopped it. Moreover, the duo was frustrated by the account executives' inability to persuade clients to accept good ideas. Conceding that it did not happen often, Hunt nevertheless recalls that it occurred 'enough to annoy us'.[37] As their frustrations mounted, Hunt and Trembath saw exciting developments in London. They were not only inspired by the creative work coming out of Britain, they were also impressed by those responsible for it. Upon learning that these boutique creative agencies comprised 'a writer and an art director and they would deal with the clients', Hunt and Trembath recognised their opportunity: 'we don't have to go through this middle layer of ... incompetent account service people. We can just do it ourselves.'[38] It was the art director Trembath who first decided to start his own boutique agency. Hunt was reluctant to leave his well-paid position at Masius but happily moonlighted for Trembath, whose business rapidly grew. Work largely came from other agencies looking for creativity rather than from advertisers. After six months, Trembath again invited Hunt to join him at what was now entitled The Campaign Palace. Seeing the opportunity to gain creative independence as well as financial security, Hunt struck a deal with Trembath that would land him a pay rise as well as half the business.[39]

The creatives' revolt was also driven by personal ambition and the opportunity to reinvent themselves as something more than mere cogs in a large agency machine. Obviously, money was a driving factor. While good creatives were already taking home large salaries, being the principal in one's own agency meant that they could earn even more. Age also played an important role in the decision to leave the big agencies. In 1968 *B&T* investigated the age of agency staff. Senior management and account service staff enjoyed long careers. Creatives were more vulnerable as 'the field of creative men thinned rapidly after 45 years of age'.[40] John Bristow, chairman of Pritchard Wood, bluntly stated that for copywriters and art directors 'I consider 50 too old. Broadly, I would say the creative peak is 35, but there are always exceptions.'[41] Singleton and Hunt were in their late twenties, while Everingham was in his mid-thirties. Copywriter Bryce Courtenay revealed that creatives were aware of the ticking clock on their short careers. At thirty-nine he co-founded Harris Robinson Courtenay. Having spent some fifteen years working for HRMcCE and JWT, Courtenay needed to take the plunge before it was too late: 'I felt that if I didn't at least try before I was 40, I might never realise an ambition. I'd always cherished to run my own advertising ship.'[42]

The founders of each new boutique promised that their agency would be different to all other agencies before them – they could hardly say otherwise. In an industry where every brand claimed to be unique, such claims were hardly novel. The founders of these new boutiques, however, were sincere in their pronouncements – they had, after all, risked their own money on being different. With little more than a handful of ambitious staff, these agencies emphasised creativity as both a justification for their existence and the key to future prosperity. Whether it was a means to an end or an end in itself, creativity was nevertheless something that these agencies felt they could offer to clients that their competitors could not, particularly the multi-nationals.

With large accounts such as Coca-Cola and Nestlé, HRMcCE of the late 1960s and 70s seemed to typify the regimented and soulless multi-national agency. Stating that 'if a company that size doesn't have discipline, you'd end up with a zoo', former account director Don Farrow nevertheless conceded that the working environment at the agency was not conducive to creative work: 'McCann is probably over-managed, and when that is reflected in individuals who are trying to win points from each other, then that's a problem.'[43] Of course, this stereotype did not apply to all agencies.

At Masius Wynne-Williams, chairman Len Reason actively fostered a positive culture, encouraging staff to socialise over a drink or four as 'the agency that drinks together sticks together'.[44] Not surprisingly, the boutique agency principals preferred the Masius model over McCann. At the Brisbane-based Jones Knowles Vinnicombe Shirley, chairman and creative director Paul Jones explained the importance of having the right environment: 'You can see from the place we create our own environment. Word gets around … we get lots of people just want to come and work here. Let's not kid ourselves, we can't get the top people out of Sydney and Melbourne to come to Brisbane. But we can get that next bunch, that non-director bunch on the way up.'[45] And the right environment might also keep them there, too.

Agencies understood the correlation between staff and environment. New boutiques were created by individuals who shared common beliefs and visions. As such, the environment was inevitably collaborative – at least initially. They actively recruited individuals who shared their ethos and had something to offer to the environment. The Campaign Palace had a clear ethos: 'we only wanted people that were brilliant. We wanted to be the best creative agency in the country, one of the best in the world … there's no magic secret to this, you've just got to hire people who are that good.'[46] Strauss sought people 'with ideas … who challenged what was going on around them' and could come up with a 'better way of doing it'.[47] At Forbes McPhee Hansen, creative director Derek Hansen wanted non-conformists: 'I looked for rebels. I looked for people that were struggling in the big agencies. I hired a few people out of the western suburbs too, hungry kids with some track record.'[48] On the other side of the fence, Ron Mather recalls how things clicked when speaking to The Campaign Palace: 'I just knew from the moment I started chatting to them … they were absolutely on the same wavelength. They wanted what I wanted. They wanted … to be slightly different, cheeky, fresh.'[49]

Financial constraints also contributed to the environment. Over the 1960s and 1970s, Sydney's advertising agencies had progressively clustered in North Sydney while those in Melbourne lined leafy St Kilda Road. These addresses were not only convenient for clients, they also helped reinforce the image of the agencies as stable and professional businesses. As few start-ups could afford the rent in these prime areas, they looked for more modest locations. SPASM's initial premises were a 'perfectly restored sandstone/sandstock (convict built) house in Burton Street Darlinghurst'.[50] Still in the earliest throes of gentrification, the area offered a hip and edgy address that was also affordable.

Success led SPASM to look for larger premises. Having established an image that connected with its environment, SPASM decided to remain in Darlinghurst. Its new premises would present an altogether different challenge. Singleton recalled that 'the "greenies" [who] didn't like offices being built in the area … Continually … sprayed our walls with such niceties as "Piss off trendies", "Homes not offices", and other inanities'.[51] Such accusations seem somewhat ironic given that SPASM was trying to avoid the soullessness of corporate North Sydney.

The Campaign Palace started out in Trembath's house on Anderson Street in South Melbourne. Hunt states that the decision to avoid St Kilda Road was 'simply an overhead issue, we didn't want to take on any costs'.[52] As it had with SPASM, growth necessitated larger premises, and it would spend $79,000 on a large Italianate Victorian building in Cecil Street in South Melbourne.[53] A significant investment, the new office nevertheless embodied the agency's creative vision. Recalling that 'We had our headquarters. The Campaign Palace. It looked like a palace', Hunt alludes to the importance of the agency's premises for its reputation.[54] The right environment would remain an abiding part of The Campaign Palace's ethos into the following decades. 'You nurture prima donnas and petunias, not creative people', explained the agency's managing director in 1984, 'All they need is the right environment – and that's where standards are respected and there is a genuine commitment (to advertising), not a commitment of convenience'.[55]

The quest for creativity had a fundamental impact on the day-to-day operations of the boutique agency. The creative department now called the shots. Although the creatives initially met directly with clients, expansion and ensuring the maintenance of everyday relationships with clients necessitated more account-service personnel. Despite the implementation of this standard practice from the big agencies, there was no question as to who was in control. Account service executives were expected to sell the creative work to the client. Echoing the ethos at Collett Dickenson Pearce, The Campaign Palace's creatives made it clear that any account executive who failed to sell their work to the client ought to look for work at another agency.[56] The account executive's task was made all the more difficult by The Campaign Palace's approach of creating a single campaign. Where large agencies offered their clients a range of alternative campaigns, The Campaign Palace only offered clients a single idea – *the* idea.[57] This simple practice was arguably the most revolutionary. By offering a single creative idea, The Campaign Palace was reinventing the client–agency relationship. Its creative credentials enabled it to challenge the agency's standing as a mere service provider and to assert its professional status. While many had called for clients to view their agencies as their partners, few agencies had the chutzpah to act on it. As we will see in the next chapter, this would not be a sustainable approach.

Regardless of the level of creative ability, personal ambition, or reformist idealism, a boutique agency fundamentally remained a business and was therefore subject to business imperatives. No agency could survive without clients. Campbell-Ewald's buy out of Hertz Walpole, for example, had been suggested by Doug Watson and Wayne McCarthy. The duo was still working for Campbell-Ewald when they were informed that they would now have to prove themselves to the agency's new partners. Angered by their treatment, Watson and McCarthy informed Hertz Walpole on a Friday that they would be starting their own agency. When they arrived the next morning to pick up their belongings and address books, security denied them access. They would have to start from scratch. Opening for business on Monday in Watson's home, the first task of the McCarthy Watson agency was simple: 'Get the business'.[58] With some experience of working on car accounts, Watson opened the telephone directory and began dialling. Others called upon former clients, mates, and acquaintances.

As an account service, art director, copywriter team, Begg Dow Priday had a clearer strategy of winning new business. In addition to pursuing the accounts that larger agencies had dispensed with in their efforts to streamline their operations, Begg Dow Priday also took on retail advertising.[59] Another business challenge that was more unique to the boutique agencies was the task of running a business. As creatives, many had been shielded from the decidedly less creative tasks associated with keeping a business afloat – from liaising with clients to paying the rent. Already in 1971, JWT's John Sharman thus observed 'that while creative boutiques have a place in advertising, their neglect of administrative particulars often foreshadows their end'.[60] Hansen reveals that there were also other stresses: 'When you're the principal of an agency and you get it wrong and you lose an account, people get fired. We didn't want that to happen … and we, too often I think, erred on the side of conservatism'.[61] To this end, it seems that the bureaucratic burdens that ignited the creative spark could also extinguish it and the hot shop with it.

Trading Media Space

The emergence of the creative boutique gave rise to the development of another specialised business – the media consultancy. In order to advertise on television, advertising agencies needed to be accredited by the Media Council of Australia. As the purpose of accreditation was to protect the media from agencies defaulting on payments, most new boutiques faced an uphill battle to meet the Council's strict financial requirements. Media consultancies, therefore, offered the small agencies an opportunity to circumvent these requirements. While media-buying consultancies had been established abroad, Australia's pioneering media agents and their new agencies followed their own path. In the process they would reinvent the media field and the relations in it. Moreover, their actions would further stimulate creativity within the agency ranks.

In 1969 Dennis Merchant was working in HRMcCE's media department. Having spent twelve unhappy months there, he readily accepted Y&R's invitation to join its new Australian operation. It would prove to be an auspicious move. Where other agencies tended to view media planning and buying as something of an afterthought, Y&R placed Merchant in the same room as the creatives: 'I felt very much part of the ... agency team at Y&R because you would never have a campaign discussion without me being there.'[62] Over his five years at Y&R, Merchant not only enjoyed making a meaningful contribution to the creative and the strategic aspects of a campaign, he also recognised that there were other opportunities to be had. Merchant believed that an agency specialising in media buying and planning now had a ready market with the 'small to medium-size Australian-owned agencies which were finding it increasingly difficult to compete with the big, mostly multinational agencies. The small guys couldn't find or couldn't afford the right people and the overheads that went with a full-service media department.'[63]

Despite the opportunity, Merchant was reluctant to take the big step. His wife, Gay, ultimately persuaded him to act on his convictions, reminding him of his age and his ambition: 'Dennis, you have to do this. I don't want to be living with you when you are 40 and you are resenting the fact of never having given it a go.'[64] With his wife's words ringing in his ears, Merchant joined forces with another Y&R colleague to form Merchant & Pettett in 1974.

In Melbourne, Harold Mitchell was working at Masius when he recognised a similar opportunity to provide a media buying and planning service to smaller agencies. He also noted that clients 'had a greater understanding of the marketing process' and wanted greater accountability for the amounts that they were spending on media placement.[65] Mitchell had tried to convince Masius to finance the creation of a media-buying agency. When this fell on deaf ears for a second time in 1975, the 34-year-old media man left Masius to actualise his plan: 'I left a very good job, a comfortable job because I just thought it was going to be the future, and that's ultimately what it became.'[66] Both men's motivations were little different to those cited by the creatives – frustration, opportunity, and personal ambition.

As Merchant and Mitchell operated in different markets, they formed a loose collaboration. Their operations also revealed various similarities. Both had strong links to the creative boutiques from the very outset. Merchant's agency shared a building with Hertz Walpole while Mitchell was next door to Begg Dow Priday. Ian Robertson recalls that the media agencies' relationships with the boutiques were strong: 'We worked with them very much the same as you would work in a normal agency ... We treated their clients ... like our own. We knew many of them ... we always went to the meetings, so they knew us and regarded us as ... part of the team.'[67] By neutralising the advantage that larger agencies enjoyed in terms of accreditation, and inspiring media buyers and planners in large agencies to branch out on their own, the media agencies also set themselves on a future collision course with the larger agencies.

The Big Agencies Go Creative

In 1962 Keith Cousins, the general manager of George Patterson, addressed a creative seminar organised by the Australian Association of Advertising Agencies (4As) in Terrigal. His comments, reported in *Newspaper News*, reveal a somewhat ambiguous attitude towards creativity. On the one hand, he 'stressed the importance of the account executive being consulted at every stage and not treated as a "hostile witness"', yet, on the other, Cousins conceded that: 'In the future, agencies would depend on the quality of their creative people.'[68] While large agencies like George Patterson clearly positioned the account service department at the centre of their operations, they nevertheless recognised the growing importance of creativity. Their business nous meant that they understood that they also needed to improve their creative output or risk losing out to the boutiques.

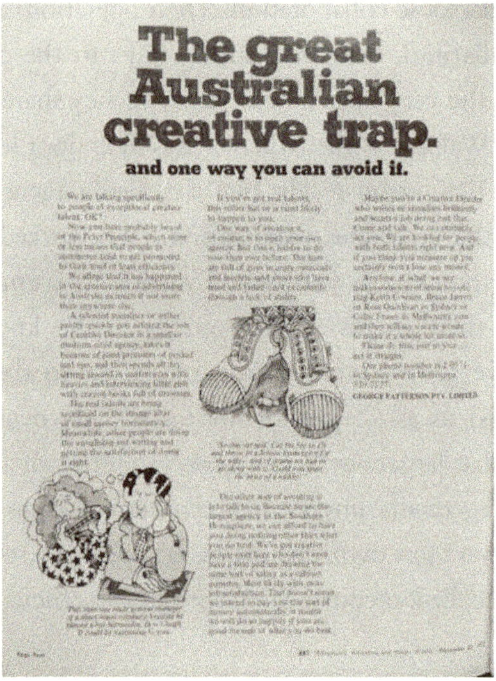

Figure 4.2 George Patterson takes on the small boutiques to attract the best creative talent. B&T, 22 November 1973, p. 4 (Courtesy of B&T)

As the number of multi-national agencies operating in the Australian market grew over the course of the 1960s, J. Walter Thompson found itself under pressure. JWT still enjoyed the second-largest billings in the country, but the others were closing in quickly. In 1967, JWT's chief executive officer John Sharman announced that the agency's Sydney offices would be restructured. It would create a single creative department that integrated copy, radio, television, art, traffic and production. Operating within the department were five separate creative groups comprising 'a creative director, a bright young writer, an art director, visualiser and production co-ordinator'.[69] Each group would work on specific accounts. Two creative supervisors from outside the agency would be appointed to oversee the department. Hoping to 'achieve the highest standard of creative end product' and to place a new emphasis on 'account teamwork, rather than departmental function', Sharman argued that JWT needed to be 'under-organised rather than over-organised – to meet the dynamic changes ahead'.[70] Months later, the agency announced that it had secured Bryce Courtenay from HRMcCE and Denis Everingham from RHE. Both men had been enticed by the prospect of converting a tired multi-national giant into a creative powerhouse. Whether they were driven by ego, their commitment to creativity, a generous salary, or all three, the successful recasting of JWT's creative credentials would be a major accomplishment for any creative.[71] Sharman also looked to incorporate a creative element into the account service department by going 'beyond the confines of our own business' to recruit people who were 'strong, durable and contemporary'. 'Advertising is not an easy business, and it is in a constant process of rapid change', he observed.[72]

Geoff Wild was despatched from Melbourne with the aim of turning around the fortunes of Clemenger's Sydney operation. The office had been in the red for almost twenty straight years when Wild arrived in 1972. After reorganising the agency, Wild looked for a way to make it stand-out. Peter Clemenger firmly believed that one should always know what the competitor is thinking. He therefore advised Wild to visit Bill Farnsworth, the head of George Patterson, to introduce himself and get some advice. Farnsworth kept his visitor waiting half an hour before letting him into the office. After Wild introduced himself and explained how he hoped that he might be able to call upon his fellow adman for some advice, Farnsworth replied: 'Son, I'm not gonna help ya, but I'm not gonna harm ya.'[73] When analysing his giant competitor, Wild found that 'while they dominated, they were not regarded as creative … They had their clients locked in on price and that sort of thing.'[74]

As creativity provided a way around Patterson's dominance, Wild duly set about establishing Clemenger as a large agency that also did creative advertising. In addition to recruiting key creatives, the agency also invested its own funds into enhancing a campaign's 'creative excellence'. Wild's strategy worked and the results spoke for themselves. In 1970 the Clemenger group was billing $9.6 million while George Patterson billed $26 million. Five years later, Clemenger's $33 million of billings was just shy of George Patterson's $40 million.[75] Moreover, Clemenger were winning creative awards for their work. Their success with awards reveals that Clemenger's creative embrace was not simply an exercise in differentiation. Clients may not have always appreciated an agency's creativity, but they certainly understood that an award-winning campaign attracted good attention for their brand. Awards also helped to attract other clients who were eager for an award-winning campaign of their own. Creativity had not only provided the basis for Clemenger's growth, it had enabled Clemenger to seriously challenge George Patterson. Looking on, Farnsworth would have regretted his promise to the young visitor from Clemenger.

A 1975 survey of clients revealed that they were also jumping on board the creative bandwagon. An agency's creativity was listed as the number-one reason for both shortlisting and appointing an agency. However, when it came to severing their association, clients were more concerned by an agency's attitude and account service than the quality of an agency's creative work.[76] By 1980, creative director Ian Nankervis observed that other multi-nationals were following JWT's and Clemenger's lead: 'Full service agencies with an emphasis on creativity are no longer a rarity. It's arguable at times some of them are better at doing ads than others, but, by and large, they all have the same philosophy when it comes to making ads.'[77] Even Patts understood that it needed to do more on the creative side. 'I was always aware … that Patts was not regarded as a highly creative agency', explains Bruce Jarrett, 'but we did do some highly creative work. The majority of the work worked.'[78] Despite having a long-standing antipathy towards advertising awards, George Patterson entered the 'Memories' campaign for OTC at the 1976 International Advertising Film Festival in Cannes. It would win the Grand Prix – the first Australian agency to take out the coveted prize.

The big agencies' embrace of creativity would have a direct impact on the agency structure. As in the boutiques, the creatives in larger agencies were now becoming the stars – and they knew it. 'Creative directors were certainly looked upon as demi-gods of the industry', notes Mike Ellis, McCann-Erickson's graphic services manager. 'They were answerable to no-one, not even the clients.'[79] Recalling that the other departments 'were all our servants', creative director John Newton reveals the creative department's growing ego.[80] Such attitudes were further reinforced by the generous salaries. As competition for creative talent intensified, agencies readily paid a premium to lure the brightest and the best. At Clemenger, Wild had the outlook that 'the fewer number of better people … the better the bottom line.'[81] He was therefore able to pay his creatives well for their work. Advertisements in *B&T* in 1976 indicate that Clemenger was not the only agency that was prepared to pay handsomely for creativity. An established copywriter at this time was earning between $17,000 and $25,000, while creative directors were being offered $35,000. For the average Australian taking home just over $10,000 per annum, the creative working in an advertising agency seemed to have it all – a high-paying job that required little more than the capacity to come up with some creative ideas.

———————————

Creativity had presented an opportunity for advertising agencies to rethink advertising. The work coming out of New York and London revealed new ways of speaking to the audience. As in the UK, the Creative Revolution was 'adapted, hybridised and indigenised' in its importation into Australia. From the 'ocker' commercials created by Singo to the more cerebral efforts of The Campaign Palace, this new wave of advertising resonated strongly with the local audiences.[82]

The impact of creativity on the role and operations of the advertising agency was perhaps less visible to outsiders but no less profound – from the formation of the creative hot shops and media consultancies to the reorganisation of the creative department and the generous salaries paid to creative staff. Arriving progressively rather than suddenly, Australia's Creative Revolution not only inspired creative staff to take action, it also provided them with the means by which they could explain and justify their reinvention of advertising to clients and large agencies alike. As the next chapter reveals, this growth in creativity would also be instrumental in providing Australian agencies with the confidence to take on the world.

CHAPTER FIVE

TAKING ON THE WORLD

Jogging along Sydney's Whale Beach in 1984, Greg Daniel met the recently retired chairman of George Patterson, Keith Cousins. As the two men chatted, the 34-year-old Daniel revealed that he was preparing to take up a position with Needham, Harper & Steers in the United States. Although George Patterson had been 80 per cent American-owned for the past twenty years, Cousins strongly cautioned the young executive against travelling to the US and urged him to meet with his half-brother, Geoff, who now headed George Patterson. After meeting with Geoff Cousins, Daniel learnt that The Campaign Palace's Sydney office was looking for a new managing director. For years Australia's most creative agency had struggled to make its presence felt in the Harbour City. Its uncompromising attitude to creativity had left Sydney's advertisers apprehensive, resulting in a regular turnover of managing directors at the creative agency. So when Daniel abandoned his US plans to take the managing director position at The Campaign Palace Sydney, it appeared that he had traded international experience for a poisoned chalice.[1]

In his new role, Daniel set about making the agency more 'client friendly'. To alleviate the concerns of prospective clients, Daniel's team set about formulating a 'narrative ... around why The Campaign Palace was like it is and why ... it's a great thing.'[2]

The agency also hoped to confirm its business credentials by hiring 'international quality account directors' who had 'worked at big agencies with big accounts'. Daniel's strategy quickly bore fruit, with the agency almost doubling its billings from $12.25 million in 1984 to $22.5 million in 1985.[3] In employing staff with international-account-service experience and adopting a more business-oriented approach to advertising, The Campaign Palace under Daniel appeared to be implementing the strategies that had helped transform agencies such as McCann-Erickson from national firms into global behemoths. However, Daniel's decision to stay put in Australia, as well as Keith Cousins's initial intervention, also revealed a different story. As contact with global advertising operations became more direct and regular, many Australians reconsidered their place in the world. Their increasing experience with, and understanding of, international practice helped foster greater confidence about themselves as professionals in a global industry, and the quality of their work on the global stage.

Globalising the International Pioneer

In February 1980, J Walter Thompson threw one of 'the most lavish agency soirees of recent times' at the Sydney Opera House to celebrate the 50th anniversary of its arrival in Australia.[4] While JWT was celebrating its pioneering role in internationalising advertising-agency operations, it was no longer a pioneer. Over the past two decades, the competition had caught up. JWT management understood that they now needed to revisit their own operations and strategies in light of those deployed by their globally focused competitors.

JWT's declining status was already evident in the late 1970s. Shortly after arriving from Canada to take control of JWT's

Australian operations in 1977, Donald Robertson set about restructuring the agency's management team. In a memo to staff, Robertson explained that the restructure of JWT's Australian operations was intended to capitalise on the agency's global connections: 'we plan to fully maximise the experience, expertise and resources within JWT-Australia and within the Thompson world. We are one-Company here and we are one-Company around the world. We fully intend to operate this way in a one-Company manner.'[5] Of course, JWT had long been operating on an international footing, with New York and London regularly providing direction on matters pertaining to client service and creative strategy. However, the Australian operation's activities following its restructure reveal a more engaging relationship between the locals and the global headquarters.

Some eighteen months after the reorganisation of JWT Australia's management, it was becoming clear that the agency was still struggling. Writing to John Sharman, executive vice-president in New York and former head of JWT Australia, Robertson stated that: 'Our market ranking has decreased from #2 to #7 in the past nine years and reversing this trend from solely national growth is difficult in the short-term.' Noting that JWT Australia was 'still known as an unaggressive, conservative yet highly professional agency', Robertson argued that the agency needed 'some major elements and evidence of dynamism if we are to change our image, rather than to just modify it.'[6] The acquisition of another agency that would operate independently of JWT, therefore, identified as a 'top priority'. Compatibility, financial stability, and growth potential were to be the basis of any deal. In a memo to the local management team, Robertson expressed his preference for a smaller agency. He felt that this would provide clients with a choice, as they could opt for the 'special attention that a small agency can give' or the 'reassurances and resources' that a large agency like JWT could provide.[7] With New York giving the green light, JWT Australia quickly moved to acquire Begg Dow Priday (BDP). Describing it as 'Melbourne's fastest growing and "hottest" agency' with a profitable clientele, Robertson was also assured by the fact that BDP's principals were '"big agency" trained' and had 'run the agency … in a sound business-like manner.'[8] BDP's decision to sell was based on the belief that the agency's 'future growth will be inhibited without access to greater resources' and that JWT offered sufficient resources and opportunity, as well as 'a reputation and people compatible with our own.'[9]

With both parties agreeing to the JWT buy-out, discussions between the two parties initially focused on the financial side of the sale. While the sale was a local matter for JWT, it nevertheless consulted with its New York office. In December 1979, Greg Reilly, the finance director of JWT Australia, sent an outline of 'our thinking regarding the possible acquisition of Begg Dow Priday' to Alun Jones, JWT's executive vice-president of finance. Reilly hoped the outline would enable Jones to '"follow our tracks" and thereby put us back on the right course when necessary.'[10] During the ongoing discussions, BDP's question regarding processes to deal with conflicting accounts was referred to New York for clarification. Responding that there were 'no automatic restrictions' and that the aim of acquiring agencies was in fact 'to bust open the conflict log jam', the New York office revealingly added: 'We may have to come back to BDP some time [sic] in the future and say, please hands off such and such an account.'[11] When *Ad News* announced the imminent deal to the industry in August 1980, its global dimensions were highlighted. *Ad News* noted that 'the purchase will form part of a second network of agencies that JWT has been putting together around the world', while BDP's Austin Begg ebulliently declared that: 'Our clients will have access to international resources, while we can strengthen our business and build it up to the next level.'[12]

BDP soon discovered the realities of merging with a multi-national giant. As the deal was being finalised, Robertson was transferred to New York – BDP's principals had been given the impression that they would be reporting to Robertson for the next three years. Robertson's replacement left BDP under-whelmed. BDP's billings nevertheless grew, enabling the agency to open a Sydney office. But Begg recalls that JWT remained uninterested in its acquisition: 'As part of their contractual obligation they undertook to oversee our financial and admin-istration and our people. Hardly ever saw them.'[13] A similar attitude was discernible in the way that JWT handled its Euro Advertising Network comprising the small, autonomous agen-cies such as BDP. 'They basically left us to our own devices because they were having problems managing their own global business', observes Begg, who sat on the Network's board. Such problems were not limited to the revelation that it had been grossly overcharging clients; billings were falling. JWT would continue to slide down the global rankings, and by 1987 the international pioneer was bought out by Martin Sorrell, an alumnus of another visionary global agency, Saatchi & Saatchi (and a globalising innovator in his own right).[14]

Going Global

'The globalization of markets is at hand', declared Ted Levitt in the *Harvard Business Review*.[15] Where international firms had previously adapted to local conditions, Levitt claimed that the modern global corporation 'will seek sensibly to force suitably standardized products and practice on the entire globe.'[16] 'Companies that do not adapt to the new global realities', he warned, 'will become victims of those that do.'[17] While Levitt's piece made no reference to advertising agencies, heads of multinational agencies who read it understood that they too needed to adopt a global outlook. One of these was Maurice Saatchi, whose eponymous agency would become the global epitome of advertising's global expansion and excess in the 1980s.[18]

Saatchi & Saatchi's dramatic rise in the 1980s took the advertising world by storm. Starting out as a small boutique in 1967, the London-based CramerSaatchi became Saatchi & Saatchi in 1970 when Maurice Saatchi replaced Ross Cramer as Charles Saatchi's partner. Over the 1970s, Saatchi & Saatchi built a reputation for creative work, such as the Health Education Council's 'pregnant man' advertisement and the 'Labour isn't Working' posters for the Conservative Party in the 1979 general election. Creativity alone, however, would not deliver the brothers' ambition of running the world's most successful agency. Combining ruthless pragmatism, resourceful innovation, and a gambler's opportunism, the Saatchis set about realising their goal.

From the outset, the Saatchis defied convention by directly approaching clients rather than adopting the discreet approach of London's advertising scene.[19] In terms of expanding their operations abroad, Saatchi & Saatchi established a European network of offices in the mid-1970s. Although the venture failed, it nevertheless taught the agency's principals the importance of offering clients a global network rather than a merely regional service.[20] Saatchi & Saatchi also looked to expand via acquiring other agencies, earning it the derisive moniker 'Snatchit & Snatchit.'[21] In 1975 the Saatchis sold their agency to the multi-national Garland-Compton in return for a 36 per cent share of the multi-national's British operations. As the largest shareholders, they effectively engineered a reverse takeover – a point underscored by the agency's new title, Saatchi & Saatchi, Garland-Compton. In addition to acquiring large Procter & Gamble accounts, the deal also provided the Saatchis with a public listing. Significantly, Saatchi & Saatchi now had a launching pad for its global ambitions.

For the Saatchi brothers, 1982 proved to be an *annus mirabilis*. After protracted negotiations, the Saatchis managed to buy out Compton Communications Inc. in the US, which provided an instant global presence. Again, the brothers demanded that their name come first in the agency's title. The deal also pioneered a new purchasing model, whereby Saatchi & Saatchi would pay for half of the acquisition in cash (sourced from the stock exchange) and the second half over a ten-year period. Over the next five years, the Saatchis would use this model to purchase some thirty-six agencies across the globe. As the Compton deal was being finalised, the Saatchis found themselves in the running for an account that required a global presence. Looking to reinvigorate its brand, British Airways's head ended the firm's thirty-six-year relationship with the multinational Foote Cone & Belding and offered the account to Saatchi & Saatchi. Now that it possessed a global network and a growing number of global accounts, Saatchi & Saatchi set about becoming a global entity in the way outlined by Levitt.

Saatchi & Saatchi entered the Australian market through the Compton network. Compton had arrived in Australia in 1962 when it bought out the Melbourne-based N.V. Nixon to access Australia's 'export drive to Far East markets.'[22] By 1980, the agency was struggling and bought out the mid-sized

Mullins Clarke Ralph (MCR). A year later, MCR Compton became a Melbourne-only operation when it closed its ailing Sydney offices.[23] By the time Saatchi & Saatchi acquired it, the office seemed conservative and moribund.[24] Needing a presence in Sydney that could also energise the Melbourne office, Saatchi & Saatchi considered a number of creative agencies before approaching Gough Waterhouse. Established as a consultancy in 1979 by expatriate British creatives, Phil Gough and Vic Waterhouse, Gough Waterhouse had forged a formidable creative reputation by the time that Saatchi & Saatchi came knocking. Asked for his views on the Saatchi approach, Gough Waterhouse's financial head, Mike Satterthwaite, demurred and suggested that the agency's mounting successes meant that it could hold out for a better deal. However, Gough felt he had little choice. '[T]here is only one Saatchi & Saatchi', he explained, 'and I want to be part of that brand.'[25] After undertaking due diligence, Saatchi & Saatchi used its standard buyout strategy for a 60 per cent share of the agency that would henceforth trade as Saatchi & Saatchi Compton Gough Waterhouse. Of course, everyone referred to it as Saatchis.

The Saatchis' attitude to managing their empire was somewhat more ambivalent than their determined approach to building it. As each buyout was finalised, senior staff in the acquired agencies soon discovered that the Saatchis were no longer interested in taking their calls.[26] Initial connections with Australia proved underwhelming. When a newly appointed manager of the Melbourne office rang London for advice on sacking his creative director, the equally new chief executive was able to offer little more than the platitude: 'do as you see fit.'[27] A senior finance officer who had been despatched to Australia shortly after the takeover would be better remembered for being a 'beautiful lunch partner' and 'raconteur' than for making any meaningful contribution to the agency's latest acquisition.[28] However, as Saatchi & Saatchi grasped the realities of running a global operation, staff began to move through the networks. Australian offices readily tapped into the global network for more appropriate staff.[29] By 1986, *B&T* was noting that 'there are people around who see Saatchi & Saatchi Compton's operations in Australia as teeming with uncontrollable pommie creative directors.'[30]

In contrast to the head office's approach to staffing, the state of the Australian operation's finances was of immediate concern. Monthly reports were despatched to London by courier, and when a telex machine was installed in 1987, the Australian operations were sending daily cash-balance updates to the head office.[31] Satterthwaite feels that this requirement was 'just a game because there was never any value in knowing how much cash there was in any particular office'. Annual reports were initially sent to London, but in later years the financial team would travel to London to present the budget in person, albeit to an often tired and uninterested audience.[32]

The agency's global outlook was perhaps most evident in its highly publicised battle to overturn Australia's local content regulations. In 1984 the Australian Broadcasting Tribunal banned the agency's latest campaign for British Airways. The Tribunal claimed that the global campaign contravened Australian local-content regulations and that the agency crew sent to work on the campaign was in fact a 'ghost crew' that did no actual work. Its commitment to producing truly global campaigns for its clients led Saatchi & Saatchi to challenge the Tribunal in the Federal Court.[33] The agency's actions were supported by multi-national advertisers and their agencies but locally owned agencies and production houses remained bitterly opposed.[34] While Saatchi & Saatchi's appeal was upheld, the government supported the locally owned firms and amended the *Broadcasting and Television Act*. Saatchi & Saatchi would, however, eventually win the war, when Australia's local content restrictions were overturned in 1991.

Sibling Rivalry

When Saatchi & Saatchi's joint chief executive, Terry Bannister, visited Australia in 1988, he asserted that the agency's Australian offices were an integral part of the network's global operations. 'If you break down the world into Europe, the United States and Asia-Pacific, if you're not making big money in Australia, you're not succeeding in the region', he explained.[35] While Saatchi & Saatchi's Australian billings were certainly growing, they were overshadowed by a more recent acquisition to the Saatchis' global empire – George Patterson. 'Unusually in Australia we are the [smaller] sibling', observed Bannister, before adding: 'We want them to continue to succeed because we're all shareholders in the same company in the end.'[36] George Patterson's unique position in the Saatchi network revealed the ongoing need for global giants to pay close attention to local conditions.

In 1986, the agencies BBDO, DDB, and Needham Harper agreed to a mega-merger that brought them under the Omnicom banner. The deal was nicknamed 'the Big Bang.'[37] Not to be outdone in their pursuit of global dominance, the Saatchis embarked on a spate of buyouts of their own. Shortly after the announcement of the three-way mega-merger, Saatchi & Saatchi acquired the Bates Worldwide network for $500 million. As part of Bates, George Patterson was now subsumed into the Saatchis' empire. Speaking to the local industry press after the announcement had been made, Patts's chairman, Geoff Cousins, took the opportunity to boast that the merger was in line with the outlook of Australia's largest agency: 'We have always believed that being number one is important ... With this move, we now hold [the number one position] worldwide ... In these days of the mega-merger, you either get bigger or get left behind. This leaves everybody else behind.'[38]

As George Patterson entered the 1980s, its management understood that the agency's growth was not limitless. 'We now have a client in virtually every category', explained Cousins in 1983. 'It's been most frustrating to have national clients approaching us to handle their business and having to say no.'[39] The acquisition of another agency provided the solution, but George Patterson rejected the idea that it should share a similar outlook to its acquisition. Reasoning that this served to diminish client choice rather than increase it, Cousins recalls that Patts was looking 'to buy businesses that aren't like us, not businesses that we bolt on that are slightly different but look like us'.

The Campaign Palace seemed to tick the right boxes. Cousins remembers not being particularly impressed by their reputation. When he looked at the advertisements created by Lionel Hunt, however, he found that they 'weren't just pieces of fluff' that were created to win advertising awards; they 'were damn good, hard-selling, wonderfully crafted pieces of communication'. Cousins arranged to meet with Hunt to strike a deal. He was not the first suitor to woo The Campaign Palace – David Ogilvy himself had expressed an interest in acquiring the creative boutique. Using every bit of the guile and persuasiveness that had taken him to the top at Patts, Cousins recalls how he encouraged Hunt to come up with idea of selling out to Patts.[40] Hunt's recollection, however, is slightly different. For

The Campaign Palace's principals, current financial issues with the taxation office and their lack of a lump sum made a buyout highly lucrative. Hunt nevertheless shared Cousins's view that opposites could attract: 'We were both the antichrist to each other … that appealed to me … because we were so different it might work.'[41] From the outside, it seemed incongruous that the two agencies would come together. MDA principal and creative director Phillip Adams thus quipped that 'the monolithic, conservative, joyless' George Patterson buying out The Campaign Palace 'was tantamount to the Vatican buying equity in the Hare Krishna.'[42]

Unlike so many buyouts, it would be the differences that made the relationship work. Hunt notes that Patts had the attitude: 'We're buying you because of what you did without us.' Cousins concurs: 'We did not interfere in their business at all.' He did not even attend board meetings. There were occasions, however, when the relationship hit rocky ground. When the Palace created a print advertisement for an insurance company featuring the words 'pedigree chump' (a play on words for the dogfood brand Pedigree Chum), Greg Daniel, the general manager of the Sydney office received a call from Cousins. 'The men from Mars are very unhappy', he told a bemused Daniel, 'and when the men from Mars are unhappy, I'm unhappy'. Cousins proceeded to explain that the Pedigree brand was owned by Mars, the agency's largest client. Daniel was forced to withdraw the advertisement, telling the insurer that they might be sued by the Mars Corporation. George Patterson's influence was also revealed in other aspects of the Palace's operations. When George Patterson established its own media-buying agency, The Campaign Palace would be among the first clients.[43] The success of the arrangement led George Patterson to increase its initial 25

per cent share of the Melbourne office to a 100 per cent ownership of The Campaign Palace in both Melbourne and Sydney.
Management changes in the 1990s meant the relationship would
become more strained.[44]

From the outset, George Patterson found its relationship with
Saatchi & Saatchi to be uneven. Ted Bates had been content to
leave George Patterson alone as long as the profits continued to
accrue. While the Saatchi and Bates networks were to be run as
separate entities, it soon became clear that the Saatchis no longer
had a hands-off approach – particularly in relation to financial
operations. At George Patterson, this influence would become
even more pronounced when the Saatchis bought out the 20
per cent share of George Patterson owned locally. New directives from London were not always possible to implement. The
requirement that rental costs be included as part of a new billing
process, for example, did not work for Patts, as it owned its own
building. Tools for assessing profitability were similarly ignored
as being irrelevant in the Australian context. Of course, George
Patterson could not simply disregard every difficult directive.
One such issue concerned profits. Having divided agency profits
evenly between the agency's expansion and shareholders, Patts
management were dismayed by the requirement that all profits
now be sent to London. Rather than fighting with the global
giant, Cousins informed the Media Council of Australia. The
Council's threat of withdrawing its accreditation saw Saatchi
& Saatchi quietly drop its requirement.[45] By the same token,
the relationship brought positives. George Patterson's leaders
understood that they could also learn from their new masters.
Cousins recalls Saatchi & Saatchi were more professional than
Ted Bates had been and they offered much more in terms of
ideas on management and creativity.

After being the 'jewel in the crown' within Bates's limited network, George Patterson occupied a less certain position within the expanding Saatchi empire. Recalling that 'It was just a new era and I wasn't quite comfortable', Cousins reveals the sense of vulnerability at Australia's largest agency. When the takeover was first announced, industry observers wondered whether Saatchi & Saatchi's relationship with Procter & Gamble would affect George Patterson's relationship with Colgate-Palmolive.[46] While the idea of a second network theoretically facilitated conflicting accounts, clients were unimpressed by the idea. Ultimately, George Patterson found themselves being forced to give up Colgate-Palmolive for the sake of Procter & Gamble. 'Colgate were very upset about it. In fact, they threw a party and gave me a gold watch!' recalls creative director Bruce Jarrett, who had spent years working with Patts's largest client.[47] While the loss of a large and beloved account left a big hole in the agency's operations, Alex Hamill proudly notes that the agency was able to absorb the blow, and not a single member of Patterson's staff lost their job.[48] Yet despite its enormous billings, George Patterson would remain the smaller sibling in the global agency's eyes. Things scarcely improved when the Saatchis merged Bates with Backer & Spielvogel and Dorland/DFS in 1987. A conscript into Saatchi & Saatchi's global empire, Patts's relationship with Saatchi & Saatchi remained ambivalent at best.

A Better Interpublic

Stating that 'we wanted to build a better Interpublic', Willi Schalk, the German-born head of Omnicom, reveals the model that had underpinned the celebrated mega-mergers of the 1980s.[49] Prior to Omnicom's formation in 1986, Schalk had spent seven years jet-setting across the globe as the head of BBDO's international operations. During this time, he had been a regular visitor to Australia. While these visits were a part of the agreement that the John Clemenger agency had with BBDO when it sold a 35 per cent share in 1973, Schalk did not consider them a mere formality.[50] He had significant respect for the agency's Australian operations and viewed them as an integral part of BBDO's global operations. The success of the Clemenger agency demonstrated that multi-national agencies did not necessarily need to be homogenous to be global.

When negotiating the sale of a third of the agency to BBDO in 1973, the management of John Clemenger made several conditions. These included 'no change of name', a refusal to 'resign any local business to take on international business unless we were happy to do so', and a refusal 'to write lengthy monthly financial reports as other American agencies demanded'. Such conditions seemed to offer little to potential suitors. 'We wanted to stay in control', Peter Clemenger bluntly observes, 'we kept our autonomy.'[51] However, the Australians' demands were not entirely inconsistent with the BBDO approach of only buying a minority share in agencies. BBDO President Tom Dillon thus accepted the conditions and the deal was done within the space of ten minutes. Significantly, BBDO remained true to its word, albeit grudgingly. 'We got the Wilkinson Sword business', recalls Geoff Wild, 'and ... they [BBDO] said you've got to take on Gillette, and we said "get stuffed" because we couldn't be told [what to do], which frustrated them mightily.'[52]

As BBDO was a relative late-comer to expanding its operations globally, it looked to its successful acquisition in Australia to help lead its entry into the Asia-Pacific region. One of its first moves was across the ditch into New Zealand. Despite having a long relationship with J. Inglis Wright, BBDO approached

Colenso, a younger, more creative agency. Colenso had already established a connection with SPASM and was considering direct connections with New York, but the New Zealanders understood the importance of a strong Australian connection and opted to give (not sell) a 20 per cent share of the agency to Clemenger. 'Money will come', noted Colenso co-founder Hylton Mackley.[53] The New Zealander would go on to become the director and finance director of Clemenger Group Limited.

In 1974, Bruce Crawford, the executive vice-president of BBDO, anticipated an expansion into Asia. Admitting that, 'We can't manage from New York', Crawford predicted that, 'If we enter these markets we would do so, not necessarily with financial assistance from the Australian company, but we would lean heavily on local management ability'. He identified Hong Kong and Singapore as the key markets while Japan was identified as 'a very difficult market' as the 'success record of American agencies in Japan is not very good.'[54]

Five years later, Geoff Wild led BBDO's charge across Asia. He based his strategy on the formula that had transformed Clemenger's Sydney office from a sleepy backwater to a giant: 'I wanted us to be the creative agency through Asia.'[55] Having identified the most creative agency in each country, Wild followed the BBDO formula of only buying a share of the operations. Hong Kong would be first, followed by Singapore, where BBDO acquired a 25 per cent share of Batey Ads in 1979. Best known for its 'Singapore Girl' campaign for Singapore Airlines, Batey Ads was renowned as one of 'the most creative agencies in Singapore.'[56] The deal provided Wild with the leverage to buy into a Malaysian agency that 'didn't know anything about BBDO, but they knew about Batey'. Although the majority of the agency's acquisitions were handled by Wild, the size and importance of gaining a foothold in the booming Japanese market saw Willi Schalk join him in the negotiations.

Other agencies had entered Japan via joint ventures with Japanese agencies, but BBDO would the first agency to buy into an established Japanese agency. Schalk muses that their 'non-American approach' was integral to sealing the deal: 'We showed more respect for the Japanese way of thinking, for the Japanese way of doing business, and we never criticised their advertising ... most Americans have never understood the kind of "childish" animated stuff in Japan.'[57] By the end of the 1980s, BBDO's eleven offices across the Asia-Pacific region were reporting to Sydney.

Although the regional and the local Australian operations of Clemenger BBDO operated separately, the former could have an indirect impact on the latter. Daniel had moved from The Campaign Palace to run Clemenger's Sydney office in 1988. While Daniel faced many of the typical issues that new managers encountered when taking on an underperforming office, he was surprised to find that the rivalry between Melbourne and Sydney was having a direct impact on his office. On multiple occasions, Daniel felt he had been prevented from pitching for large, lucrative accounts because the Melbourne office either had an account (irrespective of size) in the category or it believed that it would be acquiring one. Eventually, he discovered that the issue lay less with Melbourne sensitivities and more with BBDO's operational structure. As office heads were only responsible for the bottom line of their own operations, they had no desire to lose an account, let alone see another office in the network expanding at their expense. '[I]f there had been a grand vision, we would be all working to enhance the profitability of the group', reflects Daniel, '[but] everyone was interested in the profitability of their bit because that's what you were remunerated on and that's what you were held accountable for.'[58]

Despite the internal differences, Clemenger BBDO's billings in Australia continued to grow, and by the end of the 1980s it had emerged as the second-largest agency in Australia. BBDO's head office recognised the importance of its Australian operations. In addition to gradually increasing its share of Clemenger BBDO, it appointed Wild and Peter Clemenger to the ten-man board of BBDO Worldwide, where the two Australians offered characteristically forthright opinions and their American colleagues 'actually listened.'[59]

Australia also contributed to the Omnicom mega-merger. With the details of the merger being rapidly finalised over days rather than weeks or months, Schalk found that he had no opportunity to consult with all colleagues across the BBDO network. When weighing up the deal, Schalk used Australia as his 'test market' for the proposed merger, as his regular visits and close connections with Australia meant that he 'knew enough about the situation ... from a BBDO point of view, from a Needham point of view, from a DDB point of view.'[60] Concluding that such a merger would work well in Australia gave him the confidence that the mega-merger could work at a global level. While Clemenger BBDO had managed to make an imprint on the globalisation process, others harboured more ambitious aspirations of being leaders in this process.

Looks Good on Paper
In 1987, Don Morris, the managing director of the newly merged Mojo MDA agency, excitedly discussed the agency's plans for a London office: 'The clients that want us there, the Australian ones, want us because they want the Australianness of

our advertising. They don't want another British agency.'[61] Such comments offer a revealing insight into the Australian agency and its global aspirations. Like other multi-national agencies, Mojo MDA's global ambitions were being driven by clients as well as an unshakeable confidence in the strength of their creative work. However, the dream of an Australian-led global network did not necessarily turn out as planned.

Monahan Dayman Adams (MDA) commenced trading in 1964 when Brian Monahan and Lyle Dayman decided to open their own agency – the copywriter Phillip Adams would join them three years later. At the beginning of the 1970s, MDA was ranked twenty-eighth in terms of billings. By the end of the decade, it had cracked the top ten. MDA had acquired an impressive list of commercial clients. Adams's idiosyncratic style had also seen MDA emerge as an agency with a social conscience, creating such campaigns as 'Life. Be In It'. A 1984 feature on B&T's Agency of the Year found it 'too hard to categorise' MDA, noting that: 'It's a creative agency, but not in the English boutique style … It's one of the biggest agencies in Australia … yet it doesn't have a "big agency" (read grey) image. It's a very Australian agency, but it doesn't have the instantly identifiably "Oz" advertising style.'[62]

The acquisition of the Qantas account in 1978 would have a significant impact on MDA's operations. While the Melbourne head office and its Sydney branch shared a uniquely harmonious relationship, the latter's task of managing the Qantas account (and subsequently that of Westpac) would see it grow in size and stature. Qantas's global presence also required MDA to extend its operations beyond Australia. Leo Burnett had been handling Qantas's international campaigns – a legacy from its Jackson Wain days. Malcolm Spry, the agency's group managing director, would become actively involved in this process. Recalling that 'a lot of business was emanating out of New Zealand for Qantas' and that MDA promised to establish offices across Asia, Spry set about forming MDA's international network. 'The question … is do you buy an existing agency or start one up from scratch – and that's always a tough one', he reflects, 'it's easier if you can get an established office, that's already there, it's got clients – provided that the people you're dealing with you're comfortable with'. New Zealand's proximity and cultural similarities meant that MDA was content to buy a small, 'up and coming' agency run by two 'larrikins'. '[W]e liked them … it was as simple as that', Spry muses. Moreover, the Qantas account director in Sydney was in a position to keep a close eye on the office.

However, Singapore posed a different challenge. Aside from Batey Ads, which was fundamentally bound to Singapore Airlines, Spry could not find any locally owned agencies that would fit with MDA. A small three-person office was therefore opened in Singapore. Its primary role was the placement of Qantas advertisements across South East Asia. There was no real expectation that Singapore would pick up new clients and 'as long as the office paid its way, we weren't that fussed', observes Spry. MDA also bought out a local agency in Hong Kong 'not for the purpose of Qantas but because we were in Asia … purely from an expansion point of view.'[63]

The agency's expansionist ambitions would receive a further boost in 1984 with the bold decision to list MDA on the stock exchange. The anticipated $2.24 million float would drive the next phase of the agency's global push. *B&T* thus reported that: 'In Australia, its chief targets for growth will be agency groups specialising in particular areas of marketing such as sales promotion, while overseas it will concentrate on flying the MDA flag in Japan, the US West Coast and Europe.'[64] These plans would be interrupted, however, by the decision to merge MDA with another local agency, Mojo.

Alan (Mo) Morris and Allan (Jo) Johnston were the team behind Mojo – arguably the most 'Aussie' of all Australian advertising agencies. Mo and Jo had been disillusioned by their time at multi-national agencies during the late 1960s and early 1970s. Struggling with the regimentation of working for the big firms, they joined the exodus of creative talent from these large agencies (see Chapter 4). They started out as individual freelancers in 1975 before collaborating under the name Mojo. Mojo's trademark commercials featured catchy jingles sung by Jo in a 'rough as guts', unmistakably Australian voice. Success saw Mojo become a full-service agency in 1979 – ironically the shift was funded in part by the multi-national Masius, which had been looking to establish its own local network of agencies.[65] Far from adopting the business-focused culture of full-service multi-nationals, Mojo's elevation to full-service status only entrenched its distinctive culture:

> It was very tribal, very alcohol-fuelled, open bar, all day long and into the night – five days a week. ... Every lunch hour, they had a full-time cook ... [who] would cook seven or eight big legs of lamb for every-one ...It's all about the bloke and serving the bloke ... it was that whole blokey ethos and women hated it. They really did. Women with brains could not stand to work there.[66]

For clients (who were overwhelmingly male), the ability to drop in on their 'mates' for a chinwag and a drink or two was a relaxing way to do business. This, coupled with the agency's spectacularly successful campaigns, meant that Mojo's Paddington offices were a hive of activity both during and after business hours.[67]

As Australia's largest locally owned agencies, MDA and Mojo banded together to win the Commonwealth Government's campaign for Australia's bicentennial celebrations. While many were underwhelmed by the 'Celebration of a Nation' campaign, it nevertheless revealed that the two agencies could collaborate. Spry and Don Morris, a mate from Monash University and the co-founder and managing director of Mojo, continued talks about bringing the two agencies together. On paper there appeared to be strong synergies. The two agencies had few conflicting accounts. MDA looked to upgrade its creative reputation through Mo and Jo while Mojo was keen to get its hands on MDA's blue-chip accounts, particularly Qantas. MDA's public listing and its international offices also appealed to Mojo's management team. Excitement surrounded the announcement that MDA had formally bought out Mojo. Ian Dawson, the managing director of MDA's Sydney office, captured this anticipation in his diary: 'It is daunting to think about one year hence, but I continue to be optimistic for the simple reason … we have the best brains and there is an opportunity to build a genuine camaraderie … we'll do great, popular, talkable ads!'[68] Such hopes were short-lived, however.

As Anne Coombs's fly-on-the-wall account of Mojo MDA's first year reveals, a clash of cultures between the 'brash, colourful, ocker' Mojo and the 'more refined, thoughtful and low key' MDA emerged shortly after the announcement.[69] With Mojo's culture dominating the new agency, ex-MDA staff felt alienated. Many were dismissed or simply left. Frustrated and appalled by Mojo's treatment of colleagues, Dawson vented in his diary and commenced a countdown of the days left on his contract. Others adapted. John Wright was the account director for Qantas at MDA. With Mojo dismissing account-service staff as 'bag carriers' for their creative work and paying little attention to strategic planning, he faced a challenge. Unwilling to be a mere 'bag carrier', Wright continued to use the planning tools acquired from his time at JWT and Y&R. When presenting his insights to Mo and Jo, however, he adjusted his approach: 'I didn't do it in a ponderous way because I knew they hated documents, so if it was a briefing situation, I would just have one piece of paper.' He also observes that the merger boosted the confidence of those who remained. Wright was thrilled to go to client meetings with Mo and Jo's work: 'it was just like going in with a Leonardo painting ... whereas before it was always a much harder sale.'[70]

As the new agency gradually found its footing at home, it began to consider its global aspirations. The outlook was unclear, however. Hong Kong was losing money, prompting the director of overseas operations, Richard Whitington, to deliberate on the agency's strategy in South East Asia:

> Why do we want to be in those places? The answer is that, in theory, and in time, you can generate business from the network that is bigger than the business you can generate from individual offices: the whole is bigger than the sum of its parts.[71]

More exciting was the opportunity to expand into the USA and the UK. Spry had already negotiated a deal with the San Francisco agency handling the Qantas account, Allen &

Dorward, when the Mojo MDA merger was finalised. Wayne Kingston, who had previously headed the MDA Melbourne office, put his hand up to run the agency's San Francisco office. It was soon clear to him that the acquisition was not a good fit and that he faced an uphill battle: 'it's very difficult to turn a conservative, account management–led agency into a highly creative agency. It … is a cultural thing. Allen & Dorward was a conservative San Francisco agency … They were fascinated by Mojo but didn't … fully understand it.' While he spent almost a year there, Kingston offers a blunt assessment of the venture: 'I would have to say that the attempt to export this … quirky … jingoistic creative style product into Allen & Dorward in San Francisco was a failure.'[72] Amanda Moody, a creative assistant at Allen & Dorward, identifies further cultural issues. Echoing the criticisms levelled at Americans when taking over Australian offices, Moody states: 'I think the guys were a bit overconfident that they'd succeeded here [in the US]. The US has a freak-ishly diverse population … and what worked for advertisers in Australia just didn't carry here.' Recalling that 'a measure of male chauvinism [was] directed at our female employees, which came across as weirdly retro in progressive San Francisco', she revealed that Mojo's blokey culture was as problematic as the agency's creative approach.[73]

Mojo MDA's entry into New York was more ambitious. Julian Martin had returned to Australia after a stint at O&M in New York before an encounter with Don Morris saw him returning to Madison Avenue. Having just won International Agency of the Year, Mojo MDA hatched a plan that was even bigger than their award. Martin was told that 'we're going to buy Ogilvy & Mather in New York.'[74] He was to set up an office with two creatives, Scott Whybin and Rodd Martin, and was told that the 'cavalry will be coming soon'. Mojo MDA's New York dream commenced in an expensive Madison Avenue duplex. Management in Australia was unfazed by the costs as 'they thought they were going to do something bigger'. The assumption was that once the O&M deal was done, the apartment would be used for visiting executives. The 1987 stock market crash forced Mojo MDA to scale back these dreams. The three were to be sent to London, but persuaded management to keep them in New York on the proviso that they would break even by the end of their first year. Over the next year, they managed to eke out an existence winning some accounts as a small start-up that could also grandiosely claim to be the 'New York office of a multinational publicly listed Australian agency'.

Figure 5.1 Wayne Kingston sells the Australian way to the Brits.
Campaign, *21 August 1987. Photograph by Mark Tillie ©*

Mojo MDA's entry into London in 1987 was perhaps a less-ambitious undertaking than New York. While Spry thought that Mojo MDA should acquire a local agency, Don Morris favoured starting from scratch, as they would have a number of Australian accounts that were ready to switch to the new office.[75] Mo and Jo favoured the latter, and Kingston soon found himself relocating to London. His first task was to bring together a creative team. Among them was the copywriter Phil Gough, who had left Saatchi & Saatchi in Sydney to retire to Cornwall in Britain. Significantly, Kingston selected creatives who 'weren't Mojo guys, but they were very creative guys'. Kingston played on the Australian angle, however: 'We wanted to be different. We got great interest and coverage from the English trade press and that's what got most of the interest started over there.'[76] The *Times* thus reported that 'Mojo-MDA is aiming to deliver a Crocodile Dundee–style head-butt to the effete and pretentious elements of British marketing culture', while *Campaign* described how 'the rugged but debonair Kingston' played on British assumptions about Australians being 'rude and brash' to gain access to clients.[77]

While the agency managed to secure some local accounts, its dinky-di Aussie approach was a modest success at best. Campaigns were often created by Mo and Jo back in Sydney and exported to Britain. Arriving after Kingston had departed, copywriter Greville Patterson found that the British public were not interested in Mojo's trademark jingle commercials while British agencies were simply dismissive of the Australians' approach. He urged the agency to pay greater attention to British sensibilities: 'I found myself having these fights, saying it's not going to work here … but it met resistance within the agency because they wanted to create this *real* advertising.'[78]

Mojo MDA's dreams of being a major global agency came to a halt in 1989 when it sold out to Chiat/Day, an American creative agency best known for its '1984' campaign for Apple computers. Unable to land any other major international accounts beyond Qantas and the Australian Tourism Commission, the overstretched agency saw the offer from Chiat/Day as the only way of avoiding a collapse. While Mojo MDA managed to open offices across the globe that shared the Mojo ethos, the network failed. The failure went beyond misunderstanding local cultures or the inability to translate the Mojo way. Looking back on the entire exercise, Kingston suggests that the problem lay in the principals' attitude:

> I was getting the practical support and finance from Australia, but I wasn't getting the full heart and soul of "this is going to be the next major push of the agency" … Mojo was always a local Australian culture that didn't really have its heart in being a major worldwide agency.[79]

Figure 5.2 Mojo MDA embarks on its campaign to conquer America.
B&T, 14 November 1986, p. 1. (Courtesy of B&T)

In some ways, the writing had long been on the wall. Steve Gray, who had been despatched to Mojo to run its fledgling Melbourne office prior to the merger, recalls that 'they left us alone, to be honest, they didn't want to know. Alan would ring down every now and again.'[80] The network's decreasing capacity to land large multinational accounts did little to improve the management team's ambivalence. Chiat/Day wasted little time in dismantling the Mojo network – absorbing the appropriate staff in the American offices and overhauling the London office – and stamping its name upon its latest acquisition. Describing Mojo's London venture as 'ill-conceived and ill-advised', the head of Chiat/Day/Mojo's London office told *Campaign* that 'the legacy of Mojo's creative reputation as little more than a jingle shop is a problem' and that it was 'up to us to make sure it's a temporary one.'[81] It certainly had been.

————————

The 1980s had been Australian advertising's decade of confidence. Business was booming, agencies were billing more than ever before, and leading creatives and executives were earning astronomical wages. The glamorous excesses of the advertising industry were front-page news. Australian managers, creatives, and account executives were also being drawn more closely into the global advertising industry. Despite its size and distance, Australia had emerged as an important market for agencies and their global strategies. Australian staff and offices had earned a healthy respect from their international peers and sought to make the most of these opportunities. Confidence on a global scale had also helped drive the mega-mergers. The deals being made on Madison Avenue would affect Australian agencies and their everyday practices and operations – from conflicting clients to stoking dreams of an Australian-based global network. By the end of the 1980s, such confidence was beginning to wane. Globalisation saw the big clients and their agencies becoming even bigger and more powerful. In this climate, it was clear that there would not be another Mojo MDA. Australian agencies increasingly faced more-demanding clients with shrinking budgets on the one hand, and more domineering head offices on the other. As the operational and creative autonomy of Australian agencies eroded in the face of globalisation's embrace of homogeneity, it was clear that the golden age of Australian advertising was drawing to an end.

CHAPTER SIX

GETTING STARTED

Sydney's despatch boys were an entrepreneurial bunch. Scurrying from advertising agencies across the city with deliveries for print shops, newspapers and radio stations, they gathered each day in Australia Square to organise an impromptu courier service. Those who began work as despatch boys in the late 1950s and early 1960s recall swapping parcels with boys working in other parts of the city and, in an early manifestation of the business acumen that saw many of them become the leading advertising men of their generation, they pocketed the sixpence saved in tram or bus fares.[1]

So, who were these canny despatch boys? As this chapter will show, young men (and they were mostly young, Anglo men) joined advertising agencies in Sydney, Melbourne, Adelaide, Brisbane and Perth from various backgrounds, via various routes. Some had undertaken previous training in advertising-related areas, but most had not, although this changed significantly during the late 1960s as the industry gradually professionalised and began to reflect the emergence of marketing as an area of study in Australian universities. A decade later, the industry underwent another shift. Women had worked in advertising in a range of capacities from its earliest years, but from the 1970s they began to enter agencies in significant numbers. Despite their increased numbers, few women rose from support roles to the highest levels of agency life.

Background and Education

The despatch boys roaming the streets of Sydney and Melbourne in the 1950s and 1960s *were* all boys. Girls were taken into advertising agencies at entry level from the 1920s but, with few exceptions, they began their careers in secretarial support roles and, in most cases, stayed there.[2] Most of the young men who started in despatch had left school at fourteen or fifteen with few qualifications beyond the Leaving Certificate. They came from both the working and middle classes. Some working-class boys secured their first jobs by trudging the streets of the city knocking on door after door.[3] Others used the Pink Pages of the telephone directory or answered advertisements in the newspapers.[4] Some knew they wanted an advertising job[5] but most just wanted a job — any job — and discovered the advertising industry by chance because it was always close to the top of the jobs listing.[6]

With 145 advertising agencies around Australia in 1955, the industry provided young job seekers with a significant opportunity for securing work. A careers booklet produced in the 1960s advised young people that the best time to look for an advertising job was directly after the publication of the Intermediate and Leaving Certificate results. Applicants were told to address their letters to the manager of the advertising agency and that it was 'a good idea to have the letter typed'. These applicants had scant knowledge of advertising or the advertising industry, though what little they did know led some of them to imagine it as a glamorous profession. The booklet helped in this regard, advising young men not to be discouraged if they did not land a job in advertising at their first try. The industry provided 'incomparable awards in terms of job satisfaction and salary', the booklet informed them, 'many men in Australia have risen to tremendous heights through advertising. Why not you?'[7]

Middle-class boys found it easier to get a start in advertising than working-class boys. Having chosen to look for work rather than embark on the further study required for entry to the traditional professions – the law, medicine or banking – these boys often used family connections and networks to secure a job. Some benefitted from fathers employed in department stores or as the clients of advertising agencies. Others had a close relative or neighbour with the right contacts. Seeing that his brother was enjoying his work, the future copywriter Derek Hansen followed him into advertising.[8] Dennis Merchant's father had long been involved in radio station production, producing live shows for the commercial station 2UE. When Merchant joined Jackson Wain, his father was already working there in the production department.[9] John Cowper had a friend whose father worked in advertising[10] and Rod Blakeney's father, a trained accountant, was the company secretary of a Sydney advertising agency. Blakeney briefly considered journalism as a career, before joining David Jones as a trainee copywriter.[11] In the late 1960s, Reg Bryson told a mate he was interested in advertising; the mate's father had a friend in the business and set up an interview for the schoolboy. Bryson wore his school uniform to the 'terrifying' interview and was offered the job as despatch boy at Nixon Compton in Sydney.[12]

Once a job had been secured, the response of a family to the news that its offspring was to pursue a career in advertising depended on their social position. Most working-class families were simply relieved their sons had landed a job, even if they did not know what advertising was.[13] For the middle-class families, the news could be unwelcome; having invested so much into their children's education, they expected them to take up careers in more prestigious, familiar or stable professions, rather than a 'flighty' industry such as advertising.[14] Malcolm Spry's mother was shocked and disappointed that her Melbourne Grammar–educated son chose a career in advertising rather than in the traditional professions. Bryson's parents were also 'shocked' at the news of his job at Nixon Compton, which he'd secured before he told his parents he was leaving school. Like Spry's mother, the Brysons had expected their son to go to university and pursue a career in the law.

A significant cohort entered the industry at a slightly older age than the despatch boys. Some of these men – Kevin Luscombe and Ric Otton were two notable examples – had first worked for a client (Luscombe at Heinz and Otton at Nestlé) then crossed over into advertising to work as account executives, having been headhunted by agency managers. Eugene Catanzariti moved into advertising from his position as marketing manager of the French cosmetics giant L'Oréal because advertising 'looked like more fun' than working on the client side. Others began their careers in the advertising departments of retail stores such as Farmers or Anthony Hordern in Sydney, and Myer or Manson in Melbourne. Some, such as Colin Fraser and Greg Graham, began their careers in journalism but later switched to advertising, tempted by the opportunities offered by the new medium, television.[15] Many were impressed by the pay and lifestyle of friends working in the industry. While working for the pharmaceutical firm Nicholas in Slough outside of London, Spry recalls flat-sharing with Australians employed in London advertising agencies. They seemed to be having a lot more fun than Spry stuck out in the back blocks of Slough; one advertising friend even drove a Porsche.[16]

Other advertising professionals – the writers and the artists – studied commercial art, copywriting or the psychology of selling at one of the numerous technical schools, art studios and business schools scattered across the Australian capitals. Ray Black, for example, won drawing competitions as a young teen and, in 1956, secured his first job at an art studio aged just fifteen. Jack Room won art prizes at school before studying fine art then commercial design, first at the Gordon Institute at Geelong and then at Royal Melbourne Institute of Technology (RMIT). After finishing art school in Britain, Keith Aldrich wrote 'a hundred' letters to agencies asking for a break, with no luck.[17] Then, while hitchhiking during the holidays, his luck changed. He met a London art director who was looking for an assistant and who offered Aldrich the job. Ron Mather left school at thirteen and, as 'a good drawer', entered London's Hornsey College of Art. He stayed two years, then left in 1962 because 'art colleges were for the wealthy' and his mum wanted him 'to bring money in'. He found work experience at an advertising agency, CPV International. He 'loved it' there and the agency loved him back, offering the 15-year-old a job 'doing layouts and paste up.'[18] Robin Stewart studied at Caulfield Technical College in Melbourne ('a very practical course, great grounding') before joining Rickards Advertising as an illustrator.[19]

The avenues for entry were more diverse for copywriters than for art directors because the job required fewer technical skills. Most of the copywriters – John Bevins, Doug Watson, Paul Priday, Lionel Hunt, and Noel Delbridge – started their careers as despatch boys. Others took more circuitous routes.

John Box and Graham Nunn both started journalism cadetships before jumping across to advertising. Box found a job at Sydney's Fortune Advertising in 1965, recalling that 'advertising was looked down on' and he was 'ashamed of going into it'. Nunn used his journalism scholarship to study marketing, printing and copywriting at the South Australian Institute of Technology. After completing a Diploma in Commerce at Swinburne Technical College in Melbourne, Fysh Rutherford first worked as a manager for the Australian commercial and film director Fred Schepisi, then as a bookkeeper overseas before finding a job as a copywriter. Neil Lawrence 'stumbled' into copywriting at the age of twenty-seven after an arts degree at Melbourne University, followed by two years working in Aboriginal Youth welfare and a tilt at documentary film-making. His first job, in 1982, was at Melbourne's NAS Coventry Vaney agency. 'I got in because I could write', Lawrence matter-of-factly recalls. His welfare work meant that he was 'a bit negative to advertising' but he was also 'absolutely fascinated by [the industry's] creative aspects and its power. [It was] like being paid to do *The Times* cryptic crossword.'[20] Rod Bennett began his career in New Zealand radio then completed marketing and commerce studies in Australia. Bill Shannon, another New Zealander, studied at art school and worked as a designer before switching to copywriting in 1970.[21]

Only a handful of the young men who entered the industry in the 1950s and early 1960s were university-educated. Michael Ball, for example, studied at the theological college in Melbourne in the early 1950s. There he met David Wilken, a law student and Ball's future colleague at Ogilvy & Mather, who introduced him to Bob Alcock, the highly regarded creative director of J. Walter Thompson in Melbourne. Geoff Cousins, whose father

Hedley had enjoyed a successful advertising career, studied two years of arts at Sydney University before taking up a teaching position at his alma mater, Shore School. Two years later Cousins 'rang a couple of advertising agencies … out of the blue' and 'was lucky enough to get a job' (at Pritchard Wood). Box studied arts at the University of Queensland as part of his journalism cadetship but was thrown out of university for writing 'stupid things on an exam paper'. Malcolm Spry studied economics at Melbourne's Monash University. Hugh Spencer entered advertising 'by mistake'. While studying at university, he worked part time in an agency – Wellington's Carlton Carruthers du Chateau and King. The agency's copywriter Len du Chateau saw something in Spencer, taking him under his wing and 'managing' him into a copywriting career. Mentors such as du Chateau would play a vital yet under-recognised role in guiding many of the industry's highest achievers through their formative years in the industry.[22]

From the early 1970s there was a gradual increase of the university-educated entering advertising, but these men (they were still mostly men) had rarely studied advertising. Especially influential was the growing cohort of highly educated British men – mostly Oxbridge graduates who had been recruited in their final year at those institutions by the major corporations and agency networks – who arrived in Australia through global advertising networks. Chris Martin Murphy recalls being at Cambridge with the future British advertising gurus Robin Wright and Geoff Howard Spink. Corporations and advertising agencies travelled up to Oxford and Cambridge 'to poach you'. Martin Murphy was therefore 'poached' by BP Shell before travelling to London for an interview at Garland Compton.[23] Renny Cunnack, an Oxford-educated English Literature graduate, was picked up in his last term by the London advertising agency, Pritchard Wood. He started work there as a graduate trainee in 1963. This formal selection of recruits through the universities would not be reflected in Australia, with the exception of creative recruits who were often picked up through student exhibitions.

The value of a university education for those intending to work in industry and commerce had been recognised in Australia as early as 1925, when the University of Melbourne opened its Faculty of Economics and Commerce, and marketing and salesmanship was included in university courses from this period.[24] In the same year the Australian press reported that New York University was conducting courses in advertising and marketing, as well as accountancy, bookkeeping, statesmanship, banking, investment, insurance, journalism, management, and social economy.[25] It was:

> Always a difficult matter when parents are called upon to choose a career for their sons or daughters. Few professions can be mastered without incurring heavy expense, but in advertising we have a profession, which opens a wide field for the young man or woman of average intelligence.

The implication was clear: that achieving success in the advertising 'profession' was an easier prospect than doing so in the 'traditional' professions. Indeed, the AAA's attempts to add gravitas to advertising training was consistently undermined by the private business schools: the School of Applied Advertising (SAA), for example, positioned itself as 'the only school to offer individual tuition' and as an alternative to the seven years of professional experience required by the AAA for professional endorsement. The SAA courses were 'approved by the AANA' (the Australian Association of National Advertisers), which was formed in 1928.[26]

By 1960, 'average intelligence' was proving insufficient for an advertising career. Noel Adams, the director of the McClelland agency and the chairman of the 4As' education committee,told the 4As' annual convention that 'the need for people possessing a superior level of intelligence and a special range of personal attributes' had caused 'a manpower crisis' in Australian advertising.[27] Adams outlined training schemes being developed in the US and London to fix a similar problem and suggested that Australian agencies should follow these examples.[28] By 1968, however, there remained a shortage of suitable staff. One agency director described the situation:

> We have all been cannibalizing each other for staff. We hear of a good man somewhere and we let him know we are in the market for a good writer, artist or account executive, and we offer him more money.[29]

Australia enjoyed full employment in this period, which no doubt affected advertising's ability to attract good people. The article put the shortage down to the 'extraordinary growth of advertising agencies' and a 'lack of formal training facilities.'[30] Most agencies had long required some form of external training from their recruits, but, as we will see in the next chapter, it was not until the late 1960s that they began actively recruiting university graduates.

This interest in the university-trained reflected the significant expansion in the numbers of Australians attending university that had started after World War II. The war experience had drawn attention to the necessity of expanding tertiary training beyond the traditional subjects taught by the sandstone universities to include extensive training in science and technology. In support of this vision, Sydney Technical College was rebranded first as the New South Wales University of Technology (1949), then, in 1958, became the University of New South Wales.[31] At the same time the 4As increased its efforts to have advertising included in university subjects such as economics and accountancy, with mixed results.[32] As the next chapter will show, advertising professionals educated in this period would bring to the industry a new set of insights picked up in university courses.

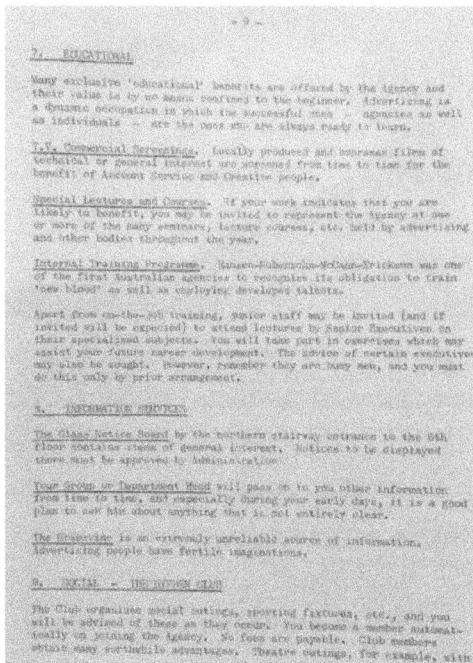

Figure 6.1. Guidelines for new staff joining Hansen Rubensohn-McCann Erickson in the early 1960s.
McCann Erickson Scrapbook.

The Interview

So who interviewed these young people and what were they asked? 'The print production manager' and 'one of the agency's directors' interviewed John Wright for his position at Clem Taylor O'Brien, Adelaide's largest agency. 'A lady' interviewed Alex Hamill for his job as despatch boy at Jackson Wain. Having met representatives from George Patterson, McCann-Erickson, Jackson Wain and JWT at his school's careers night, the 15-year-old Rob Palmer became one of eighty-five applicants for three despatch boy jobs at JWT. Palmer survived two interviews and a psychology test, and started work in January 1965. Had he been two years older, he might not have been so lucky: Alan Robertson missed out on a job with JWT because the award for a 17-year-old was too high.[33]

Dennis Merchant's father sent the future media guru out to knock on doors around Sydney looking for a job. At Canny, Paramor and Canny in the Rocks, he was interviewed by the receptionist and taken on as a despatch boy based in the checking department. He later moved to Jackson Wain as a media trainee. At McCann Erickson-Hansen Rubensohn (HRMcE) the office manager Doug Jacobs and Helen Tudehope (who had begun her own advertising career as a secretary at Frank Goldberg's agency in the late 1920s) interviewed Ian McDonald – separately – in 1964.[34] McDonald recalls that each of his interviewers was more interested in character and intelligence than McDonald's knowledge of the advertising business. Two days later they offered him the job and he started in despatch under the watchful eye of the tough-but-fair Eric Sarchfield, a former prisoner of war.[35] To secure his position in Farmer's advertising department, Graham Cox had to write an advertisement. In competition with thirty-two applicants for just one job, he was asked 'why do you want this job?' and replied that he 'liked the idea that everything is new, all the time'. Over in the United Kingdom, Cunnack recalls travelling up to Knightsbridge to be interviewed by the principals of Pritchard Wood. He 'knew a bit about advertising but hadn't researched it'. Despite his lack of preparation, they all 'got on like a house on fire' and he was offered the job.[36] A decade later, in 1971, Alwill found those who interviewed him at JWT to be 'enlightened'. Agencies no longer wanted to hire salesmen. As their clients had become better educated (especially in marketing which was a popular choice for undergraduates), agencies now required people with degrees and business backgrounds who could provide a wider spectrum of services. Alwill recalls that JWT also wanted to ensure 'he was a real bloke', and asked him whether he liked rugby, sailing and drink. He assured them that he did.[37]

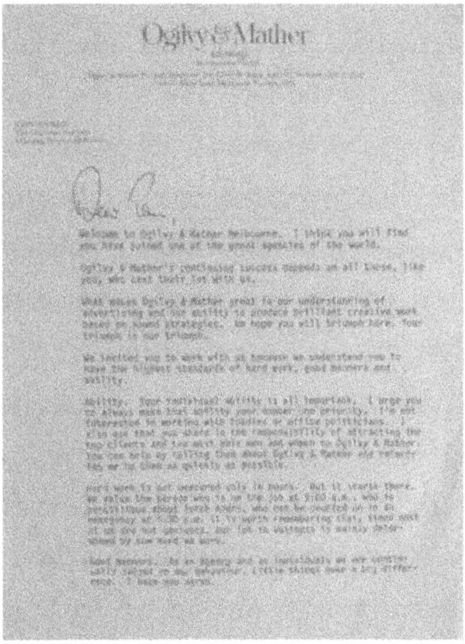

Figure 6.2 Ogilvy & Mather outline their expectations in personal letters to new staff in the 1980s. Courtesy of Toni Lawler, Barry Banks Blakeney (BBB) Collection, Box 25, Supplement.

By the 1980s, the professionalisation of the advertising industry had filtered down to its interviewing processes. Ogilvy & Mather Worldwide produced detailed guidelines for interviewing potential staff, and disseminated these to its various offices.[38] At George Patterson in the early 1980s, Eva Sellars, the Human Resources manager, interviewed the young Michael Ritchie for a job in despatch. Ritchie recalls 'a conservative approach to entering big business', 'like a law firm now'. He was interviewed three times and sat an exam before being 'given the tick.'[39]

Women's Experiences

Although most of the new entries were men, women had long worked in the Australian advertising industry and they continued to join agencies through the 1950s.[40] Their entry methods mirrored those of men. They answered advertisements, used family and friendship networks, and 'fell into' advertising through the influence of friends. In the late 1940s, the future art director Marion von Adlerstein answered an advertisement in the *Sydney Morning Herald* for a job as a junior in the advertising department of Anthony Hordern's department store. Twenty-five years later, Suzie Otten found her first advertising job in the pages of the same newspaper.[41]

Women also made use of family networks to enter the advertising business. Brought up around the industry – her father was a pioneer in the film business – the future fashion guru Joy Jobbins tried some modelling, then studied at East Sydney Art School, before starting work in the advertising department at Anthony Hordern. She moved on to the Myer Emporium and then joined the advertising agency Richardson Cox in 1955. Two years later, Paddy Stitt used a 'family introduction' to secure a traineeship at JWT, with the intention of becoming a writer. Like Dennis Merchant, Betty Quin was raised in the heart of the radio production business, performing in radio plays and advertisements throughout her formative years. Her father, Bill Smallacombe, held the first radio licence in Adelaide (5CL) and was that city's first disc jockey. After a sojourn in London, Betty worked with her brother Bill as a copywriter at the advertising agency NAS MacNamara in the early 1960s before moving into scriptwriting, first for the theatre, and later for television. Claire Nilsson followed in the footsteps of her father Frank Andrew and brother Carl by studying commercial art. She spent four years at Melbourne Technical College before starting work at the same advertising agency as her family, Thompson Ansell Blunden (TAB). When the future advertising recruitment manager Esther Clerehan was sixteen, her father organised an interview for her with his boss, the managing director of Ogilvy & Mather in Melbourne, David Wilken, and the firm's office manager, Sheila Brayne, who had been told to 'hire Clerehan's daughter'. It was, in Esther's words, 'a pretty easy way in'; at the time she thought such an entry 'was normal.'[42]

Retail fashion provided women with a reliable path into the advertising industry. June McCallum, the future editor of *Vogue*, studied graphic design and fashion illustration, first at Brighton Technical School then at Melbourne Technical College, before starting at Fortune Advertising in the late 1950s.[43] Other women made advertising careers by accident. Stephanie Borland studied languages at the University of California Berkeley for a couple of years, then 'fell into advertising' while living in Spain.[44] After completing a business course at Stott's Business College in Melbourne, Marie Jackson took an entry-level job in the media department of O&M.[45] The copywriter and creative director

Rosem'ry Bertel completed two years of a Bachelor of Music at the University of Melbourne's Conservatory before a friend of her father 'found her something to occupy her time' at the USP Benson advertising agency. She started there in 1963 as a 'gofer' and secretary.[46] Faie Davis was working as a theatre designer in Sydney in the early 1960s when she met and married an art director employed at Jackson Wain. After moving to South East Asia with her new husband, she followed him in to the advertising business.[47] Jane Caro's father worked in marketing. She had wanted to be a journalist but 'ended up in advertising.'[48]

Women made it into the Australian advertising industry in this period using similar methods to the men. Those who worked in the advertising departments of retail stores – a woman's 'natural' environment – were able to embark on the next stage of their careers, securing training, as long as they showed sufficient aptitude and initiative.[49] But those women who entered advertising agencies as typists and secretaries faced a less certain and more challenging path into the industry than their retail sisters. Young agency women had to compete for training and advancement against the young men – the despatch boys – who had been selected for their positions with their advertising potential firmly in mind.

Training

Once a job was secured, the training began. Most trainees learnt 'on the job'. In the big agencies, this meant moving around the various departments of the agency for two or three years, from despatch, through media and production, then onto the creative department and account management. For many, the first year at the agency was spent completing menial tasks: placing newspapers on staff members' desks, picking up dry-cleaning and delivering the chairman's car to the garage for repairs.[50] At O'Brien's, John Wright's job was to 'run all the despatch logistics for the agency, deliver things to newspapers, radio and television stations, clients, and check proofs'. He was the only despatch boy in the agency – the previous despatch boy had moved into the production department. John Steedman joined McCann-Erickson in Sydney as a despatch boy in 1971. The agency employed six such boys, and Steedman gradually worked his way up from number six to number one. His pay was $20 a week. Steedman received no direct training but got to know all the departments because he was 'delivering the mail'. He was also aware that 'they were assessing [his] capabilities'.

From despatch, the boys moved through the checking department where they clipped advertisements from newspapers for the production or media-buying departments.[51] For some, these departments offered them the opportunities to shine and build a career. Others were more ambitious. Steedman was disappointed when he was moved from despatch to the media department, which he considered 'the back room of advertising'. Young men like Steedman were eager to run their own accounts and work directly with clients, or they felt themselves to be 'creative' and were desperate to write the advertisements.

Australia's largest agencies – George Patterson, J. Walter Thompson and McCann-Erickson – all had training schemes for young men, starting them in despatch then moving them through most of the agency departments. John Cowper joined McCann before completing the Leaving Certificate. When his results came through he was offered a teaching scholarship, but McCann asked him to stay and offered to pay for a course in advertising at one of the local technical colleges. Cowper joined 'ten to fifteen' other despatch boys in a department that was run 'like a military operation' by Sarchfield. Cowper remained in despatch for 'twelve months to the day' then was moved into production with Warwick Bettridge, the print production manager, and Brian Ahern, the press production manager. In production, he learnt to 'mark up and set copy, talk to printers and newspapers, and semi-design ads'. For Cowper, it was a logical progression: 'we were learning the stuff that would stay with us all our lives.' Exactly a year later, he was promoted to Junior Account Executive and his career began.[52] Ian McDonald spent a month in production followed by a month in the art studio. He recalls that despatch was 'cleared out' after twelve months, to make room for the 'next mob of school leavers'. Seeing Reg Bryson 'had an appetite' for the business, Nixon Compton moved him from despatch to press production (where he was the manager while still in his teens) to media, and finally to account service, the ultimate agency job for non-creatives.

The former despatch boys remember the system as highly competitive. Many had a vague sense of being watched and assessed – 'if you took an interest in what was going on, they took an interest in you' – and the ambitious made sure they arrived first in the morning and were the last to leave at night.[53] The system did not suit everyone. The Scots College–educated John Newton, for example, found the despatch department at Patterson 'Dickensian' and felt like 'a menial servant', delivering parcels and, later, ferrying the firm's directors, including the founder George Patterson, around in a company car.

For some of these boys, formal training was compulsory and they studied at night school at the end of their day's work. Some agencies were more committed to this than others. O'Brien Publicity, for example, suggested that Wright – their only despatch boy – enrol in a four-year advertising course at the

Adelaide Institute of Technology and promised to pay the fees as long as he passed the course. Wright learnt on the job 'making and delivering advertising, and meeting clients' and studied 'theory' two nights a week. The course content was 'American based – Kleppner' and gave him 'wider exposure than just in the office, including research, media – the bigger picture of advertising.'[54] Wright did not just complete the course; he aced it, winning the Clem O'Brien award for top student in the final year. As promised, the agency paid for his tuition and books. After one year, Wright was moved to the production department, where he managed the next despatch boy, and eighteen months later, he was promoted to account service.

Reg Bryson studied advertising at Sydney Technical School three nights a week for four years. His agency also paid the fees as long as he kept passing the exams. Working as a junior copywriter at NAS MacNamara in Adelaide, Andrew Killey was encouraged to take the 4As diploma course, which was mostly run by advertising practitioners with 'real world experience'. The guest speakers and seminars provided by the course gave Killey the 'sense of an industry.'[55] At Pritchard Wood in London, Renny Cunnack spent a year moving from department to department: a month in media, a month in research, and a month 'on the road as a salesman'. At the end of the year he sat nine, three-hour exam papers set by the Institute of Practitioners in Advertising (IPA), a British professional body, which asked questions about 'creative, production, media, and psychology at a low level'. Of his five-year course at Adelaide's Institute of Technology, JWT despatch boy Simon O'Brien muses: 'I shouldn't discard it, it was a good enough course, but most of it was learning on the job.'

Not everyone was supportive of training for advertising work. Some believed (and still believe) that good advertising is instinctive rather than learned and that the industry's attempts to professionalise were in vain. Michael Ball recalls that Ogilvy & Mather favoured on-the-job training because it was 'good for building [agency] culture to train people up yourselves'. As a consequence, Ball was never particularly interested in a recruit's formal qualifications and believed that 'a three-month trial was enough'. Others were dismissive of advertising education because they considered the material taught in technical schools and universities to be out of date. John Newton, for example, remembers his TAFE course as 'totally useless' and knuckled down to learn on the job.[56] Reg Bryson found his Tech school lecturer wanting: 'the best people were out, sucked up into the growing industry.'[57]

Those wishing to improve their career prospects had a wide range of options. Training in advertising and commercial art had been taken seriously in Australia from the 1920s, as the industry sought to professionalise and improve its reputation.[58] The Advertising Association of Australia (AAA) formed its Federal Education Board in 1923 and developed a set of formal qualifications for advertising practitioners.[59] Private business colleges and public technical schools delivered the courses for the AAA qualifications.[60] From the beginning, the AAA was conscious of advertising education in the United States and Britain, comparing Australian advertising training favourably to that provided in those countries because of insistence on practical experience.[61]

Two streams of advertising education evolved: the business stream and the art stream. In the former, advertising was a small part of general studies, including accountancy. The reading lists of these various educational establishments demonstrates the reliance Australian advertising training placed on British and

American textbooks. A. P. Braddock's extensive collection of advertising texts – published as the 'Library of Advertising' series and relying heavily on Freud's psychological works – was particularly influential.[62] Copywriters learnt their trade through the business stream via correspondence courses or at night schools such as Sydney's Metropolitan Business College or J. V. Hall's School of Applied Advertising (SAA), where Michael Anderson, Marion von Adlerstein, and Rod Blakeney all took evening classes in the 1940s, 50s, and 60s.[63]

The art stream taught commercial art, photography, and illustration. Commercial art courses were established in all of the major cities from the beginning of the twentieth century and were promoted as teaching 'art that pays'. Leading commercial studios, such as Smith and Julius in Sydney, and Melbourne's Art Training Institute and Commercial Art School, trained young artists in their working studios.[64] The proprietors of these institutions sometimes had overseas experience. The former musical hall cartoonist Elton Fox, for example, ran an advertising art studio in Oakland, California, for fifteen years before returning to Melbourne in 1935 to open his Fox Art Academy.[65]

In the 1950s and 60s, public-speaking competitions became an important aspect of the development of the advertising man. Awards and scholarships remained important. Graham Cox was awarded the 4As highest student prize, the E. C. Perugini award, and in the early 70s Greg Daniel travelled to Tehran to speak about advertising and politics at an International Advertising Association (IAA) gathering, as the recipient of an IAA scholarship. George Patterson offed an annual scholarship for those under thirty: the prize was a trip to its sister agency Ted Bates in New York.[66]

Women rarely featured in these competitions: the critical mass of women in the industry was insufficient for them to make a significant impact. This started to change from the late 1970s, as the number of women entering the advertising industry began to increase significantly. Many of these women had university degrees. Julia King, possibly the most successful woman in Australian advertising, was born in Sydney in 1939, the daughter of Lebanese migrants. King attended a private school in Sydney before studying arts at the University of Sydney and the University of New England. She worked in local radio then entered advertising, starting with JWT before switching to Leo Burnett. King then took a marketing job with Lintas, which she ran from 1968 to 1989.[67]

Tania Farrelly, a graduate of the University of Adelaide, started at Concord Advertising in Melbourne in 1985 as a 'junior dogsbody'. She spent eighteen months learning on the job with no formal training before embarking on a rapid rise through account service, settling eventually on strategy planning, which she found 'most interesting'. Another high achiever, Marie Jackson also made an impressive rise through the ranks. After securing an entry-level position in the media department of Ogilvy & Mather in Melbourne, Jackson soon progressed to a position as secretary to the account management team, then to traffic manager, then office manager, and finally account manager and account director.[68]

Such speedy rises were not typical for women. Most tertiary-educated women spent far longer in entry-level jobs in agencies, as secretaries, receptionists or juniors in the media department, than did King, Farrelly or Jackson. Esther Clerehan benefitted from a training graduate programme at Ogilvy & Mather in Melbourne, which had been instituted by the managing director,

Cunnack. The process was a familiar one: she began in despatch and worked in every department in the agency before settling in the traffic department. Clerehan was unhappy there because she felt working in traffic was taking 'a woman's path.'[69] As the industry changed during the 1980s, it would remain difficult for women to find an alternative path to the higher echelons of advertising life.

Between the 1950s and the 1980s, entry into the Australian advertising industry changed in a number of ways. The types of recruits changed as it increasingly became not whom you knew, but what you knew. At the beginning of the period the young men who made it into the industry were mostly from the middle classes, and were often able to leverage family networks to secure a start. While such connections remained important, the gradual professionalisation of the industry – which reflected Australians' expanded access to university, the inclusion of advertising subjects in university courses, and the emergence of a better-educated client – resulted in a shift by middle-class recruits from entry-level to middle-ranking jobs. This freed up the lower-level jobs, which were now filled by increasing numbers of women. Once the young man or woman had secured their place in the advertising agency and completed his or her training, the climb through the ranks commenced.

CHAPTER SEVEN

KEEPING CLIENTS HAPPY

In the eleventh episode of the fifth series of *Mad Men*, the office manager Joan agrees to sleep with a potential client to secure his business for the Sterling Cooper advertising agency in exchange for a partnership at the firm. The episode makes uncomfortable viewing. It is also not particularly convincing – as Emily Nussbaum has observed, as a senior manager Joan is hardly desperate for money[1] – but there is little doubt that the personal has always been unusually entwined with the workplace in the advertising industry, as the episode implies. Before she embarked on a successful direct marketing career, Luella Copeland-Smith, for example, received a monthly clothing and entertainment allowance from her husband's employer, Ogilvy & Mather, so she could perform the role of the perfect hostess for the agency's clients. She was also expected to entertain the clients' wives while their husbands were at work.[2]

The advertising business is about relationships: the relationship between the consumer and the brand; the relationship between the 'suits' (the account executives who manage the client) and the 'creatives' (the copywriters and art directors who make the ads); the relationship between media-buying staff and the media outlets; and the relationship between production managers and their suppliers. This chapter looks at the relationship that was central to an agency's very existence: that between account managers and their clients, the advertisers, those manufacturers, retailers, and service providers with something to sell.

Again, it is a story of change. The importance of the relationship with clients to the survival of the business meant that, in the late 1950s, the account service department was considered the key area in the agency. By the end of the 1980s, this was no longer true: power within the agency hierarchy had shifted to the creatives. The ways in which account executives managed the relationship with clients also changed across these years. In the 1950s agencies often held onto accounts on the basis of strong personal friendships between agency principals and their clients.[3] These relationships were built around extra-curricular activities: sharing a drink after work, a round of golf on the weekend, a day at the footy followed by a night at a 'gentlemen's club' in the city. By the end of the 1980s, such activities had not disappeared but they had become less important. Clients had changed, becoming far more professional in their performance and their expectations, and account managers had been forced to change with them.

Women again played a part in the story. In the 1950s they were scarcely to be found in account service departments (no wild nights at the gentlemen's club for them!). By the 1980s, however, women were starting to dominate account management. Changes in marketing education had shifted the ambitions of advertising men. Their glory now lay elsewhere, and women took advantage of the vacuum to enter the account service departments of advertising agencies in their droves.

A Shifting Relationship
When Eugene Catanzariti visited Ogilvy & Mather, Rowntree's advertising agency, he could not help noticing that the agency

men lived a little better than he, a marketing manager, did. They 'drove flashier cars and were always at lunch', he recalls; their pay was 'very high compared to marketing'. Catanzariti made up his mind to join the agency side.[4] The social aspect of the advertising industry also tempted Wayne Kingston. He had made a brilliant start to his career as the marketing manager of Tooheys but found the social life at the beer giant's advertising agency Y&R alluring. There was more than the call of glamour behind the decision of clients to move across to advertising though. Kingston recalls being 'in awe of the agency' and impressed by its American managing director Joe DeDeo who 'was intent on building a new style of agency'. There seemed to be more to be learned on the agency side: besides his MBA studies and a stint at Ogilvy & Mather in New York – 'a sophisticated factory' – Kingston credits his advertising knowledge to the time he spent working with Y&R.[5]

The different skills required by the client and the agency staff could work to the advantage of the former client now employed in an advertising agency. After working on new business for Monahan Dayman Adams (MDA) in Sydney, Kingston became a reluctant account director. Though he had learnt a lot from his time as a client at Y&R, his training on the client side meant he had missed out on the thorough, department-by-department training of the despatch boy and did not understand the more arcane aspects of the advertising business such as media and production. 'Not an accounts person', he was forced to lean on the other directors for mundane advertising activities such as briefing creatives, although he later 'developed the creative side'. Kingston's strength was building relationships with the clients and, partnered with the 'intelligent' and 'charming' creative director Phillip Adams, he won two important accounts for the new agency: Qantas and Westpac. He gained respect 'as the guy who could get things done with clients – [as] a good catalyst between the agency and the client'.

Michael Anderson moved the other way, relinquishing his position as Senior Account Director at USP Benson to work for the cigarette giant Gallagher because it was 'important to have client experience'. For two years, Anderson learnt what it was like to be a client 'employing an advertising agency', a valuable experience for a future agency principal.[6]

The men who moved between the client and the agency side – men such as Kingston, Catanzariti, and the future agency principal Kevin Luscombe – were very much the minority. In some respects, the clients and the agency account managers had a great deal in common: the copywriter Graham Nunn recalls how, in 'blue blood' Adelaide, the private-school net-work provided a reliable source of clients.[7] Despite this shared background, agencies resisted hiring clients. They saw clients as a breed apart from agency men: buyers rather than sellers, nay-sayers rather than risk-takers. Lacking dynamism, former clients were expected to struggle with the pressures and intensity of agency life. Their 'blinkered vision and narrowly focused intel-lect' might hold back the agency's can-do culture. Whatever their background, most clients were not 'one of us.'[8]

Agency men might have felt quietly superior to their cli-ents but they needed to keep them happy. 'Clients were gods', according to Anderson, who ran the Qantas account at MDA Mojo for many years. For Ric Otton, account managers 'had to have relationships with clients', and his agencies – Masius then Mojo MDA – entertained clients to build trust in the relationship, which Otton calls 'lubrication'. Building a reservoir of trust in the relationship with a client 'could rectify mistakes'; errors and stuff-ups might be forgiven, if not forgotten.[9]

It is worth reflecting here on the terminology used by those responsible for 'keeping clients happy'. This agency department has been variously called account service or account management; its staff, account executives or 'handlers' working for account managers, who report to account directors. In the mid–twentieth century, different agencies called the department different things, but for Kingston there were critical differences between the two labels. The idea of 'account service' reflected the old way of doing business with clients that was hinted at (if grossly exaggerated) in the *Mad Men* episode mentioned above. If an agency failed to go to great – perhaps any – lengths to satisfy a client then its rival would, and the consequences of losing an account could be shattering, with mass redundancies, even bankruptcy and closure. In a formulation that privileged the strategic duties of the account manager over her or his servicing of the client, Luscombe described the role of the account manager: 'Account management in the ad agency business is the combined role of marketing positional analysis, internal communications interpreter and controller, service dispenser, herd rider and generalist producer.'[10] Under Kingston's leadership, the 'account service' department at MDA was refocused as 'account management', denoting a more active and less servile role.[11]

Whatever the department was called, staff continuity was crucial to maintaining good agency–client relations before the changes of the 1980s. Account managers frequently handled the same clients for many years. In the 1970s 'account managers were older' than they would be a decade later, especially in the big Australian agencies, notably George Patterson and Clemenger.

Aged in 'their forties and fifties', these men and women 'had worked on [the same] clients for years.'[12]

There were always exceptions to this. Alex Hamill became an account manager in the early 1960s aged just nineteen. In his ten years at Jackson Wain (1958–1968), Hamill experienced the 'old style' of account management. The agency principals were 'businessmen from an account service background' who had the 'foresight to lock up big clients and to hire the best creative people'. They understood that 'you grow with the client in this business'. 'Having big, successful clients and campaigns attracted other business to the agency.' For Hamill, the account executive was 'a filter', 'the middle part of an hourglass, with the client at the top and the creative department at the bottom of the glass'. A good account manager 'could get right into the [client's] company': Thiess Toyota, for example, included Hamill in its staff photos.[13]

Maintaining strong client relationships sometimes required a carefully thought out strategy employed across agency departments. Graham Cox recalls sharing with Patterson CEO Keith Cousins his concerns about the relationship between the agency and its client, the tobacco giant W.D. & H.O. Wills. Wills employed four agencies, which competed with each other for new projects, and Patterson was falling short in these battles. With the help of the creative director Bruce Jarrett, the pair developed a strategy to improve the relationship with the client by offering better creative work. As the agency's creative work improved, so did its new business success rate with Wills.[14]

The key element in the agency–client relationship was mutual respect.[15] This respect had to be built on financial transparency: Cowper describes a good agency as one that has 'good business principle, honesty and integrity [as well as] old-fashioned service.'[16] At Patterson it was 'an agency principle that no client would be disadvantaged by our charging practices. We charged all clients by the same formula and our books were always open', Colin Fraser recalls.'[17] Recalling his time at the creative boutique SPASM, Mike Strauss described the 'challenge to find clients who understood what we were about'. Clients were surprised by the agency's culture, but the agency principals 'were convincing' and successfully established strong relations with clients, such as the controversial businessman and hotelier Irving Rockman and the then Heinz marketing manager Luscombe, built on mutual respect.

Once the client respected the team, the agency could charge higher fees.[18] Gaining this respect could be hard work. John Wright recalls handling the R. J. Reynolds tobacco account while working at Y&R New York. Reynolds ran a tough business and was a tough and demanding client. Its huge budget gave it enormous power over the four agencies it employed and the client was notorious for knocking back creative work and 'demanding reshoots over something minor'. Smokers who worked on the account were expected to smoke a Reynolds product; anything else might cost them the account. Suzie Otten found agency–client relationships were usually 'fantastic' at the beginning – 'a honeymoon period' – but were likely to sour over time, as personality conflicts developed.[19] Peter Clemenger recalls 'occasional conflicts with clients' over which he 'had to take stand'. One such incident involved a client 'victimising a woman copywriter.'[20]

Being an Account Manager
The expectations of an account manager's relationship with a client varied depending on the culture of a particular agency.

At JWT, for example, clients were looked after in 'a quiet, gentlemanly manner'[21]; McCann was 'more aggressive.'[22] At Patterson, Kinsella found the culture 'peculiar', 'like a law firm or accounting firm' and not 'creative'. In contrast, Wright thought Patterson 'more contemporary, savvy, and slicker' than the 'solid, reliable [and] at times very creative' Clem Taylor, the Adelaide agency where he had started his career. At Jackson Wain in the 1960s, there was a party atmosphere but underpinning this were strong systems. The agency directors took a 'hands-on', 'account service' approach to running the agency that was 'disciplined' and 'professional'. Run by 'some very good quality people', the agency 'recognised and held onto talent.'[23] With the revered Len Reason at the helm, Masius Melbourne had 'a family feel' in the 1970s. Later, Mojo was more of a boy's club with Friday night drinks, a type of 'salon', 'a sea of interesting people': politicians, film directors, and artists.[24] As we saw in Chapter 5, Ogilvy & Mather had a conservative reputation, but that was not how it seemed from the inside. Life in the agency was 'hard work, camaraderie, and play'. Employees worked long hours in order to 'get it right'. With no room for freeloaders, the pace 'sorted the wheat from the chaff.'[25]

The most important attribute of an account director at Ogilvy & Mather was the ability to run the account smoothly; establishing a good relationship with the client came well down on the list.[26] Wright identifies MDA's strengths as networking and getting the best clients rather than strong creative. It was there he learnt that 'advertising was not just about the creatives' work but other aspects too'. When Mojo merged with MDA, Wright was ecstatic. The Mojo culture was 'Aussie, blokey, boozy, and irreverent, but the work 'held it together', it was 'just fantastic'. Later, at The Campaign Palace, Wright found his role as an account executive harder 'because creative was on top of account service' and it 'could be difficult to sell' their work. As an account executive, Wright 'was a bit more at ease at Mojo.'[27]

Despite differences in agency culture, the tasks of the account manager were broadly the same in each agency. John Cowper started work as a junior account executive at HRMcCE in Sydney in the middle of 1964. He spent three years filing and answering the telephone before completing his National Service. On his return two years later, he was promoted to account executive and his days were now filled with preparing for meetings, and writing up the minutes of those meetings as contact reports – memorandums that kept the client and the agency team up to date on the status of a project. For Cowper, being able to brief well was an account manager's key attribute. It required 'an innate understanding of the product and creative' in order to be able to draw out a 'creative interpretation of the brief.'[28]

As we saw in Chapter 1, JWT's T Square was introduced into Australia in 1957. Rival agencies developed similar tools. The New York headquarters of Ogilvy & Mather, for example, was an endless source of such tools for the Australian offices, including '"how to" books', 'magic lanterns', 'reels' and 'tapes' that showed staff 'how to create advertising that sells' and 'manage an advertising agency.'[29] Originally written by Ogilvy, the tools were later produced by the New York leadership and, by 1977, were professional, research-based, and strategic. In the 1980s Ian Strachan was sent from Ogilvy & Mather Australia to the New York office to develop 'proprietary tools' for use by the Australian offices.[30] The result was the development of a range of booklets, including a Structure and Briefing Procedure document, containing plans for creative and media briefs. The

Australian offices also utilised a range of materials produced by
Ogilvy & Mather Worldwide, including a guide for writing
memos and reports, and guidelines for interviewing and hiring.[31]
Joining Ogilvy & Mather in the 1980s introduced Suzie Otten
to 'structure' through 'the development of strategies', 'markets',
'tone', and 'restrictions.'[32]

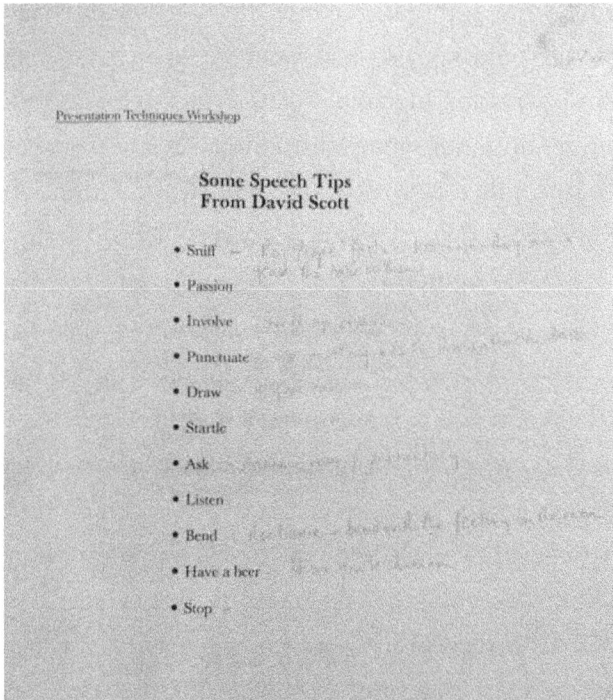

Figure 7.1 Comments on tips for Ogilvy & Mather staff on pitching.
Courtesy of Luella Copeland-Smith, c. 1980s, BBB Box 25, Supplement.

Y&R New York provided its offices with the SSO (the
Strategy Selection Outline) that local offices adapted for use,
as well as a creative work plan, 'the famous yellow book.'[33]
Sometimes the client provided its own advertising toolkit. The
cereal giant Kellogg's, for example, had a strong internal culture
and insisted that JWT use its toolkit 'The K. Way', which Cox
believes Kellogg's had 'ripped off from other agencies'. Unilever

and Johnson & Johnson also provided their own advertising toolkits.[34] For some agencies there was an inherent tension between the conservatism of their clients who wished to follow rules and paradigms, and the individual creative expression required to produce outstanding creative work. As we saw in Chapter 4, Ric Otton, for example, remained ambivalent about the idea of 'process' in the development of great ideas.[35]

Different agencies also had different account management models and reporting hierarchies, although once again these differences were minor. A Patterson account director managed three clients,[36] an Ogilvy & Mather account director four. Account executives reported to account managers, who, in their turn, reported to the account directors. Graham Cox had two account executives and a secretary working for him. An account executive's job included writing reports of client meetings: at Ogilvy & Mather the report had to be completed within twenty-four hours then faxed to client to be signed off. Budget management was a crucial task for the account managers, 'the agency costs were always set above the client budgets' and it was the responsibility of the account executive to check the creative charges.[37]

For Wright, these skills were learned gradually, a 'hands-on introduction' to the account management role while working in the production department at Clem Taylor. He knew he was being 'trained up'; his client contact gradually increased until after eighteen months in production he was given 'some smaller clients' to handle, including one he had known in production. Others learnt important lessons from senior colleagues. Malcolm Spry, for example, taught Suzie Otten 'never to show any emotion about or in [sic] conferences with clients', and to 'only write what needs to be read' in her contact reports. Phillip Adams also emphasised the need for concision. 'You need to be able to write what the client wants on the back of a business card', he advised Otten.[38]

The account director's day included negotiations with the creative director, collaboration with colleagues, and the 'stewarding of the brand'. She or he was 'the person responsible for the business' and people looked 'to the director for answers and leadership.'[39] An Ogilvy & Mather appraisal form from the 1980s outlined the key attributes of the successful account director, divided into 'professional' (a list of twelve attributes) and 'people' skills (eleven attributes), with a fair amount of crossover. The professional account director was someone who could (amongst other things) manage smoothly; execute well; be accurate, with an enquiring mind; understand marketing and the creative process; present and write well; and work well with others. Building excellent relationships with clients came (surprisingly) well down on the list (at ninth) and strategic thinking came last, which demonstrates that by now this was the job of the dedicated strategy planner. The required 'people skills' were: leadership; creativity; initiative; presence; maturity and judgement; enthusiasm and personal motivation; interpersonal skills; a positive attitude and loyalty to Ogilvy & Mather; the ability to get things done; intellectual depth and an inquiring mind; and a breadth of interest.[40] Marie Jackson 'felt quite empowered all the time as an account service person' at Ogilvy & Mather, 'but I think we always knew where the boundaries were'. The biggest challenges for the account executive were 'always about the work. That was the focus.'[41]

Getting Serious

Between the 1960s and the 1980s, there was a gradual shift away from the personal relationships that had been at the heart of the agency–client relationship towards a more businesslike, professional arrangement. Over time, the relationship became more sophisticated, more professional, and more equal: 'account management' rather than 'account service', as clients became better educated and more demanding.[42] This professionalisation started early at John Clemenger: Peter Clemenger – the founder's son and the agency's CEO from the early 1960s – preferred to work *with* clients rather than *for* them. His rules for client management were to 'learn the client's business' and to 'try to give good service', but he eschewed the old, matey style of client management that was the norm in Australian agencies. For Clemenger 'business was business'. He advised his staff to 'take [clients] for lunch but not dinner' and 'keep the personal life separate.'[43]

Figure 7.2 JWT's all-male account executives in Melbourne.
Newspaper News, *26 July 1963, p. 2 (Courtesy AdNews)*

Asked to explain what George Patterson offered its clients that differed from other agencies, Colin Fraser emphasises the partnership aspect: 'We helped our clients to identify challenges and solutions.' Nevertheless, an element of the old-style service remained. Fraser recalls that Patterson's CEO Keith Cousins was always careful to look after the clients. The General Motors account, especially, was very important for the agency, so a typical day for Fraser was spent ensuring the clients were happy. Entertaining clients remained an important tool for the account manager until 'Keating stopped us eating'[44] with the introduction of the Fringe Benefits Tax (FBT) in 1986, which shortened the long, liquid lunch.[45]

These account managers had initially been mostly men: at McCann-Erickson, Cowper's account service colleagues were all men, 'salesmen' as he calls them. While there were plenty of women working in media, finance, creative and casting, the account service department of the 1960s and 1970s was 'overwhelmingly male dominated'. At Fortune there was one female account executive; at the Murray Evans advertising agency in 1974 it was 'a bit more mixed.'[46] Over the next decade and a half, this shift would accelerate significantly. In the 1980s, the number of women account directors increased and Fraser found those women he worked with 'great, they cared about their clients and understood the business'. Women also began to handle traditionally 'male' accounts: still in her twenties, Toni Lawler, for example, became the first woman at Ogilvy & Mather to work on Shell Oil.[47]

The catalyst for these changes was the emergence and popularity of marketing as a university specialisation. As we saw in the previous chapter, the importance of marketing had first been recognised in Australia in the 1920s, but the discipline had been slow to gain a foothold in the agencies. In the late 1950s some advertising agencies began to show an interest in marketing: John Paramor (of Briggs, Canny, James & Paramor), for example, was one of the first advertising professionals to embrace the new discipline.[48] But most agencies were forced to engage with marketing only as their clients increasingly hired young men fresh from the state technical schools and universities armed with marketing diplomas and degrees. With the influx of marketing graduates, clients became smarter and began to demand more professionalism from their advertising agencies.

In 1966, Australian advertising managers from some of the leading manufacturing firms were asked: 'What makes a top-class ad manager?'[49] The main attributes they agreed were 'sagacity, toughness and a thorough knowledge of the product': the ad manager knew 'more about the product than the agency man.'[50] The following year the same magazine carried a feature article on 'The Marketing Man of the Future.'[51] The new professor of marketing at the University of New South Wales, Roger Layton, held 'the chair to which the eyes of the Australian marketing industry are turned'. The marketing degree in the Faculty of Commerce at UNSW had suddenly become 'the in thing'. Two hundred students were expected to enrol in the degree in 1968. The degree included 'the normal units of a commerce degree' at first year; Economics II, marketing principles, case studies and behavioural science in second year, plus a special option subject such as accountancy or data processing, and Economics III, marketing management, marketing research and organisation theory plus two humanities subjects at third year.

As the clients became better educated, agencies began to realise they, too, had to work smarter. The British advertising agency Saatchi & Saatchi began recruiting business and marketing graduates from the firm's inception. Over the next decade, Australian advertising agencies followed suit and a more disciplined, sophisticated style of account management evolved.[52] Young people entering the industry became more disciplined and better educated.'[53] Advertising began to grow up; with 'more intelligent, university-trained people in it', it embarked on becoming a 'responsible profession.'[54]

Account managers began producing more informed and insightful strategies. They were expected to think strategically, to be able to write a brief that told creatives what the client required, and to understand and sell creative work.[55] Interviewees remember account management in the 1970s as 'more rigorous than expected later on'; 'suits' were yet to become mere 'bag carriers' – that is executives who merely delivered creative work to clients rather than strategic thinkers who influenced the direction of creative work.[56]

This new attention to strategic thinking was accompanied by a push to recruit more graduates into advertising, which, it was hoped, would lift the industry's status.[57] Eventually, the Advertising Federation of Australia (AFA) set up a graduate training programme for the industry. An intern in the first AFA intake in 1981, Julian Martin recalls that Melbourne's agencies greeted the new training programme enthusiastically. One of sixteen trainees (a fairly even mix of women and men, most of whom would become account managers), Martin was sent to USP Needham for a nine-month 'helicopter view' of the advertising business. A senior staff member was assigned to look after him as he followed the well-worn trainee path through the agency's departments: starting in account management, then production, creative, media and back to account management. His mentor, a 'perfectly turned out' English account director named Richard Jenkins, would take the young Martin to lunch with other account directors. Lunch started with a scotch and dry, and was 'quite boozy'. It was, as Martin says, 'a different era.'[58]

Over the next decade, however, the business became increasingly serious. A growing emphasis on discipline, strategic thinking and planning led to some account managers special-ising in these areas and leaving the handling of clients and accounts to others. Strategy planning had developed first in the UK in the 1970s and, by the 1980s, Australians were aware of its growing importance to the industry. There was some resistance to this specialisation in Australia – Mo and Jo, for example, were never fans – and it would not be until the late 1980s and early 1990s that planning gained a foothold here, led by the US agency Foote, Cone & Belding and the Sydney branch of The Campaign Palace.[59]

When Ogilvy & Mather arrived in Australia in 1967 it did not establish a separate research department (unlike its own US and UK offices, and the Australian offices of the big global agencies, such as Hansen Rubensohn-McCann Erikson). Strategic thinking was central to the agency's approach, how-ever: Norman Berry, Ogilvy & Mather's New York–based creative guru, insisted on the importance of 'tightly-defined strategies' for producing creative excellence.[60] Over the next decade, Ogilvy & Mather's Australian offices began to use focus groups to test their ideas and, with the help of the 'O&M New York Research and Planning staff', introduced the Values Segmentations Studies, which were later picked up by the Roy Morgan Research Centre. These studies were 'descriptions of major patterns of values and motives' and were useful in 'defining magnitudes, understanding trends, planning actions, and conceptualising issues, threat and opportunities.'[61] Jackson recalls: 'We were obsessed by the consumer, absolutely obsessed by the consumer.' Research groups were really important: 'That was Ogilvy. Before you wrote a creative brief, you researched the proposition, concepts, and issues. You had to understand where the consumers were now and where you were taking them.'[62]

Wright's experiences reflected the gradual uptake of research and strategic thinking by agencies, as well as their ambivalence towards it. During his first stint in London in the early 1970s, he worked as an account representative at JWT. There he was well schooled in marketing disciplines. Working on 'classic packaged goods', Wright was amazed by the amount of data the agency collected, including research, sales data, competitive information, and media information: 'I'd never seen anything like it.' He attended monthly presentations by the research company Nielsen, and was introduced to 'new and different data' and learned how to make use of it. On his return to Australia, to work for Y&R Adelaide, Wright brought a new emphasis on consumer research and strategy. Hired by MDA to introduce his knowledge of processes and his discipline to the Qantas account, he found there was 'not the discipline' he'd been used to in his previous agencies; the agency was 'eclectic, do your own thing'. The merger with Mojo brought another shift. Wright wanted to continue doing strategic planning but 'Mojo didn't have that'. As we saw in Chapter 5, Wright decided to 'keep doing it my way' but informally, 'not in a ponderous way.'[63]

The Campaign Palace's Reg Bryson had been enamoured with the strategic side of the advertising business from his first years in the industry working with the Nixon Compton agency in Sydney. There he had been 'lucky' enough to be mentored by 'one of the best account directors'; an account director who was 'strategic' not just a 'charming, grey flannel suit' only interested in 'the party scene, which was then common in the industry'. Advertising was a social business, Bryson recalls, but his mentor 'was not caught up in the social [aspect]'. 'Intense' and wanting 'to know what was happening in the marketplace', he taught Bryson 'to drill down', 'think strategically' and 'look at things differently'. At Masius in London, Bryson worked closely with the planners (then called researchers). He found them to be 'good thinkers' and together they achieved great success for their clients. On his return to Australia, Bryson hoped to maintain this depth of strategic thinking, but a brief sojourn at USP Needham proved disappointing. There was 'not much strategic thinking' there. He found the work shallow and short term because the agency focused on profit rather than the product. Without planners doing the hard work developing the appropriate strategy, clients were presented with several ideas, all of which followed category conventions. Good strategy required long planning and worked to involve 'minds and ideas' with the brand; it was not just 'selling bombardment style.'[64] At the Palace in Sydney, Bryson was able to pursue strategy planning in earnest – and to great success – thanks to the support of like-minded colleagues such as the copywriter Jack Vaughan.

By the mid–1980s, strategy was the buzzword in the Australian advertising industry, but agencies struggled to define it and harness its power.[65] A document produced by Kevin Luscombe provided guidance for those confused by the nascent discipline, emphasising the depth and breadth of understanding, as well as the single-mindedness its successful execution required.[66] In fact, Luscombe refused to employ a dedicated strategy planner. The speciality might have a place in the larger agencies but he felt it was not really appropriate or, indeed, financially viable for a smaller agency such as Luscombe and Partners. Luscombe expected his account managers to be able to 'read research and have an intelligent conversation with the client' and he did not want to employ 'message carriers.'[67] Some account managers were attracted to strategy planning because they found the day-to-day activities of handling an account 'incredibly repetitive'. Catanzariti, for example, found planning was 'a saviour' for him; 'the best part of account management'. Focusing on the consumer's point of view – 'bringing the consumer to the table' – and the problem solving involved was far more rewarding than the traditional work of account service.[68]

From the late 1980s the tasks became increasingly separated with specialist strategy planners setting up their own departments and the return of the dedicated account service person, whose sole job was to keep the client happy: Luscombe's 'message carriers'. Cunnack describes account management as 'the last male bastion' because 1970s Australia was 'ocker' and 'blokey.'[69] This was certainly the case for Laura Henschke. Henschke had commenced her advertising career at JWT in Lima before migrating to Australia in 1977. At FCB in Sydney, she was the only female account executive. While she was 'flabbergasted with the amount of drinking', she did not feel excluded from the agency. However, when she fell pregnant, the agency determined that she would not be returning to work: 'It ... hit me hard.'[70] At the same time, there was a sense in Melbourne at least, 'women were increasingly everywhere', and in the 1980s and the advent of the strategy planners, 'women often got those jobs', as 'ex-researchers' and 'ex-account' people.[71] This may well be true but the emergence of planning as a separate discipline was not entirely beneficial for ambitious advertising women.

With many male account managers now aspiring to be strategy planners, a vacuum emerged which young women (often over-educated for the relatively menial tasks of the account executive or 'bag-carrier') began to fill, and many of them would find themselves stuck there.[72] There were exceptions. The account manager Tania Farrelly chose to switch to strategy planning in the early 1990s when she had her first child. The move suited her family commitments and, like Catanzariti, she had always found planning the most interesting part of the job. It also suited her problem-solving skills. The demands of account service were less conducive to child rearing. Creating good client relationships meant socialising after hours. This was not Farrelly's style and 'she didn't feel comfortable with it'. After consulting with Jackson (her 'amazing' mentor), Farrelly made the move to strategy planning.[73]

————————

Martin Sorrell, the CEO of WPP, a global advertising and public relations giant, has described the evolution of agency–client relationships in the digital era. Clients, he argues, are driving major changes in the relationship as they demand superior measurement techniques and favour digital advertising over more traditional forms. Agencies are struggling to keep up.[74] As we have seen in this chapter, the role played by the client in driving industry change is not new. By enthusiastically embracing marketing education in the 1960s and 1970s, clients forced advertising agencies and their account managers to educate themselves and professionalise. In the 1980s, O&M's creative head Norman Berry drew the attention of his colleagues to the important contribution clients made to the agency's creative success, and reminded them to give clients the credit they deserved.[75] As we will see in Chapter 9, clients drove even more significant changes from the late 1980s, as they began to question the financial structures at the heart of the relationship. Relationships remain 'very important' in the advertising business today, 'if not as disclosed [as they used to be].'[76]

Throughout these shifts, keeping the client happy remained the account manager's key challenge. A breakdown in the relationship with the client could have severe consequences for the agency and the individual account manager.[77] The clients had to trust the agency and feel respected. But they also had to be given advertising that worked, that persuaded consumers to buy their product or service. This involved another agency department, the creative department. One of biggest changes to occur between the 1950s and 1980s was the power shift from account management to the creative department. In the 1960s account management led the relationship and still 'had the upper hand', but over the 1970s creative directors became 'the main players'. As 'the industry matured', creative became increasingly important. In the late 1970s, agencies such as The Campaign Palace and Ogilvy & Mather began to produce consistently strong creative, which forced the more account management–orientated agencies such as Patterson and Clemenger to improve their creative product.[78] By the 1980s, creative directors had become 'the heroes of every agency'; the highest-paid group in the agency.[79] How this shift came about is the subject of the next chapter.

CHAPTER EIGHT

RULING THE ROOST

By the late 1980s, Ogilvy & Mather's creative department was placed firmly 'on a pedestal' in a 'hierarchical' internal structure in which the agency's departments operated as 'siloes'. Creatives – the copywriters and art directors who wrote and visualised the advertisements – 'did not appreciate account service' and often behaved badly towards account managers. Caught between the creatives and the client – 'the meat in the sandwich' – the account manager Tania Farrelly found this atmosphere 'always tense'. When she failed to sell a campaign to the client, the creative department would tell her to 'go back' and try again. At the same time, she was expected to make money for the agency, and Farrelly often 'felt sick' from the pressure.[1] By the late 1980s, this tension between creatives, account managers and their clients was common. But it had not always been this way.

This chapter traces the internal power shifts within agencies from, account managers to the creatives that began in the 1960s. At the start of the decade, writers and artists were atomised: writers would develop an advertisement's concept, headline and body copy before passing it on to an artist for visualisation. By the end of the 1980s, agencies had undergone a creative revolution. Writers and artists were now paired into teams – copywriter and art director. The team shared an office, worked on creative briefs together and, as the powerhouse of the agency, treated account management with disdain. Looking towards New York and London for inspiration, these Australian creatives used international agency networks to travel to those glamorous cities (and others) in order to enhance their advertising skills and experience. Hundreds of British creatives travelled in the opposite direction, tempted by the promise of endless sunshine and better pay. This hierarchy held relatively briefly in Australia (from the early 1970s to the end of the 1980s) but, while it lasted, the creatives reigned supreme.[2]

Frank Palmer, co-creative director of Leo Burnett, Sydney, with writer Dierdre Brierley.

Figure 8.1 As creativity emerged as the lifeblood of an agency's operations, creative directors assumed a more influential position in the agency hierarchy.
Advertising News, *3 November 1978, p. 10 (Courtesy of AdNews)*

Art Versus Science

Agency power struggles between account managers and creatives were rooted in debates over whether advertising was an art or a science. These debates went back to the very beginnings of the industry. Opinions on this matter have shifted with each generation. In 1904, the American copywriter John E. Kennedy, for example, defined advertising as 'salesmanship in print'. Basing his copy on thorough research of a client's business, he insisted on testing the copy before it ran. Ten years later this 'hard sell' approach gave way to Theodore McManus's famous 'soft sell' long-copy ad for the Cadillac, in which the brand of the car was not even mentioned and no 'reason why' was proffered to induce the consumer to buy it. Instead, the reader was left to imagine the feeling of superiority that would come from owning such a car.[3] Again the fashion moved back to 'hard sell' with the publication of Claude Hopkins's *Scientific Advertising* (1923), which argued for research-based advertising that was tested and accountable through the use of market devices such as coupons.[4] Advertising men around the world, including in Australia, picked up these ideas and continued to debate the benefits of these competing approaches throughout the first half of the twentieth century.

There was regular commentary on the topic in the Australian industry press, usually coming down on the side of rigour rather than inspiration: 'It is not magic which conceives the successfully unorthodox advertisement, not a sudden brain wave; it is investigation and concentration';[5] and 'Advertising is printed salesmanship.'[6] The *Advertising Careers* booklet told school leavers: 'Yes, advertising is an art but today it is a science as well. The writer thinking up a headline for a *Woman's Weekly* advertisement is quite likely to be spending his [sic] evenings studying for a psychology degree.'[7]

Many of the copywriters and commercial artists who wrote and visualised the advertisements in the first half of the century were only lightly invested in this debate. With little support for the creative industries in Australia before the establishment of the Australia Council in 1967, many painters, poets and playwrights were thrown back onto the advertising industry to support themselves, their families and their creative pursuits.[8]

Advertising had long provided a safe haven for artists and writers. A roll call of Australian creative talent who shined in the advertising industry but could not be contained by it tells the story: the novelists Peter Carey, Morris Lurie and Bryce Courtenay; the journalist and broadcaster Phillip Adams; the playwrights Mona Brand and Barry Oakley; the film directors Fred Schepisi and Bruce Beresford; and the artists Elaine Haxton and Ken Done.[9] The copywriter Hugh Spencer recalls working with 'clever people … who didn't have anywhere to go', people such as Adams and the future dual-Booker-prizewinner, Carey. These were 'bright people' and advertising was 'an area where you could meet other bright people.'[10] As late as 1975, John Newton found the agency Leo Burnett in Sydney to be 'a close, warm group of people … who went on to other things; poets, writers, etc. The place you went to get paid for doing such things.'[11] Many of these artists and writers imagined a creative future beyond advertising, producing great art and literature, but the new advertising began to offer creative people the possibility of increased satisfaction through their work.

In the early 1960s, the majority of writers and commercial artists worked separately.[12] Some writers are rumoured to have

191

pushed their finished copy under the door of the artists' studio for the advertisement to be drawn up. At this time, influential agencies such as Melbourne's Thompson Ansell Blunden (TAB) employed writers and designers who worked separately and only one art director, Betty Blunden, who ran the studio.[13] The art director Ray Black recalls a 'union demarcation' between the copywriter and art director when he started in the business in 1963.[14]

There were some exceptions. In 1960 *Advertising* reported that Goldberg Advertising in Sydney had implemented a group system whereby teams worked on each account. The result was that 'the copywriters … actually work in conjunction with the artists and visualisers, as a concerted, coherent, unified team to give a united, coherent advertising plan.'[15] Melbourne's Paton Advertising (led by Phillip Adams and Len Reason) similarly appears to have been ahead of its time, with Adams bringing 'writing and art direction together' before 1965.[16] But when Graham Nunn started work at the end of the '60s, some Australian agencies still did not have separate creative departments. Andrew Killey, then a junior copywriter, found the art studio and the copy department at NAS MacNamara in Adelaide 'very siloed', which provided 'an opportunity for tension.'[17]

Despite the influx of overseas agencies outlined in Chapter 1, Australian creatives' knowledge of US and British advertising was still patchy in the 1960s. The art director at Sydney agency Rodgers Holland Everingham (RHE), Arthur Holland, had 'his American magazines airmailed to him before everyone else' but, in general, the influence of the US was slow to filter through.[18] As a copywriter working at TAB in the mid-1960s, Carey recalls having 'no idea about what was going on in the US.'[19] The copywriter Rosem'ry Bertel agrees: 'the overseas influence was not so strong [as now] because of the limits of communication technology' … 'Creatives could not easily access overseas ads even if they had wanted to.'[20]

This soon began to change. With New York's creative revolution and its emphasis on advertising that entertained the consumer with humorous copy and engaging visuals, DDB's use of creative teams to achieve this style of advertising became increasingly influential and reached Australia in the late 1960s. Graham Nunn joined Y&R, the 'new agency in town', and was impressed with its culture: it had a separate creative department and 'felt like it was ten years ahead' of Australian agencies.[21] The man behind the creative revolution in the US, DDB's Bill Bernbach, appeared to have the last word on the art-versus-science issue, saying, famously, that: 'Advertising is fundamentally persuasion and persuasion happens to be not a science, but an art.'[22]

Bernbach spelled out his argument more fully in a speech delivered to the 4As in 1980. Science and art could not be separated, he argued. 'Even science' became 'an art at the very top': 'in the magic sphere of greatness, in any field, art takes over.'[23] Moreover, emotions were crucial to any endeavour. A speaker who touched only people's minds would be unlikely to move them to action or to change their minds, the motivations of which lay deep in the realm of the passions. Facts [were] not enough, Bernbach declared. Advertising professionals should forget words like 'hard sell' and 'soft sell', and ensure they had something of substance to say, something that would serve and inform the consumer. 'Research was important', he continued, because 'the heart of an effective creative philosophy was the belief that nothing is as powerful as an insight into human nature, what compulsions drive a man, what instincts dominate his action. If a copywriter knew these things she or he could touch a reader at the core of his [sic] being, because only feeling led to action. Even among the scientists – men who were regarded as the worshippers of facts – the real giants had always been poets, men who jumped from facts into the realm of imagination and ideas. An advertising writer had to be sure that she or he said [the message] like it had never been said before.'[24]

By placing originality above facts, Bernbach changed the internal structure of the advertising industry. For the first time, the creative department sat above account management in an agency's pecking order and the new fashion for pairing up into copywriter–art director teams gave the creatives a stronger power base than they had before.[25] Yet as we saw in the previous chapter, 'suits' were gradually becoming more educated in marketing in response to their clients' higher standards, taking the business more seriously and using research to produce more insightful creative briefs. Bernbach's observation that advertising was both an art and a science would become commonplace,[26] but the changes he and the New York school (including Mary Wells Lawrence of Wells Rich Greene) introduced set up a conflict that would affect agency culture in Australia and around the world.

Australia's New Creatives
An article in *Advertising in Australia* in 1965 set out the vision of the new copywriters.[27] First, they demanded more respect from account executives and more access to clients: creatives were sometimes kept away from clients because agency management feared their unpredictable behaviour. The account executives were 'getting in the way of good ideas'. Their briefing was 'half-baked' and they set 'themselves up as judges of copy when they

[were] often illiterate'. They were also too conservative: many refused to accept an exciting idea unless the creatives could show them 'the same approach in an overseas advertisement'.

Teamwork was the key to the new advertising, the article continued. The days of the 'one-man bands of yester-year who could pluck entire campaigns out of thin air' were over. Brilliant and 'spectacular' as they were, these 'prima donnas … wouldn't last five minutes in a modern advertising set-up'. As advertising 'expanded' and became 'more interlocked', so a copywriter 'had to be able to work with other people'. The 'single biggest step forward in advertising' had been the turn to research, and individual inspiration was no longer sufficient. Now that advertisers could 'find out what people want and then whether they wanted it', agencies had become accountable for their ads, and it was too risky to 'play a hunch.'[28] The new copywriters were especially keen to work in teams with art directors because this 'achieved better results'. But copywriters needed a new type of art director to work with, one who was more than a gifted illustrator or strong designer. This new type of art director needed to be 'a good strategic thinker' and to understand 'the importance of readership to the success of an advertisement.'[29]

Bernbach's revolution brought a new level of excitement about what was going on overseas. Through the industry press and the show-reels sent out to the multi-national agencies and shown at cinemas in Melbourne and Sydney, Australian creatives were exposed to the new advertising and saw fresh possibilities for their work. Inspired by Bernbach and others, this new generation of writers and artists had an unusual confidence about them. The emphasis on creativity made the industry more fulfilling for those with creative aspirations. Convinced that their contribution to the advertising process – the production

of outstanding creative work – was the key to advertising success, they were more inclined to commit wholeheartedly to the
industry than previous generations had been.

An advertising career now offered the promise of creative
satisfaction, and creatives began to celebrate this new confidence
through associations and awards such as the Melbourne Art
Directors Club (MADC), AWARD, and the Caxtons, which
mushroomed in the 1960s and 1970s, influenced by Britain's
Design & Art Direction (D&AD) and New York's One Show.
These creative awards would become 'the backbone of [creative]
standards', the measure of a creative's success. This contrasted with
the commercial purpose of advertising work – selling product
and building brands.[30] The copywriter Stephanie Borland, for
example, considered creative awards 'fun' but 'irrelevant'. For
Borland, 'selling for big companies was what mattered.'[31] The art
director Keith Aldrich gained 'great satisfaction' from helping
a company grow. He gives the example of the mid-1980s 'Is
Don. Is Good' campaign for Don Smallgoods: 'We felt we had
helped that company grow … [I was] most proud of that.'[32] The
campaign also won awards.

Australian creatives had travelled overseas to work from the
first years of the advertising industry, but as we saw in Chapter
2 and Chapter 3, they began to leave the country in increasing
numbers from the mid-1960s, usually returning after a couple
of years working in British or North American agencies. The
copywriters Jack Vaughan and Peter Carey, for example, set off
for London; the art director Robin Stewart travelled to Europe,
London, then on to Toronto.[33] All returned in the early 1970s,
looking to apply what they had learned to Australian advertising.[34]

At the same time, the number of creatives arriving in Australia
from overseas began to increase. The copywriter Lionel Hunt

('a wordsmith like no other'[35]) had first arrived in Australia from Britain in 1963. After a stint back in the UK, he returned in May 1970 to work at Masius Melbourne before establishing Australia's premier boutique agency, The Campaign Palace.[36] Paul Priday – also a copywriter – arrived in Melbourne in 1968. Priday had trained at JWT London, 'the University of Advertising', which he found to be 'a very polite environment', with 'aristocrats as account directors' and 'a benevolent attitude to the arts'. In contrast, Priday found 'the dynamism of Australian advertising seductive', largely because of the opportunities offered by commercial radio and the larger number of television networks than in Britain. Unable to secure a job as a copywriter, Priday joined Masius Melbourne as an account executive. Masius had recently bought out Melbourne's oldest local agency, Paton Hughes, to form 'a new global agency'. The agency's gifted managing director Len Reason assembled a group of star creative talent – Hunt, Gordon Trembath, Carey and the copywriter Terry Durack amongst them. These stars worked in teams (as they had at Paton Hughes), which was a revelation to Priday, who recalls his time at Masius as 'an amazing period'. Creatives also moved across from New Zealand, looking for increased opportunities in Australia's significantly larger advertising industry. Graeme Kinsella recalls that 'many professionals and university-educated people' left New Zealand between 1972 and 1975 because of the 'difficult economic time'. Kinsella, then a copywriter, was one of them, moving permanently to Sydney in 1972.[37]

From the mid-1970s through to the mid-1980s, a steady stream of British creatives – 'the English invasion' – arrived in Australia via formal and informal networks, tempted in the main by promises of sunshine, better pay and opportunity.[38] These individuals brought with them 'intelligent advertising', inspired by the hot-shop London agencies Collett Dickenson Pearce (CDP), Saatchi & Saatchi, and Boase Massimi Pollitt (BMP), and focused on the creative possibilities advertising now offered.[39] The English sensibility of advertising was more highly regarded in Australia than the US version. Neil Lawrence judged the English to be more adaptive than the Americans to 'Australian informality' and a lot of English people were very successful here in the 1970s and 1980s, including The Campaign Palace writer John Turnbull, Saatchi's creative director Phil Putnam, and the typographer Mike Chandler. This 'Pommy Mafia' helped transform Australian creativity.[40]

The art director Ron Mather arrived in Australia in 1978 after fifteen years working in London agencies, including time at the new hot-shop Saatchi & Saatchi.[41] Mather had briefly attended Hornsey College of Art before landing a job at CPV International in 1962. There, and later at London Press Exchange, he learned his craft doing 'the odd layout' and 'paste up', and 'changing water pots'. Mather's apprenticeship had convinced the young art director that good advertising was 'all about ideas', so when he moved to Australia (a place he 'knew nothing about'), he sought out like-minded creatives. Needing sponsorship, Mather had taken a job with Masius Melbourne. He 'loved Australia straight away', partly because the advertising budgets were small: 'You had to have good thinking – 'you couldn't rely on big production.' Aldrich also found Melbourne's advertising scene exciting. He had left London for Australia in the early 1980s, having also worked in the US, and enjoyed Melbourne's 'faster process' and the increased opportunity to make television commercials.

Despite enjoying the pace and opportunity Australian advertising offered, both Mather and Aldrich were frustrated by the locals' fixation on the bottom line. Mather had discovered 'good pockets of people: Magnus, Nankervis and Curl; Leonardi and Curtis', and Masius was 'good but not great', he found that advertising in Australia was 'mostly about the money'. When Hunt and Trembath opened The Campaign Palace, Hunt rang Mather to talk to him about working for them. Mather 'liked their stuff', and 'just knew straight away they were [all] on the same wavelength'. In Hunt and Trembath, Mather had found like-minded creatives who were more focused on creative excellence than they were on the bottom line.[42]

In the dominant agencies of the late 1970s and 1980s, these new, more confident, creatives – British and Australian – held sway.[43] Mike Strauss, who had himself arrived from South Africa via London in the early 1960s, recalls SPASM as 'revolutionary', a 'one-stop shop offering research, PR and film production – a communication supermarket'. Yet decision-making was 'primarily in the creative department'. The agency focused its energies on creativity, basing its work on a deep understanding of 'how the consumer thinks', and the creative staff dealt directly with the client. [44] As we saw in Chapter 4, the confidence of the new Australian-owned agencies such as SPASM had a distinctly nationalistic flavour to it, motivated by a desire to offer an alternative to the increasingly influential US-based global agencies (and fed by anti–Vietnam War sentiment).[45]

Generating Ideas

As the new advertising took hold in Australia, creatives paid increased attention to the ideas that lay behind advertising campaigns – the insight into consumer thinking that helped an advertisement to stand out from its competition, be remembered by the consumer, and, hopefully, motivate her or him to buy the product. Working at Hertz Walpole in the late 1960s, Doug Watson realised for the first time that advertising was 'all about the idea.'[46] It was a revelation. But the process of generating these memorable ideas varied greatly across agencies. Sometimes the personality of an individual creative drove the process. For example, Fysh Rutherford recalls that Phillip Adams, then the creative director at MDA in Melbourne, worked 'phenomenally fast' and advised the younger creatives not to 'labour' the ideas process. Other agencies had strong internal cultures that transcended the influence of individual creative directors. At Clemenger, for example, the process was everything, and creatives and account management alike were encouraged to take their time settling on final concepts.[47]

The generation of outstanding ideas required trust at three levels: between the creative director and the creative team; between the creative department and account management; and between the agency and its clients. All of these trust relationships required careful management. Creative directors were the 'hero[es] of every agency'; 'the demi-gods of the industry, not answerable to anyone, even the clients.'[48] The worship was sometimes deserved: the role of the creative director could be challenging because of the balance it required. Neil Lawrence explains this challenge: 'How much are you the star? How much are you there to encourage the work of others, filter, edit and fine tune them?' He observed creative directors trying to do too much of the first, unable to put their ego aside: 'You need to be happy if a member of your team has a great idea.'[49]

Account managers were in an equally difficult position. As we have seen, they were caught between the clients and the creatives, trying to keep both parties happy. Creatives had to be treated with sensitivity and care; the good account manager would notice when creatives were under pressure and respond accordingly. Michael Anderson found 'creatives, writers and artists a different breed', and recalls with good humour the conflict between creative and account service 'for not recognising their [the creatives'] brilliance' or 'the beauty of their work.'[50] For Ian Strachan, 'the key internal skill' of an account manager was 'probably ... to build up credit with the creatives', so this credit could be drawn upon later.[51] Marie Jackson, who worked as an account director at O&M Melbourne, agrees. It was up to the account director to gain 'the confidence of the creative department as a person who can grasp concepts and recognise excellent creative work.'[52] The successful account director then 'had to be able to push those ideas through by strategic thought and argument.'[53] Borland recalls 'a natural tension between account [management] and creatives', but thinks this could 'be helpful and stimulating.'[54] Again Jackson concurs: '[The tension] is as it should be ... as long as it's always about the ball and not about the man, you never minded it.' By the 1980s, 'creative was seen as king' at Ogilvy & Mather Melbourne, but it was the account managers who 'held the business together.'[55]

At long-established agencies the relationship between creatives and account management could be more fraught. John Newton joined JWT in Sydney in 1969 as a junior copywriter paired with a junior art director. 'Creatives viewed account service as enemies or fools', he recalls, and they competed with the account managers to present their work to the clients, as the latter preferred to meet the 'glamorous' creatives. 'The creative department were really in charge of the agency', the other departments were at its service.[56] At JWT Melbourne, too, the creatives looked down on account service, and the creative department 'pulled the strings.'[57] But agency cultures varied enormously in this regard. At Compton there was 'not much of a wall between account service and creative' but at McCann-Erikson, account service was 'on top.'[58]

Great work required everyone – creatives, account managers and clients – to be flexible and willing to take a risk. Doug Watson describes developing an iconic campaign for Qantas. After receiving five pages of briefing material from account management, the creative teams at Mojo (including Watson) immediately whittled these down to 'the key ideas'. Then, for eight days, the teams came together 'every hour on the hour' to review their ideas, eventually settling on a concept based on the insight that 'Australia was the most cosmopolitan country on earth'. This was presented to the client, but Watson then 'came up with' a new 'more radical idea' – that is, filming Australians singing Peter Allen's hit 'I Still Call Australia Home' in locations around the world. Demonstrating his flexibility and his trust in the agency team, the Qantas manager James Strong took 'a leap of faith' and gave the campaign the go-ahead. In twenty-nine days filming was completed. Watson remembers it as 'the biggest thing' he had ever done; it was, he recalls, 'thrilling.'[59]

Advertising Craft

The best advertising might be 'all about the idea', but craft – clean, balanced art direction and precise, engaging writing – has always been important. And, as the standing of creatives improved through the 1960s and 1970s, so did attention to their craft. 'Sincerity was essential in copy', wrote Phil Singer of the Sydney advertising agency Hansen-Rubensohn.[60] 'The craft was everything' in the 1970s, and Bennett remembers the era as a time when 'copywriters could really write.'[61] Copywriting went beyond words. At Brisbane's Le Grand McCann-Erickson, Allan Hartley found himself literally writing to measure. Measuring spaces and font size, Hartley explains that 'you'd work out how many words you actually had to write … not only did you have to make something of the copy but you had the discipline of fitting it in that space – to the character.'[62] From the industry's earliest days, advertising copywriting in Australia gradually shifted from descriptive to persuasive copy, as writers responded to the new psychology of advertising and increasing consumer engagement offered by new technologies, as first radio, then television, outpaced the traditional print and outdoor media. As early as the 1920s, industry journals began to advise writers to speak to directly to 'her', the consumer (as well as to compose their ads on 'The Perfect Table for Copywriters'!).[63]

In the 1940s and 1950s, the popular radio soaps, both local and imported, influenced copywriting craft. Starting his career in the 1940s, Lloyd Bassett honed his skills writing ads for the 'Westralian soaps', but only after twelve months 'writing the continuity program' for a 'community singsong' from Fremantle Town Hall. This involved 'putting the ads into the program', and was a 'hard learning experience'. But it taught Bassett to 'appreciate the value of every spoken word'. He learned that 'brevity' was the main factor for writing for radio: 'a hard lesson but worthwhile.'[64] Valwyn Wishart recalls a similar training in writing for radio at the Melbourne agency Richardson Cox.[65] By the 1970s, the model for good copywriting came from the London agencies. Derek Hansen recalls returning to Australia from England and training copywriters 'to write as it was done in England'. For Bill Shannon, the legendary US copywriter Ed McCabe was 'a great influence', inspiring Shannon to avoid 'safe' advertising and strive for work that 'broke through.'[66]

Figure 8.2 Combining art directors and copywriters revolutionised the creative process. Thompson Ansell Blunden promotional brochure, c.1964, courtesy of Claire Nilsson, BBB Box 24, Supplement.

Australian art direction had its roots in the commercial art studios of the early twentieth century: Smith and Julius in Sydney, for example, and the Art Training Institute and Fox Studios in Melbourne. For the illustrators who worked from these studios, advertising was of secondary importance, only useful as a source of income to support their own artistic ambitions. There was little psychological insight behind their work: these artists simply produced pleasant visuals to illustrate the efforts of the copywriters.

The emergence of the Art Director as a distinct role and title in Australian advertising agencies is hard to pinpoint, but is closely connected to the rise of the creative team. Agencies continued to use commercial studios: Faie Davis recalls working for an art studio in the early 1960s, a kind of 'creative consortium' named Jon Hawley & Associates, which was used by

JWT Sydney.[67] At Hertz Walpole in Sydney, there were 'no art directors as such'. Three senior designers and three finished artists sat in the studio together, and the copywriters went there to 'try out ideas.'[68] There was a discernible rise in the arrival of creatives in Australia who identified themselves as 'art directors' rather than 'artist', 'designer' or 'illustrator' (from two in 1966 to eleven in 1967), and the term seems to have subsumed other titles from this point forward.[69] A few creatives worked as both copywriters and art directors. In Mather's view, 'good creatives should be able to do both'. Black agrees. Thinking he could 'write better headlines and copy' than his agency's writers, Black 'drifted into doing both: art directing and writing own stuff, like a one man [band]'. This approach to the creative process would underpin the structure of AWARD School, the training scheme for creatives Black established in 1983.[70]

The Power of the Team

Most creatives were not able to write *and* draw, however, and from the beginning of the 1970s they increasingly found a new strength in teaming up together: copywriter with art director. When Derek Hansen arrived in London in 1965, 'working with an art director was just beginning to happen'. Art directors had previously sat in a different room, assigned to an account not a copywriter: when Priday joined JWT London in the late 1960s, copywriters and art directors were still working separately. At the British creative powerhouse CDP, however, Hansen was assigned an art director, Ron Collins, and the pair became a team. From then on Hansen wanted to work with 'a conceptual art director', and always tried to build successful art director–writer teams, where if one half of the team left the agency, the other half went too. The first time Ken Done teamed up with a writer – Llewellyn Thomas – was at JWT London in 1965. Back in Australia at the end of the 1960s, Done found another writer he 'could work with': Richard Walsh, the future editor of the counterculture magazine *Oz*. When Walsh left for London, Thomas travelled out to JWT Sydney to partner Done again.[71] Killey found working in a team 'a revelation'. For it to be successful, the writer and art director needed to think the same way about the creative process, and if the collaboration worked, the relationship could become a kind of 'mental marriage'. Aldrich also likened the creative team to a marriage: like a 'husband and wife' the writer and art director 'had to get on'. Together, the team would 'go into war', presumably against competing teams, account management, and the client.[72] The naming of Mojo in 1979 – an agency whose work epitomised the new, more confident Australian advertising – reinforced the importance of the creative team. The agency's name was formed from the first letters of the agency's founders, the creative team Alan Morris and Allan Johnston. Tellingly, it ignored the agency's third principal, Don Morris – a suit who was also Morris's brother.

Finding the right partner could be serendipitous. The art director Jack Room returned to Australia in 1979 after trying his luck in advertising in London and design in Los Angeles. He had opportunities lined up at the global advertising giants FCB and JWT, but a recruitment agent – Claire Worthington of Apple International – persuaded Room to meet with the creative director of a local agency, Berry Currie, who was looking for an art director. The outfit held only a couple of small accounts, but Worthington thought Room might hit it off with the creative director. She was right: Room met with the copywriter and creative director Rod Bennett and, over the next twenty years, the pair would build a reputation as one of Australia's most influential creative teams.[73]

By the mid-1980s the creative team had become the power-house of the agency. No longer atomised, creatives now promoted themselves as 'teams', many carefully crafting their professional reputations as hardworking obsessives, advertising mavericks or troubled geniuses in order to give themselves a point of difference. The teams moved agencies together and many spent more time with each other than they did with their families. Management indulged these star teams, giving them enormous leeway, which the creatives sometimes exploited. Advertising had always been a hedonistic business: Watson recalls his years at Hertz Walpole in the late 1960s as 'drunken, insanity, fantastic'; Strauss remembers the early days of SPASM as 'a wild time' with 'pot smoking and drinking'; and Noel Delbridge penned the famous 1975 Liberal Party campaign 'Turn on the Lights' at the pub. In the 1980s, however, indulgence of creatives attained new heights in some agencies, which tolerated unashamedly unpro-fessional behaviour – including onsite drug abuse, alcohol abuse, and workplace bullying – in the hope that such indulgence would result in memorable campaigns.

Research and Creative: 'An Unhappy Relationship'
Though agencies indulged creatives throughout the 1980s, a shift had begun in the 1970s that would, over time, diminish the power of the creative department. This shift had two key causes. First, in response to the 1973 oil crisis and the end of the post–World War II 'long boom', a new approach to business had emerged, one that emphasised economic account-ability.[74] Second, the high cost of producing television in

comparison with print and radio meant campaigns increasingly 'had to be right first go'. [75] Bertel recalls that 'all of a sudden people started hedging their bets' and 'the relationship with clients changed'. With clients demanding more for their money, agencies gradually became 'profit centres' and 'more careful about budgets.'[76] In turn, 'the agencies lost their control over the client.'[77]

This new accountability demanded a more disciplined approach to advertising. Many agencies responded by turning to research and eventually, as we saw in Chapter 7, the shift to strategy planning.[78] Agencies and their clients tried to limit the risks associated with expensive advertising campaigns by 'measuring' the likely success of an advertising campaign at two stages – in the development of the creative brief and testing the effectiveness of a completed campaign. The use of surveys, focus groups and strategy planners became increasingly important to an agency's bottom line, as the area developed into a costly service for which agencies could charge their clients.

How would creatives respond to this new discipline? Some rose to the challenge. Newton, for example, found concentrating on the psychological motivations of consumers revealed by research – 'selling an experience rather than a product' – made him a better writer: the long-copy advertisements he developed for Dunlop were the result. But he also resented the shift to research: '[Before the change, developing] strategy was some-thing you did with your art director.' By the time he moved to Leo Burnett as the creative director in 1986, that role and the power it entailed had been taken from the creatives and given to the strategy planners. For Newton 'research was [now] a bugbear' and the creative process 'not as much fun as before' because it had taken away the risk, which was essential to good advertising.[79]

When he moved to Connaghan & May in 1988, the agency's internal research requirements continued to be a source of tension. Watson, too, was unimpressed with the rise of strategy planning, describing planners as 'creatives who can't draw, paint or have an idea', whose presence constructed 'another barrier' to great creative. For Rutherford, the shift to accountability through research encouraged clients to 'get in the way of creativity' because they now wanted 'to look the same as everyone else'. The challenge for creatives then became how 'to be different', how to stand out from the crowd.[80] Done has a similar take on the impact of research: 'Good creative people don't believe in research' because 'they are trying to do something that is new, that hasn't been researched.' Research tries to eliminate risk but as a creative person 'you've got to take that risk.'[81]

The thirty years spanning the 1960s, 1970s, and 1980s were, arguably, the glory days for advertising creatives. Copywriters and art directors gained new power in agency hierarchies as their contribution took centre stage.[82] At first, lifting creative standards became an important tool in attempts to re-engage a generation that had become disillusioned with consumer culture, by producing more entertaining campaign ideas, copy and visuals. Over time, an emphasis on creativity provided agencies with a way of differentiating themselves from the pack: the Palace's reputation for sacking clients who rejected their brand of creativity is just one notable example of this. Combined with the awards system, the emphasis on creativity also gave some individual creatives and creative teams a mystique they were able to leverage to maximise their bankability.

These copywriters and art directors represented a new category: the professional advertising creative who found a satisfactory creative outlet in producing the new, more creative advertising campaigns. But many gifted Australians continued to keep a foot in both camps, supporting themselves through advertising but from outside the agencies, working as suppliers: illustrators, designers, photographers and freelance writers. As the next chapter will show, these professionals were part of a large industry support staff – located both inside and outside the advertising agencies. This support staff kept the advertising business operating from behind the scenes, without the flamboyance of the 'creative kings'.

CHAPTER NINE

SUPPORTING THE 'STARS'

In 1965 an opportunity came up in the television production department of USP Benson in Melbourne. Management
plucked a young man from the agency's accounts department,
where he was 'opening envelopes', and gave him the job of
film projectionist. Nineteen years later, that young man, Mike
Reed, became the first living inductee of the Federation of
Australian Commercial Television Stations (FACTS) Hall of
Fame.[1] In the intervening years, Reed had built a thriving business, Mike Reed Partners Post-Production (MRPPP). He had
edited hundreds of Australian television commercials, employed
scores of Australians, and enthused generations of advertising
practitioners with his passion for 'the great idea'. Yet, reflecting
on his career, the modest Reed perceived himself as an outsider
to the main advertising game, someone who was 'looked down
on' as a supplier to the industry.[2]

This chapter explores the contributions and experiences of
those whose expertise was crucial to the success of the advertising
industry, but who were employed outside of the key departments of the agencies: the creative and account management
departments. These experts stepped into view at various stages
of the advertising process. They provided the research on which
the creative brief was based, bought the space in which the
finished advertisement appeared, typed the copywriters' scripts,

and managed the account directors' diaries. They assembled the film-ready art, negotiated with the print-production companies, managed the budgets, and ensured the deadlines were met. They illustrated the advertisements with pen, airbrush, or camera; crafted the type; shot the footage, and, like Reed, edited that footage into shape. As this chapter will show, the significance of each of these experts – often invisible but essential to a successful agency – shifted dramatically between 1959 and 1989, as advertising agencies grew and became more professional. Some moved from the backrooms of the agency to take a starring role in the advertising process. Others disappeared completely, obliterated by inexorable technological change that enveloped the agency business.

The Headhunters

In the 1950s and 1960s most people had found their way into the advertising industry through the Pink Pages or the newspapers, as we saw in Chapter 5. By the end of the 1980s, however, a new service had emerged and consolidated its place in the industry: the advertising recruitment agency. Specialised recruiters had been operating in the market place since the mid-1960s, but their role in the advertising process took on increasing importance as the industry professionalised and internationalised.[3] Melbourne's most influential recruiter, Claire Worthington of Apple International – 'a wonderful spotter of … young creative talent'[4] – had begun her career as an art director. Her successor, Sydney's Esther Clerehan, had started in the traffic department of O&M Melbourne.[5] These recruiters were advertising insiders; they understood the special needs of an expanding industry, dealing with increasing specialisation within agency ranks. By the mid–1980s they had become the confidantes and advisors of a generation of advertising professionals.

The Researchers

Australian clients were at first sceptical about the value of market research (for example, understanding consumer buying habits) and media research (that is, determining the size and demography of specific media audiences). Only the multi-national advertising agencies – Unilever's agency Lintas and JWT – pursued research seriously in the first half of the twentieth century.[6] Australia's post-war economic boom led a growing number of advertisers and agencies to engage independent research firms to assist with their marketing issues.[7] As noted in Chapter 1, McCann-Erickson's arrival in 1959 signalled a renewed effort to move research closer to the centre of advertising practice. Research would provide brands with an edge in the market place and help ensure that advertisements reached the right target audience. An integral part of the advertising process, research was increasingly employed by most large manufacturers and their advertising agencies, some of it bought in from specialist market research suppliers such as McNair, some of it produced in-house by agency researchers.[8] Hansen Rubensohn-McCann Erickson's research department initially operated with some six or seven staff before it was converted into a separate entity, Marplan, in 1961.[9]

Understanding the research data called for an educated workforce, and researchers were the first group in the advertising industry for whom a university degree was essential. Most had completed commerce or economics degrees.[10] Margaret Boston, an Australian who spent her career working in advertising research in London, completed a commerce degree in Melbourne before working at the London School of Economics, conducting social surveys. In 1957 she took a job at London's Mather & Crowther advertising agency to do similar work. The agency had a 'fully functional research department, its own interviewers and did its own research', employing people (such as Boston) 'who went out and found things'. Importantly, Mather & Crowther's research department at this stage was run as a service centre, not a profit centre. This would change over the next decades.[11]

Figure 9.1 Television schedules at Lintas's Sydney office.
B&T, *31 January 1963, p. 17 (Courtesy of B&T)*

Malcolm Spry, the future managing director of MDA and Mojo, left Australia for London in 1965 armed with an economics degree from Monash University. Spry took a job at Nicholas, the UK pharmaceutical company 'who were collecting an enormous amount of research' and 'needed someone to do analysis of all the market research data'. When he shifted back to Australia later that year, he looked for a job in advertising, not as a researcher but as an account executive. At USP Benson in Melbourne, his degree was an advantage as there were few university graduates employed at the time. Spry felt confident about the research aspect of his job: 'my skill was distilling information ... the more complex the better', but he 'was intimidated by the mechanical side of advertising' and learnt this aspect of the business 'on the job.'[12]

Paul Gaskin, also a university graduate, joined the research department at JWT Sydney in 1969 as a research executive. Agencies initially relied on quantitative research, but from the early 1970s, qualitative research became increasingly important. Gaskin recalls the influence of two mentors at JWT Sydney, the researchers John Brown and Hugh Mackay, who taught him the importance of balancing quantitative and qualitative research, and of applying intellectual rigour to his work.[13] Mackay's approach to research was particularly significant, influencing a generation of researchers and account executives. Mackay encouraged them to tie their strategies to 'a groundswell of demography', understanding the role 'feelings' played in purchasing decisions, keeping up with 'changing cultural norms', and paying attention to 'underlying cultural and social movements.'[14]

The transformation of agency research departments into planning departments proceeded slowly in Australia. In 1971 Gaskin was sent to JWT London to investigate that office's account (or strategy) planning department and decide whether to introduce account planners to the Sydney and Melbourne offices.[15] He found the London research department to be 'full of Oxbridge, numerically trained people'. The agency's most influential 'thinker', Steven King, had 'created account planning' and his book *What is a Brand?* (published in 1967) was at 'the centre of everything that went on at JWT London and Australia'. Gaskin decided the Australian offices were 'doing everything that London account planners were doing anyway' – 'we didn't need to re-label it' – and recommended that JWT should not open planning departments in Australia, thus missing the opportunity to set up separate profit centres in the agencies. It would be another fifteen years before McCann-Erickson introduced 'strategy planning' to Australia, after which the sub-discipline became mainstream.[16]

The Media Buyers

Between 1959 and 1989, as the industry became more professional, the media department gradually moved out of the shadows and into the spotlight, poised to take centre stage in the 1990s.[17] Such a shift would have been difficult to predict in the late 1950s when the media department was 'seen and not heard.'[18] Buying media space was a clerical job, performed by people (often women) viewed as 'number crunchers' or 'pencil pushers'; hidden away at the back of the agency; deemed unglamorous compared to the account managers; and not interesting enough to meet with the clients.[19] Gaskin's first job in advertising – as an account co-ordinator at Rodgers Holland Everingham in 1965 – included buying media space. He recalls having 'no say in [developing] strategy'. His job was to get good exposure, using TV survey data followed by 'Dutch auctions' between the three commercial television stations, Channels Seven, Nine and Ten.[20]

The clerical nature of the work meant that women dominated media departments at all levels.[21] When the 19-year-old Ian McDonald moved from despatch to the media department of Hansen Rubensohn-McCann Erickson in 1966, his response to the women-run department reflected the sexist attitudes of the time. He saw media as 'a backwater'; 'like a retirement home' staffed by older women. The print buyer Dorothy Smith was in her fifties; the TV buyer Sybil Hunter in her late forties. Joy Young, who McDonald found 'fabulous', managed the department, which he describes as 'very clubby, with tea served on silver service, very formal'. The women were seen as passive and unprofessional: there was no negotiating, no bargaining with the clients.[22] In the 1970s, Jane Mara moved through secretarial work at Coudrey-Campbell-Ewald into the media department at Madison Advertising, a smaller 'father and son' agency. Starting as a media assistant, she was promoted to media manager within three months, aged just nineteen.

With the introduction of television in 1956, however, the low standing of the media department had begun to change, albeit glacially. Clients were becoming more astute and demanding, increasingly aware of what advertising could achieve for them.[23] As the power of television grew, it became clear there was big money to be made through commissions for placing advertisements in this increasingly costly media.[24] The world of media buying was becoming 'much more aggressive', and ambitious young men began to see its potential for a career. Realising their power in the new advertising era, these young men perceived women media buyers as old-fashioned amateurs who could be easily brushed aside.[25]

By the mid-60s the media departments were poised for change. McCann replaced Joy Young with a man (Terry Connaghan) in 1966. Over the next decade the media department grew from ten people to thirty-five, fuelled by a new, more aggressive approach to dealing with the media. The new media men – men such as Ken Chesterfield, Don Farrow and David Baker – came with 'great contacts with the research companies.'[26] They were consequently more astute at identifying and contacting target audiences. Moreover, they considered themselves to be dealmakers, selling the agency's capabilities on the one hand and securing the best deals with the media on the other. They made it their business to stretch the client dollar. They worked hard and they played hard. Despite media's increasingly central role in advertising processes, agencies were yet to embrace integrated communication plans; at McCann, for example, the media was removed from the creative, production, and account management departments, and located on a separate floor. Media also remained 'an afterthought in creative pitches'; McDonald recalls sitting outside and waiting to be called into the pitch.

Dennis Merchant was another of the ambitious young men who spotted media buying's potential in the mid-1960s. Merchant had started in the checking department of the Sydney agency Canny Paramor & Canny (CPC) around 1960. Although checking was more often a way into the industry for young women, his experience in this department would provide a valuable grounding for the future media star. The agency received two free copies of any newspaper in which it had placed an advertisement. One copy was for 'tearing' (that is, attaching to the client invoice) and one was for filing. Under the watchful eye of the woman manager, Merchant would check an advertisement had appeared as scheduled, cut it out from the newspaper and attach it to the invoice to be sent to the client. Merchant spent more than eighteen months in this department and by the time he left he 'would have known every newspaper and magazine in the country'. CPC was a small agency and Merchant was sometimes sent along to a rival agency, Goldberg's, to collect spare tear sheets from the woman manager there. Merchant recalls that it was a less competitive era: 'There was a spirit of cooperation around the agencies at that time … [agencies] were always happy to help one another.'[27]

With his checking experience under his belt, Merchant took a job at a larger agency, Jackson Wain, as a media trainee. He found that he loved his work 'with a passion' and started to take it very seriously – 'I could never learn enough' – taking industry-led training classes, entering public-speaking competitions, even enrolling in Toastmasters because he wanted to be able to present his own work. The most significant aspect of Merchant's approach to buying media space, however, was his incorporation of creativity into the process. Inspired by the gifted art director Arthur Holland, who told Merchant that 'creativity was not the divine right of artists and copywriters', he came to see that media people could be 'creative and intelligent'. He started to reflect on the compatibility between the advertised product and its audience, and realised that there was more to media buying than numbers – that psychology and creativity were important, too. Incorporating 'the clerical and the creative', Merchant 'adopted a completely different approach to media than anyone else working in media at the time' and was 'rewarded with a management position at a young age.'[28]

Around the same time, another bright young man was also seeing the possibilities of media buying. Malcolm Spry met the media manager at USP Benson in Melbourne, Harold Mitchell, in 1965 and found him to be 'a really good operator'. Mitchell's career in advertising had commenced in 1959, when he travelled in from country Victoria to secure a job in despatch at Paton Advertising. Like Merchant, he had embarked on a meteoric rise through agency ranks, respected by everyone who worked with him. As we saw in Chapter 4, Merchant and Mitchell would revolutionise the Australian advertising landscape.[29]

Media's new status as a crucial part of the advertising process was underpinned by its role in driving the introduction of new technology into the agency. Gaskin gives the example of data being bought from dedicated research companies such as Roy

Morgan and Nielsen, which then needed to be manipulated by the agency media buyers. In the late 1970s, the data was printed out and used manually; by the late 1980s, media departments could arrange online access via dedicated telephone lines, computer to computer.[30] Media's rise within the agency hierarchy was also helped along by the arrival of the global advertising networks and their more enlightened attitude towards media. When Mara joined Ogilvy & Mather, it was the first time she had participated in client meetings. As the media director at Y&R in the late 1960s, Merchant felt that he was a valued part of the team. Some of the global agencies were slow to embrace media's new status, however. In 1973, two young despatch boys at McCann, John Steedman and Greg Graham, hoped for careers in account management and television production respectively. Both were moved to the media department, however – 'the backroom of advertising' – where Steedman recalls working for 'a Canadian woman … a pencil pusher', filling out media schedules manually: 'a very mundane task.'[31]

With hindsight, it seems inevitable that the improving status of media buyers would, eventually, lead to their break from the agencies, but when Dennis Merchant left Y&R to set up his own independent media-buying shop Merchant & Partners in 1974, it was a bold and perceptive move. Despite the new emphasis on creativity in this period, advertising was (and remains) a business first and foremost, and 'media [was] always where the power has been, far more than creative agencies'. Small, creative agencies struggled to compete with the media-buying power of the bigger agencies, such as George Patterson, who used its 'might and power' to buy up media space 'without doing anything with it': in other words, buying up great swathes of media space to keep smaller players out of the game.[32] Merchant's aim in setting up his own shop was to 'level the playing field', by 'aggregating the media spend of the smaller agencies'. Rising media stars such as Alan Robertson, then at JWT, viewed Merchant's move as 'exciting', 'the next big thing', and Robertson joined Merchant & Partners in 1979.[33] One of the first agencies to close its media department and outsource its media-buying, O&M, gave its business to Merchant & Partners.[34]

Over the next decade, a 'fundamental change' took place as media buying received increased recognition, even in the more conservative, large agencies.[35] There was 'far more integration', especially 'more collaboration and socialising with the creative department' who 'knew that working with media would help them'. Despite this integration, media remained 'very much third in line' in the agency pecking order after creative and account management.[36]

A further shift was underway, however. A voluntary code of media accreditation had long permitted agencies to generate income from media commissions, which were rebated from media operators and based on a percentage of their advertising expenditure.[37] Agencies were not allowed to rebate media commissions to their clients; if they did they lost their accreditation. The service fee could be negotiated but not the commission: this was 'worldwide practice.'[38] From 1968, the Media Council of Australia had administered this accreditation system through its subsidiary the Australian Media Accreditation Authority. In 1975 the Trade Practices Commission (TPC) began to investigate the system on account of suggestions that it was anti-competitive and, therefore, against the public interest. The proprietors of the country's largest advertising agencies vigorously defended the existing system, warning of increased overheads and lower advertising standards should the system be abolished.[39] The TPC subsequently endorsed the existing system with only minor changes to the regulations, in order 'to promote competition among agencies and stability in the fee-system.'[40] Media companies were guaranteed payment within forty-five days for placed advertising, but only from agencies deemed to be financially sound by the Media Council. [41] In return, the media company was required to pay a commission to the agency that placed the advertisement.[42]

Media buyers had always felt downtrodden in agency hierarchies, but from the 1980s they found themselves being taken more seriously. The new media independents 'grew like topsy' and began to undermine the 'very cosy media and agency [accreditation] system' outlined above.[43] Mike Satterthwaite recalls Merchant approaching Gough Waterhouse in the early 1980s, offering to buy media space for the Commonwealth Bank for the media commission alone, without a service fee. Merchant took 5.5 per cent of the media commission and the Gough Waterhouse proprietors 4.5 per cent. Seeing the opportunities on offer, media directors jumped ship from the big agencies and started their own media shops: Total Media – founded by the media buyer Ian Bennell and the managing director of Pritchard Wood, Don Fox – was one prominent example.[44] These independents worked through accredited agencies. Robertson recounts Merchant's close partnership with the advertising agency Hertz Walpole, where the media agency operated 'just like their media department': it was even located in the same building. The new independents had 'neutralised the media game' for their clients, and media buyers' salaries doubled as their importance to the formation of advertising strategies increased.

By the late 1980s, the media accreditation system was 'crumbling.'[45] In 1995 the Australian Competition and Consumer Commission abolished the system, arguing that 'the industry [had] changed' and that the accreditation system had become 'a shackle upon the capacity of the advertising agency to adjust to changing circumstances, including the emergence of specialist agencies.'[46] Agencies were now to work on a fee base (usually 17.5 per cent) rather than on commission for media placement.[47] For the industry, this decision 'was a hell of a blow' and working on this fee basis would affect the profitability of agencies.[48] Media departments subsequently disappeared from most agencies and the new independent media companies began to drive the communication process.[49] Some view this shift in power as 'a disaster for the advertising business', which lost its main source of income.[50] Colin Fraser, the former Channel Seven executive and the creative director of George Patterson in the 1960s, also argues that 'the seriousness of advertising' – that is 'understanding what makes the customer buy' – was 'destroyed by the decision to give the media-purchasing rights to the independent media buyers.'[51]

The Administrators

While the creatives and the account managers reclined in their glamorous offices, the administrators worked behind the scenes, holding together the everyday operations of the agency.[52] The finance (or accounts) department beavered away in the backrooms, issuing the invoices, paying the bills, and trying to balance the books. Once again, women often performed these essentially clerical tasks, using the bookkeeping training provided by most of the secretarial colleges. To an ambitious young man, these women seemed to be from another era. Rob Palmer recalls the 'old ladies' in the accounts department at JWT Sydney dousing their company-supplied hand towels with 4711 Cologne.[53]

Again the story from the late 1950s to the late 1980s is one of increasing professionalisation, with university-educated finance men such as Mike Satterthwaite replacing these women bookkeepers, as increasingly complex takeovers by global networks required a new, higher level of financial literacy.[54] The university-educated Satterthwaite began his career at the accountancy firm Price Waterhouse in London and then moved out to its Sydney office in 1979. Soon after he arrived he took a job as the finance director of Sydney creative hot-shop, Gough Waterhouse. In theory, an advertising agency was just another business to someone from a finance background – Satterthwaite found his role in the agency to be 'reasonably insular' and that he was 'not as connected to [the] business as others [in the agency]'. But advertising could throw up its own unique challenges, especially in the profligate 1980s. Foremost for Satterthwaite was trying to rein in dissolute spending: 'I've cut up so many credit cards in my time.' Because entertaining was tax-free, 'it made sense to go out for lunch every day', but agencies 'were still paying for half of it'; they were 'not getting it for nothing'.

Satterthwaite's role changed with the purchase of Gough Waterhouse by the London-based network Saatchi & Saatchi in the mid-1980s, but perhaps less than might have been expected. He was now required to report daily cash balances back to Martin Sorrell, then Saatchi's London-based finance director, but in reality 'no one [was] brought in to keep an eye on [the Australian operation]'. Neither Maurice nor Charles Saatchi ever visited the Sydney office, which repeatedly upgraded its premises 'to look like the Establishment'. This was 'the nonsense of Saatchi', as Satterthwaite recalls. The Sydney office 'upgraded everything without Saatchi & Saatchi [London] stopping them', and the Saatchis 'were not the financial geniuses they were professed to be.'[55]

The skills required for agency support roles – the work of the receptionists, secretaries, and personal assistants – differed little from the skills required by other businesses for similar roles, although it was likely to be more fun.[56] As elsewhere, women trained at Australia's numerous business colleges usually performed these roles. Such women had worked in the Australian advertising industry from its earliest days. Most left when they married, but others took the opportunity to show what they could do, especially in retail advertising departments, and moved through to managerial positions. As we have seen, some moved from secretarial work into finance or media buying, and, later,

Figure 9.2 The typing pool provided a common entry point for women entering the advertising agency business.
B&T, 27 November 1969, p. 21 (Courtesy of B&T)

225

account service. Technology would close this entry route at the end of the 1980s, when the introduction of personal computers dispensed with the need for secretaries.[57]

In the mid-1960s, however, the gendered division of labour remained firmly in place. Most young men moved through the administrative departments on their way to a more rewarding career, but the women lingered, performing these menial tasks year upon year, unable to move on for a range of reasons, no doubt including their responsibilities at home. Newly aware of their own privileged place in the agency hierarchy, some young men dismissed these women as peripheral to the 'real' business of advertising. Rob Palmer recalls joining the checking department at JWT in Sydney in 1965 on his way through from despatch to account management. Run by 'Mrs Ryan' with 'a steel rule', the department seemed to the young Palmer to be 'a collection of women, lesbians, housewives, and grandmas' all of whom 'fussed over every boy'. There was 'cake for everything'. The work was 'mindless, repetitive, boring'. Palmer dealt with 'tens of thousands of newspapers' in his nine months in checking and, like Merchant, learned a lot of 'media stuff' on his way through. Perhaps most importantly, though, Palmer learned 'how to get on with people', especially 'middle-aged women.'[58]

On the way through to 'something else',[59] many ambitious young advertising people – men and women – spent two or three years in 'traffic' or 'control', a unique advertising role designed to ensure advertisements were delivered to the media on time and on budget. In the biggest agencies – JWT London, for example – the control department could comprise scores of people.[60] The smaller agencies might have just a handful of people doing the work, most of them multi-tasking. Traffic managers were responsible for the distribution of briefs, the collection of materials, plotting deadlines, and liaising with the production departments and the print media. The job required exceptional organisational and time-management skills, as well as the ability to handle intense pressure and inflated egos on a daily basis.[61]

A too powerful traffic department, however, could stifle creativity. At USP Needham in the late 1970s, Reg Bryson found the intervention of the traffic staff in the relationship between creatives and account management 'frustrating'. Creatives came up with several ideas, which would then 'go back through traffic' rather than directly to account managers, and clients would be 'presented with several possible advertisements, all following category conventions'. The power of traffic reflected the agency's emphasis on profit over product knowledge, the exact opposite approach to advertising to that later employed by Bryson and his colleagues at The Campaign Palace in Sydney.[62]

Securing a position as a traffic manager depended largely on the personality of the applicant. Lee Harrington, for example, won her break into the advertising industry because of her 'large personality'. Harrington grew up in country Victoria and rejected a teaching scholarship for advertising, starting at a finished-art and photographic company that provided overflow support for agencies.[63] She had demonstrated 'an innate ability' for organisation from childhood and her talents were ideally suited for the traffic manager's role: 'organising people, talking to people, motivating people … [and] bringing them together to complete a project'. Within two years, Harrington was the traffic manager at MDA in Melbourne. She crafted an advertising career spanning more than thirty years – demonstrating that no matter what technological and financial changes wrought in the industry, the need for exceptional organisational skills remained.

Harrington is unusual in having built a long and successful advertising career around traffic and project management. Most of the people in traffic were on their way through to what they anticipated would be a more stimulating and rewarding role in another part of the agency's operations. Many of these ambitious young people – John Wright and Doug Watson are just two prominent examples – embarked on the next stage of their advertising education by working in a department that would, in the decade beyond the scope of this study, the 1990s, undergo change as seismic as that experienced by the media-buyers.

The Producers

Since its earliest days, print had been the dominant medium in Australian advertising. From the 1920s, however, radio gained increasing importance and, while most radio advertising was produced at the broadcast stations, the largest agencies began to set up their own production units. From 1956, with the introduction of television, a shift away from print and, especially, radio began. Although print and radio production would remain in the mix, the big money from the mid-1960s was being invested in television production because of the inflated cost of television media space. Nevertheless, within the restricted world of the advertising agency, there was often little delineation between print and broadcast production. In the smallest agencies everything was integrated: print production managers might traffic, check and despatch their own work, as well as oversee broadcast production.[64]

Rob Palmer left the JWT's checking department behind in 1967 and moved on to the production department – the place 'where they made the ads'. In a world before computers, finished artists assembled the advertisements 'physically' from bromides (photographic paper with typesetting on it), which were 'stuck together' on 'big bits of cardboard'. The finished art was photographed and became the 'image that found its way into the newspaper'. When Palmer first joined the production department, the whole process was 'a mystery' to him, but in his time there he 'learned all about' the agency's suppliers – the typesetting houses – and the 'incredibly labour-intensive process' involved in getting an advertisement into print in the years before 'cold metal' phototypesetting began to replace 'hot metal' linotypesetting, around 1975.[65]

The young John Wright spent a year in despatch at Clem Taylor Advertising in Adelaide before moving into the production department in 1965. The department comprised four men: 'the director', the production manager, the junior production manager (Wright) and one other. Wright's job was to collect the advertisement's copy and layout from the creative department or the account executive; go to the files and select the relevant blocks, stereotypes and mattes; and insert the elements into a bag or an envelope. Then either Wright or another despatch boy would deliver them to the newspaper or the printer. Wright would look over the proofs at the newspaper at 7 pm that night, checking the copy and layout, ensuring the prices were correct, and, time-permitting, returning with the proof to the agency for the approval of the account executive. Wright learned to do corrections on the spot, 'like a proof reader'. Junior production manager level was 'the last opportunity to take the work to the medium', and he would perform a similar role for the small broadcast production group at Clem Taylor, taking tapes to the television and radio stations.[66]

The copywriter Doug Watson also began his advertising career as a print-production manager at Sydney's V.H. Freeth agency. Fired when he mistakenly ordered 500 stereos instead of 500 mattes (one matte could produce ten or twenty stereos), he learned an early and valuable lesson: 'always get the order in writing'. Watson went to the US-owned FCB as the traffic manager and worked as an audio operator 'on the side'. Following the advice of 'a visiting [audio] engineer', he moved to another agency where he could 'do the sound work full time'. Watson consequently joined Hertz Walpole as control engineer in the recording studio (like Reed, Watson was also the projectionist, but 'was no good at it'). The studio at Hertz Walpole was 'really important', a place where the creatives could try out ideas, and it was here that Watson met Allan Johnston (Jo of Mojo). After helping Johnston to complete a jingle, Watson, too, became a copywriter.[67]

Most despatch boys had ambitions beyond the production department. An exception to this was Roger Rigby, Clemenger Sydney's production manager in the 1970s and 1980s. Growing up around the advertising industry – his parents were both commercial artists – Rigby had fallen for 'the smell of printing ink'. He moved into the production department at Sydney's NAS McClelland after eighteen months as a despatch boy. After two years at 'the more modern' advertising agency Jackson Wain, and a brief return to NAS, Rigby joined Clemenger in 1970, staying until 1998.[68] Over this time his work evolved from the standard production of press and television advertisements to managing the agency's site relocation and the implementation of the Clemenger computer systems.

By the end of the 1970s, the industry's professional drive meant that most young people who joined agency production departments and in-house studios possessed some type of formal qualification.[69] Eighteen-year-old Greg McIntyre, for example, studied for the Certificate of Business – Advertising at RMIT. The course was full-time for the first year then part-time at night for the subsequent two years, while students gained industry experience. They were given some creative training, but the course concentrated mostly on media–buying and print production with no account management. McIntyre's first job was at a small Melbourne advertising agency, Moffatt Sharp, as a production coordinator.

Mike Ellis's first job was also at a small agency. In his early thirties, Ellis had trained as a print artist at Prahran College of Advanced Education, completing the Certificate of Applied Art in 1982. At Parker Davidson advertising agency in South Melbourne, he started as a finished artist putting 'print ads together', doing 'some drawing', and organising bromides. Ellis moved to the multi-national McCann-Erickson in 1985, where he found there was 'a department for everything': 'logo design, package design, [a] photographic department … [a] print studio'. He stayed at McCann for twenty-six years, becoming the graphic services manager, a role that 'combined print production with studio manager.'[70]

In his twenty-six years at McCann, Ellis witnessed the disintegration of the advertising industry as he knew it. When he joined in 1982 the agency employed 160 staff. When he retired in 2011 there were just twenty-five. The key change behind this downsizing – the media deregulation of the mid-1990s – sits beyond the scope of this study. But the digitisation of advertising processes – the change that would revolutionise the work practices of Ellis and McIntyre – did start within this period, at the very end of the 1980s. McIntyre recalls being shown 'a massive IBM computer' back in 1980 during a college visit to George Patterson, but from about 1988 agencies began to take computerisation seriously, recognising how it might save them time and money.[71]

The McCann-Erickson in-house studio introduced its first computer in 1989, and this opened up 'a period of stress for print', as the agency was now doing work – for example, typesetting – that outside suppliers had previously undertaken.[72] Clemenger Sydney moved from paste-up to electronic finished art across just four days. Rigby considers this shift the most significant change of his career, as taking this work in-house increased agencies' revenue. Rigby made sure he was prepared for the new era with extensive reading but production managers who failed to keep up with these changes were quickly sidelined.[73] McIntyre recalls spending two years out of the business while travelling overseas and returning to find the industry had digitised in his absence.

The digitisation of print production raises the issue of the uncomfortably close relationship between some agency pro-duction managers and the print companies, such as Markby's and Show-Ads in Melbourne, which 'kept a grip on the ... industry' in this period of transformation by providing its clients with 'dreadful software' (Milestone), rather than the superior Quark and Adobe. As Ellis and McIntyre had moved on in responsibility during the 1980s, from press advertising to the more lucrative print buying, both became acutely aware of the importance of building and maintaining relationships with these companies. Agency production managers – some of whom had previously worked in the print industry – were 'feted' by the print companies, who were 'after their business' because of the large amounts of money spent on big print runs.[74] This 'feting' consisted of gift hampers, parties, and free lunches, but there was, of course, 'no such thing' as the latter: the print companies were buying the loyalty of the production managers and expected to receive all of their business in return. In some cases this even extended to providing new companies with two years of credit in order to lock in their future business or to placing the print company's own person into the agency as production manager.[75] Agency management in the former position would try to dictate which suppliers a production manager could use – 'the mates rule' – which 'always led to problems', with suppliers going round the production manager to the management.[76]

Although the occasional woman might be found at a drawing board, the print-production department and art studio were largely male enclaves. This was not true of broadcast production. Women had long been employed in radio production, where literacy and clerical skills were valued. They wrote the continuity scripts and chose the music for the sponsored dramas at both advertising agencies and radio stations back in the 1940s and 1950s.[77] As agency broadcast departments grew, women managed the budgets and trafficked the production of commercials. Joy Young managed radio production at Sydney's Hansen-Rubensohn agency in the mid-1950s, then spent three years working in the US, including stints at the United Nations and McCann-Erickson New York, where she received training in television production. On her return to Australia in 1961, Young was responsible for both radio and television production at the newly merged Hansen Rubensohn-McCann Erickson (HRMcCE) before being appointed media manager. Women television producers were often recruited from in-house secretarial staff, and chance could play a role in their move into production. The television producer Helene Nicol, for example, started work at Melbourne's Carden Advertising in 1974 while still a student at the Swinburne Film and Television School. She had applied for a job as a copywriter, but the television producer was leaving and Nicol was offered her job. A decade later, Ann Miles completed an advertising course at RMIT then joined McCann-Erickson where her father was a client. She worked as a 'Girl Friday' for six weeks before being appointed head of TV aged just twenty-one.

Warren Fahey's early career demonstrates the flexibility of movement in the broadcast production area both inside and outside of agencies in this period. Fahey started in despatch at Jackson Wain around 1961 but was keen to move out and up. After six months in the typography department (where a dozen people worked), Fahey bumped into the broadcast director Neville Merchant (Dennis Merchant's father) in the lift. Fahey introduced himself telling the director: 'I want to work for you and I'm only interested in radio', thereby giving himself a point of difference from everyone else who was eager to work in the more-fashionable television production. Fahey was given a chance in radio production under the wing of a 'nonchalant' broadcast director. It was 'a baptism of fire' because the director gave Fahey 'all the work', and the latter cut his teeth putting together White Wings commercials, producing jingles at the sound studio, and working with voiceover talent. The director then asked him to help with television production for White Wings and Sunbeam, and Fahey found himself producing live commercials, a process he describes as 'nerve-wracking and sim-plistic'. He was 'good at pre-production': 'getting from the script to the costings; allocating the producer and director; and getting quotes from different film studios' and soon received an offer to work for HRMcCE. Here, he was responsible for 'allocating scripts to the five full-time directors, producing radio com-mercials, liaising with film studios, talent and the directors'. At both Jackson Wain and McCann, Fahey found the relationship between production and the creative departments to be one of 'us and them': the creatives were 'zany people, not of this world'. The artists would go out for a three-hour lunch – the account executives, too – and come back 'sozzled'. Fahey, too, endured 'massive lunches' with people 'who wanted to get his business', and he was 'useless' after them. The day would often end at the media-industry haunt, the 729 Club in St Leonards. They were, as he says, 'different days'.

The Suppliers

The advertising industry relied on teams of experts located outside of the agencies to supply services beyond the scope or the budgets of the agencies themselves. Rather than invest in the necessary equipment and expertise, agencies used that of the radio and television stations, the print-production companies, and broadcast production and post-production companies.

As the industry grew, the number of freelancers – the art directors, designers, copywriters, illustrators, and television producers – increased. These workers could do their jobs from home, or from temporary desks within an agency, without the investment of vast sums for equipment. Art and photographic studios had long supplied design, illustration, and photographic services to the advertising agencies, when the agencies' in-house studios had 'overflow' work.[78] Ken Done started his career at such a place – Jon Hawley Studios in Sydney in 1959. After a couple of years at Hawley's, Done opened his own small freelance studio in Sussex Street. It was, he recalls, 'somewhat rare for a design person to be working outside an agency'. The ability to freelance was especially useful for those who wished to travel overseas. In the mid-1960s, Done picked up freelance work – sometimes 'as an illustrator', sometimes 'as a designer'

– for McCann-Erickson in Los Angeles and New York, and for JWT in London, where he worked with the agency's legendary creative director Jeremy Bullmore and met the copywriter Llewellyn Thomas.[79]

The life of a freelancer could be uncertain. Advertising has always been an insecure business, and, as well as the retrenchment of employees, the loss of a large account could mean that freelancers did not get paid. The graphic designer Alex Stitt (who created the 'Life. Be In It' campaign character Norm) worked as a freelancer and recalls agencies asking him to revise his invoice and resubmit it at a lower rate. The agency would then send his original invoice to the client but pay Stitt on the second lower, invoice and pocket the difference. According to Stitt, freelancers 'wised up on this' and began to 'inflate the first invoice', and, in order to lock the freelancer into a fixed (and lower) rate, McCann-Erickson introduced a contract document.[80]

Without a system of fixed rates, deciding what to charge clients for freelance services could be a challenge. Bruce Lauchlan, an illustrator and designer who freelanced for Australian advertising agencies for forty years, disliked this aspect of the job. Lauchlan trained at Swinburne in the early 1960s, studying a mix of commercial and fine art. In his final year both Clemenger and the ABC offered him a full-time job: he chose the latter because at this point (1965) the pay was better at the ABC. After three years at the ABC, Lauchlan travelled to Germany to work at the Frankfurt office of the US giant Ted Bates. There he learned the new illustration technique of airbrushing and spent a month working at the London office before returning to Australia in 1971. Although he never again worked in an advertising agency, he did work for most of the big agencies, including USP Needham, MDA, and Clemenger. As with most freelance suppliers, Lauchlan found his work through word of mouth. But he also advertised in the influential publication *Creative Source Australia* (later *The Wizards of Oz*), which came out annually from 1982 and was packed with advertisements for photographers, illustrators, and production companies.[81] Lauchlan was kept busy producing illustrations and television storyboards – only with the introduction of computers did the flow of work reduce – but dealing with the agencies could be tricky, especially when it came to getting paid. It 'usually worked out okay' though, with the exception of the occasion when a client refused to pay for the artwork and Lauchlan tore the illustration up in front of him.[82]

The size of the agency could affect the freelancer's experience. The copywriter Derek Hansen ran a freelance consultancy in the late 1970s, working for both big and small agencies. Hansen found that the small agencies gave him 'good, clear briefs' and were 'good payers', but several agencies were 'slow payers', including JWT, and he 'had to resort to tricks to get paid.'[83] The copywriter John Newton also freelanced, using advertising as 'the bread-and-butter work', while he tried his hand at writing short stories and film scripts. He, too, faced the 'great challenge of freelance', that is 'getting paid.'[84] Despite this difficulty, some creatives preferred working freelance. Keith Aldrich found that he became 'stale and fidgety in an agency'. Freelance work offered variety and put him in control of his hours. It also meant he could sidestep 'the insecurity of the agency downturn.'[85]

The life of a supplier in a collaborative industry such as advertising required a large amount of tact: Mike Reed describes his editor's role as 'fence sitting' between the advertising agencies and the film-production companies. From the mid-1960s, the post-production companies that edited film footage and prepared it for broadcast had become an integral part of the advertising process. Reed would be at the forefront of this change. After working as a projectionist at USP Needham and 'falling in love with film and with advertising', he studied film and television at RMIT, then worked with two film-production companies, Cambridge Films and Senior Films. In 1970 he travelled to London, where he found work as a sound editor. He also visited the US and witnessed the 'magic' achieved by the post-production companies there.[86]

Returning to Australia in 1974, Reed saw an opportunity to improve Melbourne's poor post-production services, which were not only languishing well behind those he had seen in America but were inferior even to those available in Sydney. The film production industry had long been centred in Sydney: Walker reports that 80 per cent of commercials made by Melbourne agencies before 1964 were produced in Sydney, although this had reduced to 40 per cent by 1967.[87] In Reed's view, Melbourne's film-processing laboratories provided 'woeful' and 'unprofessional' service, and looked down on advertising because it was not a proper 'art form'. Reed, who was free-lancing at the time, decided to do what he could to change this situation. Encouraged by Alan Dobell from the Melbourne Editorial Service he set up MRPPP, a post-production company that would be responsible for the complete post-production job from start to finish. He borrowed $20,000 and supplemented it with a friend's $3,000 to buy 'an editing machine, benches, video recorder, [and] monitor'. MRPPP opened for business in 1975. When Reed sold up in 2010, the business had forty-two staff across two offices. In the intervening years, Reed had helped navigate the Australian advertising industry through numerous technological advances, not least the shift from film to video, which began in the late 1970s. In the 1980s, as video made the production of commercials faster and more viable, Reed's business 'grew and grew.'[88] The most revolutionary shift in post-production, however, would come after our period, in the 1990s, with the introduction of digital video.

Changes between 1959 and 1989 affected advertising's support staff as much as they did those who worked at the industry's core. Higher education levels, increased travel opportunities and, especially, technological developments affected researchers, media-buyers, production and administrative staff, and creative suppliers to various degrees. Some, like the media-buyers, moved closer to centre stage, as advertising (prompted by its clients) adopted more serious and more professional attitudes to all aspects of the advertising process. Most felt the impact of technological innovation, especially those working in print and television production, whose jobs would change inexorably in the second half of the 1980s, and the secretaries, many of whose jobs did not survive the introduction of the PC.

It is impossible to separate these developments from the context of the expansion of global advertising networks we saw in Chapter 5. Individuals travelled through these networks and picked up new skills and trained in the new technologies. The impact of these networks on the everyday work of support staff, however, appears to have been minimal. Most of these groups continued to do things the Australian way, incorporating and adapting international developments when required. One agency group, however, had to deal with these developments in a more direct way. These were the agency principals: the CEOs and managing directors who were at the forefront of Australian advertising-industry globalisation, and whose experiences handling these changes are the subject of the next chapter.

CHAPTER TEN

RUNNING THE SHOW

L en Reason, the managing director of Masius Melbourne in the 1970s, epitomised the old-style manager. In the words of his acolyte and successor, Ric Otton, Reason was 'enormously personable' with 'a great deal of integrity'. The former Queenslander 'valued people' and brought 'a family feel' to the business. 'Nice, wise and brave', he 'backed risky decisions', for example, dropping Schweppes as a client when they tried to change the remuneration system. From Reason, Otton learnt that the culture of an agency mattered. He learnt to step back and think about things. He learnt that trust was important, that if a manager allowed people to 'find what they are good at', it would 'repay, in work and loyalty.'[1]

The management of an agency set the culture of that agency and their approach could influence generations of executives.[2] So who were these agency principals in the years between 1959 and 1989? Where had they come from? And how had they reached the acme of their chosen profession? This chapter examines shifts in the nature of agency management in the years between 1959 and 1989.

At the beginning of the 1960s, most agencies were run by larger than life characters (such as Reason) who were often self-educated and whose names frequently adorned the agencies' front doors. By the 1980s, these names had disappeared – the largest agencies were branches of international organisations and the principal might well be a recent appointment from New York. This chapter records the origins and nature of the leadership philosophies employed by Australian agency principals in these years, then reveals the ways in which these men (again, they *were* all men) sought to deal with the challenges and shifting expectations prompted by the demands of globalisation and professionalisation. It shows that successful leaders built strong agency cultures through a careful balance of stability and flexibility, retaining the best features of the 'traditional' entrepreneur model of agency leadership and combining these with a new, more professional and intellectually rigorous approach to advertising production.

'Gentlemen with Brains'

The handover at Masius from Reason to Otton in the late 1970s provides an ideal example of the shift in agency management in this period. The form of the management might be similar – inclusive and warm – but it would, as we will see, differ in its content. Some interviewees perceived this difference as a shift in emphasis: from making money to producing quality advertising.[3] However, the recollections of chief executives who felt increasingly pressured, especially by overseas owners, to improve profits contradict this assessment. Advertising was a business in the 1950s and it remained so beyond the impact of globalisation and professionalisation. The agencies still needed to make money. What changed was the seriousness with which they went about making it.

Agency management before the 1960s had been largely performative: entrepreneurs kept business through the force of their personalities and the depth of their friendships with clients, friendships that were built and maintained across the dinner table, at the football, and on the golf course.[4] The men with their names on the door were often gregarious characters from eclectic backgrounds and with idiosyncratic personal styles: Frank Rickards and Basil Carden in Melbourne, for example, and Frank Goldberg and Sim Rubensohn in Sydney. From the mid-1960s, however, to be picked out from the pack for management grooming increasingly required university qualifications.

The best of the agencies retained the family atmosphere but combined it with an atmosphere of inquiry driven by tertiary-educated executives, with spectacular results. John Clemenger and George Patterson were both the standout examples of this balance. David Ogilvy articulated perfectly this new ideal – a hybrid of the old and the new – when he declared that he wanted to hire 'gentlemen with brains', which he later adapted pragmatically to 'gentlemen and ladies with brains.'[5] His modification was optimistic. When Chris Martin Murphy left Ogilvy & Mather in 1991, he wrote thirty-two letters to agency principals across Australia, three of whom were women (and two of these women were the only ones who wrote back!). Ten years earlier, he believes, there would have been just one woman principal.[6] The figures seem to back him up, although it is not clear who that single woman might have been.[7]

Ogilvy may well have discovered his perfect hire when he met the Australian Michael Ball in 1961.[8] In a familiar pattern for the industry, as aging advertising principals passed down their business philosophies to the chosen few, Ogilvy selected Ball to be groomed for international management. The young Australian epitomised Ogilvy's 'gentleman with brains' maxim, bringing an analytical and efficient mind to the network's expansion, while handling employees in an affable, if somewhat-remote, manner. One of Ball's contemporaries thus remembers him as 'an interesting manager, enormously experienced, efficient [who] didn't give feedback face to face, but wrote comments in red on a plane'. [9] From Ogilvy, Ball learnt three lessons that would underpin one of Australian advertising's most successful careers: the value of blending research depth with creative excellence; the importance of timely decision-making – 'there is some consensus but at the end of the day someone has to make a decision' – and the need to maintain a company's culture. O&M's company culture was underpinned by the philosophy of 'one agency indivisible across the world' and, as we saw in Chapter 2, a commitment to the staff training that was integral to achieving and maintaining this. Ball grew the O&M business in Asia by training local staff with materials sent out from New York. He set the tone for O&M's future Australian executive hires and, in his turn, provided mentoring to men such as Renny Cunnack, who were themselves urbane and well educated. Cunnack acknowledges the importance of mentoring to his development as an executive, first by Jimmy Benson in London, then by Jock Elliott who replaced Ogilvy as chairman and whom Cunnack 'adored'. But it would be Ball who provided the 'most lasting – if mixed – influence' on Cunnack.

In contrast to Ball, Peter Clemenger learnt the business of running an agency 'from the ground up', in the family business established by his father Jack. It was, he recalls, 'not a bad way to do it'. Clemenger commenced his training by running messages for the agency. Then, sent to London and the US in 1951 to 'learn and build contacts', he met the principals of the global agency BBDO in New York, a connection that would later pay dividends for his agency.[10] Geoff Cousins also started his career at a 'family-affair type business', Pritchard Wood in Sydney, and, establishing something of a trope for budding agency principals, was impressed by his boss John Bristow's car, an E-type Jaguar. The Mercedes owned by the principal of Tom McFarlane's first agency likewise impressed the young copywriter. He was less impressed with the agency itself. Melbourne's Handbury Advertising was another family business, but the 18-year-old McFarlane found Mr Handbury and his agency of twenty-four 'old-fashioned and formal … [with] old clients', especially in contrast to McFarlane's next agency, Thomson White & Partners, whose principal Tony White was 'cool' and 'well connected.'[11] The family-business style of agency required an authenticity to be truly successful, and this was not easy to replicate. Despatched north to invigorate Clemenger's long-struggling Sydney office in 1971, Geoff Wild struggled to build the family atmosphere he had experienced at Clemenger Melbourne. The strain of looking after the clients and the staff, especially the creatives who were 'childlike', proved too much.[12]

The family feeling in these agencies ensured that once a young man had been picked out from the pack, the full force of the agency's support would be placed at his disposal. Pritchard Wood noticed that Cousins was 'special' and fast-tracked him through the usual apprenticeship, which, as we have seen, involved a gradual progression through most of the agency's departments.[13] At his next job, at George Patterson in Sydney, Cousins was again earmarked as a potential leader and sent to build Patterson's business in Brisbane. Cousins found the task 'terrifying' but learnt 'a very important aspect of advertising': that 'what drips out of the bucket must be replaced' and set out successfully to pin down 'a lot of new business.'[14]

Like Ball, Cousins's business philosophy was formed under the tutelage of an older, more experienced advertising man – in

Cousins's case the legendary Patterson CEO Bill Farnsworth. He picked up 'a very valuable business tool' from Farnsworth: to position George Patterson as 'absolutely the leading agency beyond any question in anyone's mind'. This positioning became essential to Cousins's *modus operandi* and every decision he subsequently made was designed to ensure Patterson continued to occupy the number-one position in Australia. The agency remained the biggest, but Cousins also wanted it to be the best, and worked to make it more professional, using techniques employed to build clients' brands to position the agency. For example, when Farnsworth died unexpectedly, Cousins and his colleagues undertook a positioning test to tease out the core of the thriving business that the long-time CEO had built – what Cousins calls the agency's Unique Selling Point or USP. While the survey found that George Patterson was viewed as being expensive,[15] it also revealed that the agency's USP was its 'direct, prompt service to the client', and Cousins would focus on continuing to deliver this service underpinned by 'honesty, integrity [and] good business practices'.

At the heart of it all, though, was, again, a strong commitment to the agency family, its staff. George Patterson would commit to 'sharing the wealth' with valued staff in order to keep and reward them: they were helped to purchase shares in the company, giving them 'a sense of ownership' in the business and reaffirming the 'family business' approach,[16] as would its competitor Clemenger with its Share and Purchase Assistance Trust.[17] The agency also provided mentoring to staff members with potential, much as Cousins had received from Farnsworth. And, again like Clemenger, the agency ensured it made money: as Cousins notes 'a business is not a craft workshop'. Unlike most other agencies, Patterson would own the buildings from which it operated, enhancing its sense of familial stability. Significantly, its superior liquidity meant that any loss of business did not result in retrenchments: Cousins remains proud of the fact that he never retrenched anyone.

Not all employees found Patterson's culture conducive. Bruce Harris, who worked there as an account executive for three years in the early 1970s, found it a 'less gentlemanly' environment than Lintas, his previous (and subsequent), employer. Ironically, an assertive creative department led not by 'a gentleman' but by a woman, 'Bobs' Tree, was the cause, at least in part, of Harris's discomfort. Harris found that, in contrast to Lintas, the contributions he tried to make to discussions of creative work were 'chopped off'. Difficult creative people and 'clients pushing what they wanted' made Harris's time at Patts the 'least happy time of his life' in advertising, and he was relieved to be 'inveigled' back to Lintas. The atmosphere there he found more collaborative and much less combative, the agency's founding client Unilever having encouraged 'gentlemanly behaviour' because of a belief that 'how you dealt with people in business affected your future career.'[18]

The inclusive cultures valued by home-grown agencies such as Patterson and Clemenger gained significant validation when contrasted with the more cut-throat culture of some of their US rivals, most notably McCann-Erikson. A number of interviewees mentioned McCann's reputation as a rather ruthless and hard-headed environment, where staff members were less happy than they might be.[19] McCann-Erikson's former creative director, Bryce Courtenay, warned a young Peter Hamilton to manage carefully his career with the agency because it was

Figure 10.1 George Patterson chairman Keith Cousins (left), account director Graham Cox (centre) and creative director Ross Quinlivan (right) review a new campaign.
Advertising News, *10 June 1977, p. 7 (Courtesy of AdNews)*

'notorious for dumping people after three years.'[20] Courtenay later told John Bevins that McCann was 'a hate agency' that did not look after its people as well as other leading agencies.[21]

Courtenay's assessment of McCann's culture was, of course, informed through personal experience, but there is evidence that its American roots lay behind perceptions of the agency as hard-nosed and profit-driven. That the culture of a local branch reflected the pressures the global head office placed on it is unsurprising. But agency cultures were affected by overseas business cultures in other ways. Like Peter Clemenger, most of the CEOs had been influenced by early trips to overseas agencies. Michael Ball was appointed deputy managing-director of the new O&M office in Toronto aged just twenty-five in 1961, and commenced his globetrotting role just four years later. Peter Rankin joined Clemenger in 1959 aged twenty-nine. He was sent to New York and, influenced by the systems he saw there, introduced timesheets to the Melbourne agency on his return. Wayne Kingston was studying for his MBA when he joined Y&R – a 'hot agency' run by the American Joseph DeDeo – 'the new breed from the US', which showed Kingston the importance of creativity to good advertising. Later Kingston spent time at O&M New York where he learnt about the disciplines of account management and planning, and how to write briefs for the creative and media departments. He used these lessons at MDA Melbourne, where he became a managing director 'on the job', bringing the discipline of O&M New York to Melbourne.

As the manager of Lintas Sydney, Max Gosling tried to recreate the culture he had experienced working at JWT London in the 1970s – a civilised culture that encouraged pride in the job 'but not arrogance.'[22] Reg Bryson travelled overseas in 1974 and found that 'the mannered approach of England' he experienced working at Masius in London was more in line with his own ideas than 'the mercantile approach of America'. The Masius advertising staff would 'look for creative ways to change the rules' and involve researchers in problem solving. Bryson 'came to understand the power of good advertising' in the UK. Advertising seemed to have social currency there; people would discuss it on the train, in the pub. UK advertising aimed to 'surprise the mind' and Bryson decided he 'wanted to be part of that'. Back in Melbourne at the helm of The Campaign Palace, however, Bryson found that Australia's small market meant keeping an eye on the bottom line could not be sacrificed for creative excellence, and decided that a combination of the British and US approaches to advertising production would in fact 'work best in Australia.'[23]

Bryson's pragmatism reflects the general response of the best Australian principals to the new leadership models offered by the globalisation of advertising processes and practices. Eager to embrace the new intellectual rigour and higher professional standards, they tempered this enthusiasm with an understanding that Australian advertising had its own culture, much of which was worth retaining. In particular, this meant resisting the hierarchical, often aggressive, corporate structures favoured by the Americans and retaining Australia's model of a family-style business led by a benign autocrat. Australian principals believed that astute business practices and a happy workforce – in other words, combining intellectual rigour with gentlemanly behaviour – was the best way forward for business success.

The Challenges

For Clemenger's Peter Rankin, the 'number one challenge [was] to keep the business.'[24] As agencies professionalised during the 1960s in response to the demands of their now better-educated clients, this became increasingly difficult. There was fierce competition amongst agencies for lucrative business and, though they remained important, friendships with clients could no longer be relied upon. A new type of principal – university-educated in economics or commerce, sometimes with previous marketing experience and equipped with 'the capacity to think' – became increasingly valuable to agencies wishing to provide themselves with an edge in their new business pitches.

Peter Charlton was a pre-eminent example of this new breed.[25] A graduate in Economics and Commerce from Melbourne University, Charlton became a fixer who was repeatedly brought in to introduce new levels of professionalism to failing agencies. In 1972 SSC&B: Lintas pulled him in from the marketing department of ICI to fix its ailing Melbourne branch. In 1976 Charlton moved across to McCann-Erickson to 'fix its structures' and improve its 'professionalism.'[26] His next challenge was McCann-Erickson Sydney, which he found to be overstaffed. He shifted the agency to Sydney's North Shore, away from its long-time home in Caltex House on Kent Street, which Charlton describes as 'the boulevard of broken dreams' when he arrived. The agency had lost its core staff – Bryce Courtenay and the two Davids, Sherborne and Baker – and the resulting shift of culture demanded a fresh start. Charlton left McCann in 1985, 'tired of the relentless emphasis on the bottom line' and the 'figure-men's' constant demand for better profits.

For Cunnack, too, making money was a constant challenge. It was 'easy to overspend' so 'self-regulation' was crucial in his view. Management needed to keep an especially close eye on the creative department who were 'not necessarily the best money managers in the world.'[27] Rankin recalls money problems with some accounts because the client refused to pay up. The consequences could be dire: 'If you've spent a quarter of a million, the client *must* pay you.'[28] David Mattingly's biggest challenge in the early years of his eponymous agency was 'paying the bills' because he and his partners had acquired 'a massive debt at 20.85 per cent interest' in order to get the agency off the ground. Later, Mattingly had 'two main concerns – keeping the client and the work', both of which became more difficult once agencies began discounting their rates after they had 'gone public' and were required to pay dividends to shareholders.[29]

Asked to reflect on what made a good advertising agency, Wayne Kingston replied 'it [was] all about the culture.'[30] Almost without exception, his contemporaries in agency leadership concurred. They emphasised the importance of building a strong agency culture in order to retain valued staff, which they saw as essential for achieving long-term business success: 'People are the one element that can make or break an agency.'[31] Or in the words of Alex Hamill: 'staff, first; clients, second; profits, third. It always works.'[32] Advertising people were, however, notoriously mobile, and agencies required strategies to pin down their loyalty.[33] Faced with the problem of competitors trying to steal his staff, Mattingly went out of his way to ensure his agency was 'a happy place' which staff members were reluctant to leave.

A similar problem led Cunnack to initiate the Advertising Federation of Australia (AFA) training scheme in 1980, with the help of Mike Strauss, Jamie Aitkin and Peter Clemenger. The scheme aimed to get agencies to take on trainees to encourage 'more bright people into the business who would not normally come' and became a permanent fixture in the Australian advertising scene.[34] For Hamill 'holding [onto] staff' was 'formulaic'. The answer was consistency, building a strong culture over time, with 'lots of little things' adding up to broader success: the leadership walking the agency each day (as Reason did), for example, or ensuring that office doors were open. Providing staff with little things to keep them attached – small gifts and Christmas cards – also helped build and reinforce a supportive culture, as did holding regular staff meetings.[35]

The last of these 'little things' seems to have been especially significant with a number of the interviewees, emphasising the importance of promoting harmonious relations between the agency's departments. For Peter Clemenger, it is 'the art of business.'[36] Ball and Kingston have similar perspectives: 'One of the arts of training and managing [in advertising] is to help staff understand both account management and creative aspects', argues Ball, while Kingston believes 'a good principal fosters across departments', encouraging each department to have its say and preventing any one department from dominating, because 'a good idea can come out of any department.'[37] For Bryson, a good agency required the people who ran it 'to work together'. This meant adhering to an overarching vision and philosophy: 'to know you are in business and what your purpose is'. 'A year out of advertising' working at USP Needham had helped Bryson realise that his purpose was the opposite of that agency's leadership which privileged 'the profit motive' over the end product and was prepared to give 'the client what[ever] they want'. At The Campaign Palace – an organisation that was 'heart, soul and spirit driven' – Bryson realised *his* purpose: working with others who shared a commitment to producing great advertising, an end product that 'inspired' and 'fascinated', and paying less attention to making a profit.[38]

Managing an agency of diverse skills and talents, some of them creative and flamboyant personalities, provided many agency principals with a significant challenge. Each principal approached this problem in his own way, although many of the leading CEOs operated, necessarily, as autocrats, notably Peter Clemenger, Michael Ball, and Keith and Geoff Cousins.[39] Such autocracy needed to be tempered by a passion for the business and the ability to act as 'a decent human being.'[40] Ian Alwill took the advice of a mentor, Peter Jacklin, and learnt to adjust his management style to suit the circumstances. 'Your job is the handling of people', Jacklin told Alwill. 'Change gears, change hats, depending on who you are communicating with.'[41]

At Mojo, Ric Otton relished the challenge of 'managing a big mix of people half of whom [were] crazy'. He found office politics to be rife in the agency: 'a huge on-going problem' that was 'best managed by the charismatic leadership of Mo and Jo'. 'Excessive ownership of creative outcomes' manifested in a tendency amongst some staff to blame others for mistakes, which undermined the team. So Otton applied 'a firm rule'. He rewarded teamwork, punished selfish politics, and fired those who 'used political behaviour'. By encouraging a 'culture of karma' and emphasising the need for 'forgiveness and generosity', Otton was able to achieve harmonious relations at Mojo.[42] In 1987, readers of B&T were informed that 'Everyone feels like a member of the family – one big family' at Mojo MDA. The agency had 'striven to avoid a hierarchy, even to the extent of dispensing with business titles, putting everyone on an equal footing'. Staff members were also able to share in company profits, which no doubt heightened their job satisfaction. At Lintas, too, structures had been flattened by this period. The agency's head – Lucienne de Mestre – identified as 'a leader rather than a manager' and was 'trying to develop a collegial style of leadership with decisions based on discussion and agreement.'[43]

David Ogilvy's insistence on 'gentlemanly' behaviour sat firmly behind Cunnack's approach to management at O&M. Cunnack aimed 'to take people with [him]' by communicating his expectations clearly at staff meetings and ensuring staff members had the tools to help them deliver. He 'developed ideas and wrote notes to managers'; brought Ian Strachan over from England to oversee the training programme; and introduced an internal award, the Silver Nail, to recognise outstanding effort. The 'one agency indivisible' brand underpinning O&M Worldwide eased the chief executive's role. Behind the visual uniformity – the furniture, the carpet – lay a shared culture influenced by David Ogilvy that emphasised the exchange of knowledge and ideas. Cunnack argues that this shared culture transcended any Australian parochialism, what he calls the 'not invented here syndrome'. The provision of training tools from New York reinforced this sense of a global identity, as did the convention of managers attending three international board meetings a year. Cunnack took every opportunity to 'fly the flag', 'push the philosophy', and 'promote what O&M was about'. He wrote personal letters to each new member of staff in the mid-1980s and tried to meet with them all. He also promoted an atmosphere of trust through his willingness to delegate – 'I was very good at delegation' – leaving staff to identify and sort out problems. By the time the boutique agencies of the 1980s began to emerge in Australia in response to the merger madness of the 1960s and 1970s, the founders of these agencies had imbued the business value of a happy, stable workforce. John Bevins, for example, had experienced the combative (McCann-Erickson) and the gentlemanly (O&M), and chose to go with the latter when he opened his own shop in Sydney in 1982, providing staff with a supportive, inclusive environment in which they felt valued.[44]

Whatever an agency's distinctive culture, two circumstances challenged a manager's ability to preserve and maintain it. First, merging with another agency (a common occurrence in this period as we have seen) could throw an agency's culture into turmoil. The mergers between FCB and SPASM, and Mojo and MDA are, arguably, the most instructive examples of this problem. Bringing together such diverse agency cultures required careful management. Issues included the duplication of staff in key roles (and the subsequent retrenchments), as well as the inevitable cultural clashes that arose from differing manage- ment styles, agency structures, and advertising philosophies. As the managing director Mike Strauss remarked following the FCB–SPASM merger in 1980, it was like 'a meeting of oil and water … they didn't mix at all … SPASM people wondered why we had got together with *those* people. The people interac- tion was totally wrong. You could smell it.'[45] The Mojo–MDA merger foundered for similar reasons. Two very different cultures clashed head-on. Brash Mojo did not respect the subtler creatives of MDA and 'wouldn't let the marriage really succeed.'[46]

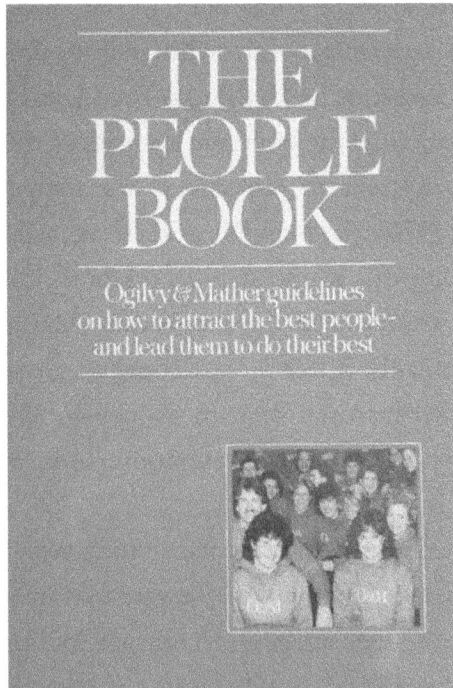

Figure 10.2 O&M's guidelines ensured that management strategies were consistent across its network
Courtesy of Toni Lawler, c. 1980s, BBB Box 25, Supplement.

A further challenge for agency principals was rapid and strong growth. The Campaign Palace Sydney is just one example of this, having to navigate carefully through periods of strong growth in order to keep intact the very culture (in the Palace's case, a perceived 'edginess') that had attracted the growth in the first place.[47] An imperative for the successful manager was to lead the agency in securing new business, without which 'business transformation' (i.e. growth) became unachievable.[48] In the early days of his leadership, Peter Clemenger found growth to be his single biggest challenge. Over time, he learnt the importance of the managing director becoming 'part of your city'; of meeting and getting to know people in order to keep abreast of new business opportunities. This approach was unique to Clemenger and gave him an edge over his competitors. The agency's dramatic growth in the late 1950s was built on exactly such a relationship when the agency secured Viscount Cigarettes, a client who dealt only with the managing director. As Peter Clemenger notes, he likes 'to work with clients not for them'. Clemenger's subsequent growth and success was achieved through maintaining a balance of flexibility and stability. Peter Clemenger recognised that his agency had to learn to cope with new problems and 'change with the times', but a 'rock solid' team of four at the top provided the stability required to make the most of new opportunities thrown up by the changing times. Fifty years later, the agency remains in the hands of the Clemenger family: 'we are still running the show. We've worked to stay in control and not be taken over as others were.'[49]

Shifting Expectations

As the industry professionalised, the costs of the business pitches required for an agency to grow increased significantly: less welded to an agency, clients looked more often at moving their accounts and took the process of selection more seriously than before.[50] The clients' new professional standards prompted agency principals to up their game. O&M's insistence on a worldwide approach to training reflected the new seriousness with which principals now approached the advertising business. At Clemenger Sydney, Geoff Wild embraced this push to 'intellectualise the business' that developed from the late 1960s, producing a series of booklets dealing with various aspects of Clemenger's business in order to position it as 'the thinking agency'.

The arrival of DeDeo to manage the local Y&R outfit was particularly stimulating for local competitors, offering a new model of leadership and brand differentiation for other agency principals to emulate. Y&R's managing director in the 1970s and 1980s, the Cambridge-educated Chris Martin Murphy, describes the agency as 'very hierarchical in its dealings' but believes that this type of organisation 'made sense'. To this end, account managers were required to work closely with finance directors who, in their turn, had close links with the agency heads back in the States. Job numbers and job bags were used to show profitability, and detailed budgets were provided on a monthly basis. Such efficiency and financial accountability provided Y&R with its own point of difference.[51]

By the mid-1970s most agencies understood the importance of differentiating their brand philosophy from those of their competitors. The challenge then became turning that philosophy into a convincing narrative that could be communicated to prospective clients, as Greg Daniel would discover a decade later at The Campaign Palace in Sydney. Sydney clients appeared to be put off by the Palace's unflinching creative vision, interpreting it as arrogance. To counter this, Daniel developed a communication strategy that aimed to explain to clients why the Palace took the approach it did, and how it would provide clients with better results.

The demands of a more intellectual approach to advertising required better-educated executives. In the 1960s, agency principals with MBAs were rare in Australia, but in New York they were becoming more common and had begun to 'infiltrate the advertising business.'[52] From the early 1970s, this shift reached Australia, as more university-educated leaders took control of the business – men such as Malcolm Spry, for example, who was 'interested in the management of corporations' and 'read a lot', including the *Harvard Business Review*. Sections of the Australian industry resisted this creeping professionalisation, however, seeing it as 'a threat', and continued to use 'the old world, *Mad Men* techniques' for keeping clients happy.[53] There had been a consistent presence of copywriters in the executive levels of the Australian advertising industry, but such positions became more challenging for them, particularly as the demands of being a senior executive in a multinational agency increased. Bill Shannon, briefly the CEO of O&M Melbourne in the mid-1970s, struggled to balance the business and creative demands of the job and considered his time in the role as 'an experience not to be recommended.'[54] And when Tom McFarlane became Creative Director at JWT in the 1980s, he found he was inexperienced at managing both people and finances. Firing people was 'horrible' and, as a manager, McFarlane was 'expected to show manners to visitors' even though he did not 'feel it'. He did the job for four years, believing he was 'not very good at it', and it 'broke him in the end.'[55]

The technological changes that had provided support staff with numerous challenges and opportunities had less impact on the CEOs. Ball mentioned the shift to colour film, Cunnack that from film to video, and Mattingly emphasised the importance of the fax machine, which saved his agency money, as it 'no longer had to fly ads all over Australia for approval'. With one important exception, however, the majority of our interviewees who had spent their careers as agency principals or network executives – with teams of people available to them to perform the mundane tasks using new technologies – reported that technological change had little impact on their day-to-day tasks.[56] The exception was the time spent travelling by these executives. The globalisation of the advertising industry would have been impossible before the availability of regular flights in and out of Australia, but Ball recalls that in his early career it still took three days to fly from Melbourne to New York. From the end of the 1970s, airline travel became increasingly faster, a change that was 'important for management'. *B&T*'s regular 'Newsmakers' columns reveal a drop off in recorded lengthy overseas trips by agency principals – no doubt as international travel became easier and more common.[57] From 1966, the column switched to recording the arrival of overseas professionals and Australian professionals' attendance at overseas conferences, although the 'world trips' of leading advertising men such as John and Peter Clemenger, Bill Currie and Bruce Harris were sometimes noted.[58]

———————

Australian advertising's chief executives might have been the least affected of agency personnel by the technological advances of the third quarter of the twentieth century, but they were, arguably, more affected than other personnel by the relentless forces of globalisation. In many ways, their day-to-day lives barely changed. They still chased new business, nurtured their clients, and worried about retaining good staff and balancing the books. They did all this, however, in a larger, far more competitive framework, especially after the arrival of the new, slicker US agencies from the late 1960s. Armed with higher levels of education than the previous generation of principals, the new CEOs responded to the demands of their equally well-educated clients by applying a new level of professionalism manifested in the application of a conscious intellectualism and a more rigorous management style. They also began to apply the strategic approaches they took to their clients' business to their own businesses, seeking out points of difference from their competitors in strategy and creative style that could give them an advantage in the increasingly competitive push for new business. The more successful of these principals approached the challenges of massive change in this period by constructing a careful mix of flexibility and stability within their agency operations, keeping the best of the industry's past – the family-business style that took seriously the importance of a happy workforce – and combining it with a systematic, intellectual approach to the production of advertising that would provide the professional standards, insight and efficiencies demanded by a truly global industry.

CONCLUSION

As each of our interviews drew to a close, we asked our subjects what they considered to be the secret to a good agency. In his interview, Geoff Cousins observes that: 'Most people would probably answer your question by saying "creating great ads"', before stating, 'No, not creating great ads. Sometimes, you're telling people don't make any ads.' For Cousins, a good agency was 'like most business – good business practices with people, having a clear understanding of what you're trying to deliver, and then the money turns up.'[1] Lionel Hunt expands on these points: 'You've got to have very good people and an environment that is fun and helps them produce great work.'[2] Both responses point to the central theme in this study, namely the professionalisation of the advertising agency and all aspects of its operations. Such professionalism had been integral to the advertising agencies' growth in size, stature, and profitability over the course of the 1960s, 1970s, and 1980s.

Keeping the client satisfied had long been one of the foundation stones of the agency business. This not only intensified from the 1960s onwards, in the face of growing competition between advertisers on the one hand and agencies on the other, it would also be instrumental to the agencies' professionalisation. As advertisers expanded their operations internationally, they increasingly expected their agencies would be in a position to handle their account in these new markets. Well aware that an international network was essential to maintaining large clients and, indeed, enhancing income, advertising agencies readily followed their clients across the globe. Of course, this was not necessarily a post-war phenomenon – General Motors had led JWT into Australia in the 1930s. However, McCann-Erickson's arrival in Australia in 1959 at the behest of Coca-Cola, and the subsequent stream of American and British agencies commencing Australian operations to service their clients' needs, signalled a new orthodoxy within the agency business. International networks had become the norm. Australian agencies' subsequent entry into South East Asian and Pacific markets similarly adhered to this new order.

As Australian agencies gained more direct access to the latest developments in client service, many discovered that they were becoming more than mere producers of campaigns. Agencies could offer clients general marketing advice. Market research, for example, was not only used by agencies to identify creative opportunities, it could also be used to examine broader marketing issues such as product development and packaging. Others impressed their clients by drawing on their agency's global reach and its worldly 'know how'. As agencies employed university graduates who had studied marketing and commerce, they were also able to offer more informed advice to their clients. Technology further reinforced this position. Transport and telecommunications technologies facilitated client–agency interaction, while computers provided more accurate details on campaign costs that also helped eliminate errors. This commitment to client service also encouraged agencies to embrace creativity. As client requests for more memorable and distinctive campaigns increased, agencies responded by investing more time and money into their creative capacities.

For their part, clients were willing to pay – sometimes directly, other times indirectly – for the services that agencies were offering them. The great boom of the 1960s and early 1970s had meant that it was a buyers' market, and they needed the agencies' expertise to secure their share of this market. When the boom slowed, they again looked to the agencies to maintain this share. The media landscape similarly reinforced their dependence on the agencies. Television was the most dominant medium and few advertisers possessed the capacity to produce their own commercials, let alone the all-important media accreditation that would enable them to buy airtime. Agencies recognised their unique position and went to great lengths to assure clients that they were getting the best service, from the best lunches to the best price for media space.

Over the 1960s and 1970s, the agencies' ability to meet their clients' needs effectively enabled them to reposition themselves from being a mere service provider to becoming a trusted partner in the client's operations. Perhaps the clearest indicator of the importance that clients ascribed to their agencies was the dramatic increase in advertising expenditure. George Patterson's billings went from $24 million in 1969/70 to $680 million in 1990. Over the same period, JWT billings went from $18 million to $135.6 million, while McCann-Erickson's $16.5 million grew to $167.2 million. Such figures dwarf the standard inflation rate of 9.3 per cent over this twenty-year period.

The professionalisation of advertising practice was greatly assisted by the advertising agency's profitability. In addition to the clients' increasing levels of advertising expenditure, agencies received a highly lucrative income stream from media commissions. Australian content regulations similarly enabled agencies to build up their production capacities while passing on the costs to clients. While the agency profits soared, the enormous amounts being spent on advertising coupled with the cutthroat nature of the agency business required agency chiefs to pay serious attention to improving their own operations and enhancing their professionalism. Training of staff at all levels was identified as an essential aspect of this process. Although training was largely conducted on the job, agencies progressively implemented more formalised systems of improving staff skillsets. Agencies with global networks could send staff abroad to attend seminars and to spend time in key offices. They could similarly import overseas expertise to assist local operations. Globalisation was therefore crucial to the industry's professionalisation – both driving it and responding to it. By interacting directly and indirectly with the global advertising industry, local advertising professionals also developed a deeper understanding of their own role as well as an ability to enhance or improve their effectiveness. The account service department thus embraced strategy planning, the creative department sought to enhance creativity, and the media department asserted its role in delivering effective campaigns.

The professionalisation of agency practice was also evident in the agencies' efforts to recruit the right people and to establish the right environment. Those who entered the business in the 1950s and 1960s often had little idea about the advertising industry. It was still something of an obscure, backroom operation. Over the coming decades, agencies emerged as a glamorous business. Agency staff enjoyed generous salaries and enviable working conditions that seemed to involve little more than talking about ideas over long lunches or hobnobbing with the rich and famous.

The opportunity to travel internationally did little to detract from this image. As the competition to enter this glamorous industry duly intensified, agencies were able to recruit the brightest and most creative young men and women. It is hardly surprising, then, that a generation of Australian novelists, artists, musicians, business leaders, and media personalities started out in advertising. The money flowing through the agencies as well as the absence of a fringe benefits tax also enabled them to embark on and maintain an expensive bidding war to poach staff from the competition and, indeed, from clients.

The recruitment process illustrated other aspects of the agency's professionalisation. In a c1960 introduction to the agency business prepared by the Australian Association of Advertising Agencies, aspiring admen and adwomen were informed that advertising was a meritocracy: 'In an advertising agency you make your way by your own ability. There is no automatic promotion. If your ideas are good ones, if your judgment is sound, you will quickly build up into a lucrative and satisfactory position.'[3]

Education, social status, and gender were less important than ability and dedication. However, this meritocratic principle began to weaken. As education provided a means by which agencies could better serve their clients, they progressively employed young men and women who had matriculated and, later, completed a university degree. Connections were also becoming important. Many had managed to enter the industry on account of a family member either being in the agency business or an allied industry. While education and connections helped open doors to the agency, subsequent progress remained subject to hard work and commitment. Gender presented a more complicated perspective of the agency's meritocracy. Agency employees were generally evenly split between males and females. However, the young men circulating through the departments were given greater opportunity to demonstrate their abilities than their women counterparts, who were often restricted to a single department or role. Yet over time, a growing number of women not only managed to impress their superiors with their acumen and ideas, they were able to enter male-dominated areas, most notably the account service department. However, the glass ceiling effectively prevented the vast majority from taking on senior positions.

Over the 1960s, 1970s, and 1980s, the operations, practices, and structures of Australian agencies were fundamentally shaped by professionalisation and globalisation. Such changes had seen the advertising agency business grow in size, scope, influence, and profitability. However, this 'golden age' of the Australian advertising agency was to be fleeting rather than permanent. The good times came to an abrupt end with the recession of the early 1990s. A closer reading of the features of this 'golden age' reveals that the very factors that had underpinned the agencies' dramatic rise would also consume them.

Recognising the importance of marketing, agencies had sought to enhance their understanding of the concept and pre-sented it to clients as part of their service. Yet the realisation that marketing went beyond advertising led many clients to pay closer attention to their marketing practices. Like the agencies, they employed marketing graduates, who, in turn, advised them that marketing went beyond advertising. The appointment of marketing managers fundamentally changed the clients' relation-ship with their agencies. Where agencies had previously dealt with the key members of the client's executive team, they were now dealing with the client's marketing manager. As marketing managers considered advertising to be part of a broader strategy, agencies found themselves subjected to the whims of the client's marketing manager with little capacity to increase their influence. So when the money finally ran out in the 1990s, it was the marketing manager who reminded agencies that they existed to service the clients' advertising needs. Clients have maintained this outlook through to the present.

The enormous profits enjoyed by the advertising agencies began to attract adverse attention from clients. Many questioned why their agent was earning more than they did. Clients called for greater accountability for each dollar, while marketing managers readily reduced their advertising allocation. Moreover, the abandonment of the Australian content regulations meant that clients could cut out the Australian agencies altogether by airing commercials produced overseas. It was the emergence of the media agencies, however, that posed a more profound challenge to the agencies' operations. They successfully outmuscled the full-service agencies by offering cheaper media space to clients and creative boutiques. The full-service agencies eventually capitulated, closing their media departments and outsourcing their media buying and planning to the media agencies. As the media commission stream dried up, advertising agencies found that they needed to do the same work for clients but with smaller budgets. With less time to devote to each campaign, creative standards would decline.

The realities of operating in a globalised industry were apparent from the early 1960s. Within a few years of McCann-Erickson's arrival in Australia, overseas-owned agencies had already displaced local operations as Australia's largest and most profitable agencies. Although local agencies were able to compete against these foreign firms, they were simply unable to do it on a long-term basis. Of course this did not deter agencies such as Mojo from dreaming large. But Mojo MDA's fall demonstrated all too clearly that globalisation favoured the largest agencies and the largest clients. Australia's foray into South East Asia revealed a similar story. While American and British firms were happy to have Australians overseeing a developing region, they were less comfortable to leave the more advanced (and profitable) areas, such as Japan, in Australian hands. Tellingly, the economic rise of Singapore and Hong Kong in the 1990s would see many agencies relocate their Asia-Pacific headquarters away from Sydney. Global alignment of accounts remained a contentious topic – those who secured lucrative accounts were happy with the process, while those who lost out were inevitably frustrated by it. Such realignments not only underscored Australia's peripheral status in global deals, they also undermined the industry's vaunted meritocratic principle.

As their income and influence began to erode, so too did the glamour and the fun. From the 1990s, the advertising agencies were forced to become more accountable to their clients for every decision and every expense. Clients also reminded agencies that they could easily move their account if they were unsatisfied with the quality of service on offer. Agencies were therefore expected to deliver the same service but on leaner budgets. The time and resources allocated to client lunches, ideas development, and advertisement production consequently dwindled. While agencies continued to identify themselves as a dynamic and vibrant creative industry, the agency business had become more like any other service industry.

Summing up the period, Andrew Killey reflects that: 'In the '60s, it was always about service, the account service guys and the client ... It then went to the craziness of 1980s, where creative was king … and then, I think, the [1990] Recession just stopped everything.'[4] In this tough climate, clients were focused on the bottom line and marketing budgets were ruthlessly slashed. Advertising agencies were put on the back foot – 'beaten down' – and clients have kept them there ever since.[5] Other factors would also contribute to this status: the ongoing rise of the media agencies, the digital revolution, and the emergence of specialised communication professions have all undermined the advertising agency's influence. While there has always been a place for innovative and effective advertising agencies with creative ideas and an ability to meet the client's needs, the reality is that it is difficult to see the glory days of the advertising agency ever returning.

NOTES

Introduction

1   Michael Ball, interview with Rosemary Francis, 13 March 2015; E.
    Williams, 'The Admen', *Age,* 7 October 1968, p. 4.

2   G. Whitwell, *Making the Market: The Rise of Consumer Culture,*
    McPhee Gribble, Melbourne, 1989, pp. 26, 29–31, 51–66.

3   See A. Mattelart, *Advertising International: The Privatisation of Public
    Space,* Routledge, London, 1991; M. Tungate, *Adland: A Global History
    of Advertising,* Kogan Page, London & Philadelphia, 2007; J. Sinclair,
    Advertising, the Media and Globalisation: A World in Motion, Routledge,
    Abingdon, 2012.

4   See D. Sutton, *Globalizing Ideal Beauty: How Female Copywriters of the
    J. Walter Thompson Advertising Agency Redefined Beauty for the Twentieth
    Century,* Palgrave Macmillan, Basingstoke, 2007; R. Davis, '"Through
    Thompson Eyes": A Global Analysis of Advertising in the J. Walter
    Thompson Agency, 1928–1945', Unpublished Manuscript, PhD
    Thesis, University of Sydney, 2008; S. De Iulio & C. Vinti, 'The
    Americanization of Italian Advertising during the 1950s and the
    1960s: Mediations, Conflicts, and Appropriations', *Journal of Historical
    Research in Marketing,* vol. 1, no. 2, 2009, pp. 270–94; S. Nixon,
    Hard Sell: Advertising Affluence and Transatlantic Relations c.1951–1969,
    Manchester University Press, Manchester, 2013; F. Fasce & E. Bini,
    'Irresistible Empire or Innocents Abroad? American Advertising
    Agencies in Post-war Italy, 1950s–1970s', *Journal of Historical Research
    in Marketing,* vol. 7, no. 1, 2015, pp. 7–30; S. Nixon 'Looking
    Westwards and Worshipping: The New York 'Creative Revolution'
    and British Advertising, 1956–1980', *Journal of Consumer Culture,*
    doi:10.1177/1469540515571388, 2015.

5   See J. Meron, 'Putting Foreign Consumers on the Map: J. Walter
    Thompson's Struggle with General Motors' International Advertising
    Account in the 1920s', *Business History Review,* vol. 73, no. 2, 1999,

pp. 465–503; J. P. Woodard, 'Marketing Modernity: The J. Walter Thompson Company and North American Advertising in Brazil, 1929–1939', *Hispanic American History Review*, vol. 82, no. 2, 2002, pp. 257–90; C. E. Hultquist, 'Americans in Paris: The J. Walter Thompson Company in France, 1927–1968', *Enterprise & Society*, vol. 4, no. 3, 2003, pp. 471–501; J. E. Moreno, 'J. Walter Thompson, the Good Neighbour policy, and Lessons in Mexican Business Culture, 1920–1950', *Enterprise & Society*, vol. 5, no. 2, 2004, pp. 254–80; V. Pouillard, 'American Advertising Agencies in Europe: J. Walter Thompson's Belgian Business in the Inter-war Years', *Business History*, vol. 47, no. 1, 2005, pp. 44–58; R. Davis, 'Negotiating Local and Global Knowledge and History: J. Walter Thompson around the Globe 1928–1960', *Journal of Australian Studies*, vol. 36, no. 1, 2012, pp. 81–97.

6   L. McFall, *Advertising: A Cultural Economy*, Sage, London, 2004, p.3.

7   S. Nixon, *Advertising Cultures: Gender, Commerce, Creativity*, Sage, London, 2003, p.4.

8   J. Spierings, 'Australian Advertising History: A Research Note', *Media Information Australia*, no.31, 1984, p. 101.

9   J. Sinclair, *Images Incorporated: Advertising as Industry and Ideology*, Croon Helm, London, 1987.

10 R. Crawford, *But Wait, There's More… : A History of Australian Advertising, 1900–2000*, Melbourne University Press, Carlton, Vic., 2008.

11 J. Dickenson, *Australian Women in Advertising in the Twentieth Century*, Palgrave Macmillan, Basingstoke, 2016.

12 P. Fridenson, 'Business History and History' in Geoffrey Jones and Jonathan Zeitlin (eds), *The Oxford Handbook of Business History*, Oxford University Press, Oxford, 2007, p. 10.

13 R. Perks, 'The Roots of Oral History: Exploring Contrasting Attitudes to Elite, Corporate, and Business Oral History in Britain and the U.S.', *The Oral History Review*, vol. 37, no. 2, 2010, p. 218.

14 R. Perks, '"Corporations are People too": Business and Corporate Oral History in Britain', *Oral History*, vol. 38, no. 1, 2010, p. 36.

15 See http://www.oralhistoryaustralia.org.au/files/oha_journal_ indexes_1979–2015_secured.pdf.

16 H. Marsh, 'Exploiting Marine Wildlife in Queensland: The Commercial Dugong and Marine Turtle Fisheries, 1847–1969', *Australian Economic History Review*, vol. 48, no. 3, 2008, pp.227–65; A. May, 'Ideas from Australian Cities: Relocating Urban and Suburban

History', *Australian Economic History Review*, vol. 49, no. 1, pp. 70–86; C. Davila & J. C. Davila, 'The Evolution of a Socially Committed Business Group in Colombia, 1911–85', *Australian Economic History Review*, vol. 54, no. 2, 2014, pp. 164–82.

Chapter One: Arriving in Australia

1   Editor, 'Huge US Agency to Open up Here', *Broadcasting and Television*, 15 May 1959, p. 4.
2   'Aust., U.S. Agencies in Merger', *Sydney Morning Herald*, 29 September 1959, p. 9; Carl Spielvogel, 'Advertising: McCann is Invading Australia', *New York Times*, 28 September 1959, p. 45.
3   'Minutes of Meeting of Directors held on 30 June 1925', SAM 3/1 Minute Book, 1912–1948, Samson Clark & Co Ltd (Box C), History of Advertising Trust, UK.
4   *The Samson Clark Staff Gazette*, no. 242, 19 February 1926, p. 2, SAM 1/4/1, Samson Clark & Co Ltd (Box A), History of Advertising Trust, UK.
5   '£50,000 Merger', *Sydney Morning Herald*, 27 March 1930, p. 6.
6   'Law Notices', *Argus*, 24 May 1943, p. 11.
7   'Big Advertising Venture', *Sunday Times*, 8 September 1929, p. 2.
8   R. Welch, 'Notes on the American Invasion', *Advertising News*, 3 October 1980, p. 10.
9   'Memorandum to Mr Kinney', 14 May 1928, The Papers of James Webb Young, Box 2, International Branch Notes – Miscellaneous Data Concerning Organization of Foreign Offices, 1928–1930, Rare Book, Manuscript and Special Collections Library, Duke University, North Carolina, USA.
10 Representatives Meeting, 8 October 1929, '1929, May – 1930, August, Minutes of Representatives' Meetings', Box 2, Rare Book, Manuscript and Special Collections Library, Duke University, USA.
11 W. R. McNair, 'The Establishment of J. Walter Thompson's Offices in Australia and New Zealand, International Office Histories – Australia 1963, Nov.', Sidney Ralph Bernstein, Company History Files, Box 5, J. Walter Thompson Company Archives, Rare Book, Manuscript and Special Collections Library, Duke University, North Carolina, USA.
12 'Advertising Service', *West Australian*, 14 November 1930, p. 21.
13 See W. A. McNair (ed.), *Some Reflections on the First Fifty Years of Market Research in Australia*, Sydney[?]: Market Research Society of Australia, NSW Division, c.1978.
14 'How well do you know your JWT'ers? Thumbnail Sketch – Philip

Mygatt', *J. Walter Thompson Company News*, 16 June 1952, p .4.

15 'Import Entries Passed at His Majesty's Customs', *Daily Commercial News and Shipping List*, 18 September 1931, p.6; 'Import Entries Passed at His Majesty's Customs', *Daily Commercial News and Shipping List*, 12 October 1931, p. 6.

16 Cited in Ann Stephen, 'Selling Soap: Domestic Work and Consumerism', *Labour History*, no. 61, November 1991, pp. 65–6.

17 'New South Wales Export Manifests', *Daily Commercial News and Shipping List*, 6 August 1931, p. 6.

18 'New Registrations', *Sydney Morning Herald*, 17 January 1935, p. 13.

19 'JWT Chief on McCann Entry', *Broadcasting and Television*, 8 October 1959, p. 1.

20 J. Walter Thompson Company, *The Australian Market*, McGraw-Hill, New York, 1959, p. 7.

21 Murray Goot, 'Rubensohn, Solomon (Sim) (1904–1979)', *Australian Dictionary of Biography*, National Centre of Biography, Australian National University, http://adb.anu.edu.au/biography/rubensohn-solomon-sim-11579/text20669, accessed 11 March 2015.

22 *Hansen Rubensohn-McCann Erickson Accounts at 31ˢᵗ December 1959*, Price Waterhouse & Co, Sydney, c.1960, held by McCann, Sydney.

23 'McCann's Entry Confirmed', *Broadcasting and Television*, 1 October 1959, p. 1.

24 DDB Melbourne, *50 Years in the Making*, DDB, Melbourne, c.1995, p. 12.

25 'Story Board', *Newspaper News*, 5 August 1960, p. 1.

26 'GP's U.S. Link Reflects Key Ad Trends', *Newspaper News*, 20 March 1964, p. 1.

27 R. R. Walker, *Communicators: People Practices, Philosophies in Australian Advertising, Media, Marketing*, Lansdowne Press, Melbourne, 1967, p.122; 'Cousins Takes a Bow', *Advertising News*, 3 February 1984, p. 22.

28 'GP's U.S. Link Reflects Key Ad Trends', *Newspaper News*, 20 March 1964, p. 1.

29 'We Want Readers', Views on the US Influence in Advertising', *B&T*, 4 June 1964, p. 3.

30 'The US Patter of Colonial Expansion in Advertising', *B&T*, 26 November 1964, p. 4.

31 'Bristow sees Major Ad Changes in Aust.', *Newspaper News*, 16 September 1966, p. 1.

32 'Jackson Wain is Burnett', *B&T Weekly*, 16 December 1971, p. 7.

33 V. Nicholson, 'Look Back in Anguish, but Don't Forget to Keep on

Watching', *B&T*, 3 February 1977, p. 11.

34 Michael Ball, interview with Rosemary Francis, 13 March 2013.

35 'Revolutionary Move by Sydney Agency', *Newspaper News*, 24 January 1964, p. 4.

36 Graham Nunn, interview with Robert Crawford, 21 May 2013.

37 Dennis Merchant, interview with Robert Crawford, 15 March 2013.

38 'Y&R Chief takes a Cautious View of Advertising Research', *Advertising News*, 18 August 1972, p. 10.

39 'JWT Sydney', *J. Walter Thompson Company News*, vol. xiv, no. 138, 23 September 1959, p. 3.

40 'McC-E seminar – B.&T. Nov. 10th, 1960', Hansen Rubensohn-McCann Erickson Press Cuttings Scrapbook, Unpublished Manuscript, McCann Australia, Sydney, n.d., unpaginated.

41 John Cowper, interview with Robert Crawford, 24 January 2013.

42 Graeme Kinsella, interview with Robert Crawford, 9 January 2013.

43 Renny Cunnack, interview with Rosemary Francis, 14 May 2013.

44 Doug Watson, interview with Robert Crawford, 19 April 2013.

45 Jane Mara, interview with Robert Crawford, 6 March 2013.

46 Julian Martin, interview with Robert Crawford, 23 April 2013.

47 Tania Farrelly, interview with Rosemary Francis, 23 July 2013.

48 Doug Watson, interview with Robert Crawford, 19 April 2013

49 Luella Copeland-Smith, interview with Robert Crawford, 15 February 2013.

50 Ball, interview.

51 Eugene Catanzariti, interview with Rosemary Francis, 18 January 2013.

52 Chris Martin Murphy, interview with Robert Crawford, 8 March 2013.

53 J. Briears, 'Ideas Gush from Citadel of McCann-Erickson', *Newspaper News*, 20 January 1961, p. 7.

54 B. Parsons, 'Lindley Brings his Luck to O&M Sydney', *Advertising News*, 12 May 1978, p. 16.

55 Luella Copeland-Smith, interview with Robert Crawford, 15 February 2013.

56 P. Mawbey, 'The Agency PR Game', *Advertising News*, 27 April 1979, p. 8.

57 Peter Charlton, interview with Robert Crawford, 11 February 2013; Martin Murphy, interview.

58 Mike Satterthwaite, interview with Robert Crawford, 13 September 2012.

59 Geoff Cousins, interview with Robert Crawford, 15 March 2013; Alex Hamill, interview with Robert Crawford, 12 April 2013; Bruce Jarrett, interview with Robert Crawford, 5 April 2013.
60 Bruce Jarrett, interview.
61 Ian Dawson, interview with Robert Crawford, 14 December 2012.
62 Helene Nicol, interview with Rosemary Francis, 19 April 2013.
63 Mike Reed, interview with Rosemary Francis, 1 May 2012.
64 'McCann's Entry Confirmed', *B&T*, 1 October 1959, p. 1.
65 J. Bristow, 'Find out what Consumers want – Newspaper News Sept. 1960', Hansen Rubensohn-McCann Erickson Press Cuttings Scrapbook, unpaginated.
66 Paddy Stitt, interview with Rosemary Francis, 12 June 2012.
67 Douglas West, 'From T-Square to T-Plan: The London Office of the J. Walter Thompson Advertising Agency 1919–1970', *Business History*, vol. 29, no. 2, 1987, p. 204.
68 Ibid., p. 213.
69 Alan Robertson, interview with Robert Crawford, 23 November 2012.
70 Geoff Wild, interview with Robert Crawford, 17 May 2013.
71 John Wright, interview with Robert Crawford, 16 January 2013; Martin Murphy, interview.
72 'Financial Review Jan. 5th', Hansen Rubensohn-McCann Erickson Press Cuttings Scrapbook, unpaginated.
73 Michael Ritchie, interview with Robert Crawford, 14 April 2013.
74 R. Crawford, *But Wait, There's More... : A History of Australian Advertising*, Melbourne University Press, Melbourne, 2008, p. 204.
75 'Thumb-Nail Sketch – Lloyd Ring Coleman', *J. Walter Thompson Company News*, vol. viii, no. 17, 27 April 1953, p. 4.
76 'Invitation to US Marketing Men', *B&T*, 13 May 1965, p. 14.
77 'McCann through Others' Eyes', *B&T*, 27 September 1979, p. 34.
78 'US Adman for HR-McC, Melb.', *B&T*, 21 January 1960, p. 1.
79 'O&M Australia Lowdown', *B&T*, 6 April 1967, p. 7.
80 'Top US Agencyman Looks Us Over', *B&T*, 9 October 1969, p. 9.
81 Graham Nunn, interview with Robert Crawford, 21 May 2013.
82 'Craftsmen, Buccaneers and Missionaries', *B&T*, 17 November 1977, p. 32.
83 Lionel Hunt, interview with Robert Crawford, 22 January 2013.
84 B. Parsons, 'The Imports', *Advertising News*, 13 May 1977, p. 10.
85 D. Light, 'The Headhunters', *Advertising News*, 13 May 1977, p. 14.
86 'As We See It', *B&T*, 29 May 1959, p. 3.

Chapter Two: Studying Abroad

1   *Sydney Morning Herald*, 29 July 1959, p. 7.
2   Russell McLay, interview with Robert Crawford, 13 May 2013.
3   'Agencymen Can Gain a Lot from Overseas Travel', *B&T*, 20 April 1961, p. 25.
4   G. Patterson, *Life has been Wonderful: Fifty Year of Adventures in Advertising at Home and Abroad*, Ure Smith, Sydney, 1956, pp. 8–9.
5   Ibid., p. 10.
6   F. Goldberg, *My Life in Advertising 1912–1957*, Frank Goldberg, Sydney, c.1957, pp. 15–18, 37, 55.
7   W. A. McNair, 'The Twenties and Thirties – W.A. McNair' in W. A. McNair (ed.), *Some Reflections on the First Fifty Years of Market Research in Australia, 1928–1978*, Market Research Society of Australia, Sydney, 1978, p. 20.
8   Marion von Adlerstein, interview with Robert Crawford, 14 December 2012.
9   Derek Hansen, interview with Robert Crawford, 26 April 2013.
10 Bruce Jarrett, interview with Robert Crawford, 5 April 2013.
11 Graham Cox, interview with Robert Crawford, 26 April 2013.
12 H. Wilson, 'Our Agencies Rate with Best Overseas', *Newspaper News*, 5 February 1960, p. 23.
13 'HR-McCann Executives to Visit US', *Newspaper News*, 8 July 1960, p. 18.
14 'HR-McCE Executives in US', *B&T*, 8 December 1960, p. 26.
15 'HR-McCann Executives to visit US', *Newspaper News*, 8 July 1960, p. 18.
16 'Adman Reports on Harvard Course – B&T 31/1', Hansen Rubensohn-McCann Erickson Press Cuttings Scrapbook, un-paginated.
17 'Best US Ads can Benefit Aust. Admen', *Newspaper News*, 26 April 1968, p. 17.
18 'Bill Farnsworth – the Man and His Views', *Advertising and Newspaper News* (Advertising in Australia Supplement), 22 August 1969, p. 1.
19 Graham Cox, interview with Robert Crawford, 26 April 2013; Geoff Wild, interview with Robert Crawford, 17 May 2013.
20 'Staff Loyalty a Major Factor in Agency Work', *B&T*, 18 June 1970, p. 16.
21 Ian Strachan, interview with Rosemary Francis, 9 April 2013.
22 J. Cumming, 'Basic Differences Aid US Agencies', *Advertising: The Magazine of Marketing*, July 1959, p. 20.

23 'Fewer Personnel to an Account in Australia', *B&T*, 10 June 1965, p. 17.

24 Wayne Kingston, interview with Robert Crawford, 30 January, 6 February 2013

25 Suzie Otten, interview with Rosemary Francis, 28 May 2013, 25 June 2013.

26 Geoff Cousins, interview with Robert Crawford, 15 March 2013.

27 Hugh Spencer, interview with Robert Crawford, 3 May 2013.

28 Blane Hogue, personal correspondence with Robert Crawford, 26 March 2015.

29 Robin Stewart, interview with Rosemary Francis, 5 April 2013.

30 Alan Robertson, interview with Robert Crawford, 23 November 2012.

31 'Aust. Matches World in Ad Creativity', *Newspaper News*, 2 February 1962, p. 1.

32 T. Frank, *The Conquest of Cool: Business Culture, Counterculture, and the Rise of Hip Consumerism*, University of Chicago Press, Chicago, 1997, pp. 47–8; S. Nixon, 'Sean Nixon 'Looking Westwards and Worshipping: The New York "Creative Revolution" and British Advertising, 1956–1980', *Journal of Consumer Culture*, doi:10.1177/1469540515571388, 2015.

33 'Our Account Executives Have a Big Say', *B&T*, 4 January 1962, p. 10.

34 S. Nixon, 'Apostles of Americanization? J. Walter Thompson Company Ltd, Advertising and Anglo-American Relations 1945 –67', *Contemporary British History*, vol. 22, no. 4, 2008, pp. 477–99.

35 Robbie Hall, interview with Robert Crawford, 12 December 2012.

36 Paul Priday, interview with Robert Crawford, 23 January 2013; Trevor Fearnley, interview with Robert Crawford, 8 February 2013.

37 Fearnley, interview.

38 John Newton, interview with Robert Crawford, 9 April 2013.

39 Peter Charlton, interview with Robert Crawford, 11 February 2013.

40 Mo Fox, interview with Robert Crawford, 11 September 2012.

41 Marion von Adlerstein, interview with Robert Crawford, 14 December 2012.)

42 J. Dickenson, '"Nowhere Else to Work": Advertising and the Left in Australia', *Labour History*, no. 108, 2015, pp. 17–36.

43 Ken Done, interview with Robert Crawford, 12 February 2013.

44 Done, interview, See also 'Agency Round Up', *B&T*, 29 October 1959, p. 30.

45 Alan Robertson, interview with Robert Crawford, 23 November 2012.

46 Reg Bryson, interview with Robert Crawford, 11 February 2013.

47 R. Hazelton, 'What a Creative Man gains from Overseas Seminars', *B&T*, 2 November 1972, p. 15.

48 'Are We Overawed by Madison Avenue?', *B&T*, 4 June 1964, p. 17.

49 See 'Overseas Commercial Trends', *B&T*, 7 September 1961, p. 23; 'Fewer Personnel to an Account in Australia', *B&T*, 10 June 1965, p. 17.

50 'Australia is Now a Challenge', *B&T*, 24 July 1969, p. 23.

Chapter Three: Entering Asia

1   *B&T*, 25 March 1971, p. 27.

2   A. Sobocinska, *Visiting the Neighbours: Australians in Asia*, NewSouth, Sydney, 2014, Chapter 2.

3   'The Implications of the Patterson Agency's Far Eastern Expansion', *B&T*, 14 February 1963, p. 3.

4   Sobocinska, *Visiting the Neighbours*, p. 33.

5   'Mozar George Ernest', B2455, National Archives of Australia.

6   'Publicity Co. and E.G. Mozar', *Straits Times* (Singapore), 1 December 1931, p. 15.

7   'Death of an Advertising Pioneer', *Straits Times*, 10 September 1965, p. 9.

8   J. Dickenson, *Australian Women in Advertising in the Twentieth Century*, Palgrave Macmillan, Basingstoke, 2016, p. 40.

9   Elma Kelly, interview for Radio Television Hong Kong's 'Time to Remember' programme on 30 June 1968, available at https://mmis.hkpl.gov.hk/.

10 M. H. Anderson, *Madison Avenue in Asia: Politics and Transnational Advertising*, Fairleigh Dickenson, Rutherford, 1984, p. 136.

11 'Shortage of Raw Materials Started Fortune Agency', *Advertising News*, 26 April 1974, p. 24.

12 'Blistering Report Won Account for Fortune', *Advertising News*, 26 April 1974, p. 26.

13 'Agency Round-Up', *B&T*, 25 February 1960, p. 30.

14 'Fortune Plans More Orient Expansion', *B&T*, 21 February 1963, p. 10.

15 'Fortune MD's Overseas Trip', *B&T*, 18 June 1964, p. 26.

16 'Carrying the Australian Ad Flag Across the World with Ken Landell-Jones', *Advertising News*, 12 May 1972, p. 46.

17 'Fortune Fades in Merger', *B&T*, 28 October 1982, p. 8.

18 'Aust. Agency's London Move', *B&T*, 31 March 1963, p. 3.

19 'Jackson Wain's Progress in Asia', *B&T*, 6 October 1966, p. 14.

20 'With LB-JW Acquisition A'cs Swing?', *Advertising & Newspaper News*, 13 November 1970, p. 10.

21 '$6.5 MSA Account goes to McCann Erickson', *Straits Times*, 3 December 1970, p. 5.

22 Dickenson, *Australian Women in Advertising in the Twentieth Century*, p. 45.

23 Elma Kelly, interview for Radio Television Hong Kong's 'Time to Remember' programme on 30 June 1968, available at https://mmis. hkpl.gov.hk/.

24 'Letter from E. Kelly to K. Sherrard, 21 February 1963', K. M. M. Sherrard papers, ca. 1918–1975, Further Papers, 1909–75, with associated papers ca. 1888, 1916–1932, MLMSS 2950 ADD–ON 834 (K48975–K48989) R964, Box K48982, Mitchell Library, State Library of New South Wales.

25 Hamill, personal correspondence with Robert Crawford, 30 May 2013.

26 Geoff Cousins, interview with Robert Crawford, 15 March 2013.

27 *Straits Times*, 18 April 1974, p. 9.

28 '21st Birthday Party', *Singapore Free Press*, 10 September 1949, p. 5.

29 'Changes in Benson's Malaya, HK Companies', *Straits Times*, 15 December 1961, p. 18; DDB Melbourne, *DDB Melbourne: 50 Years in the Making 1945–1995*, Melbourne, DDB Melbourne, 1995, p. 25.

30 'Advertising Firm Offers Training in Australia', *Straits Times*, 22 July 1960, p. 9.

31 'HR-McCE Head Back', *B&T,* 11 March 1965, p. 7.

32 'Australia – the Driving Force in Asian Market', *B&T*, 5 April 1973, p. 12.

33 'Jacklin, Adams Head JWT Push into SE Asia', *B&T*, 3 October 1974, p. 5.

34 'Agencies may Expand into Asian Markets', *Advertising News*, 5 July 1974, p. 4.

35 J. Light, '"It's Good to be Part of the World" – Peter Clemenger', *Advertising News*, 21 November 1980, p. 40.

36 B. Courtenay, *Fortune Cookie*, Viking, Melbourne, 2010, pp. 141–2.

37 'Local Supplements Unchallenged', *Straits Times*, 12 October 1966, p. 12.

38 Neil Lawrence, interview with Robert Crawford, 23 October 2013: Mike Reed, interview with Rosemary Francis, 1 May 2012.

39 S. Gunn, 'The Good Old Days: Memories of the Advertising

Business', *Ad Asia*, 1 January 2004, http://www.adasiaonline.com/2004/01/the-good-old-days/, accessed on 18 November 2015.

40 Wayne Kingston, interviews with Robert Crawford, 30 January and 6 February 2013; Hugh Spencer, interview with Robert Crawford, 3 May 2013.

41 'The Multi-national's Asian Lot', *B&T*, 25 November 1976, p. 28.

42 Michael Ritchie, interview with Robert Crawford, 14 April 2013.

43 Gunn, 'The Good Old Days'.

44 Available at http://cathayadvertisingltdhongkong.blogspot.com.au/2009/09/whole-old-gang-rooftop-princes-building.html, accessed 18 November 2015.

45 K. Roman, *The King of Madison Avenue: David Ogilvy and the Making of Modern Advertising*, Palgrave Macmillan, New York, 2009, p. 144.

46 John Newton, interview with Robert Crawford, 9 April 2013.

47 Cousins, interview.

48 'A New Director for Masters Ltd', *Times Straits*, 13 April 1954, p. 12; 'Advertising has a Big Future He Says', *Straits Times*, 30 September 1955, p. 14; 'Masters Get New Expert', *Straits Times*, 17 December 1957, p. 14; 'Woman Director for Masters', *Straits Times*, 7 February 1958, p. 14; 'Greater Need for Advertising Now', *Straits Times*, 11 September 1959, p. 10.

49 'Carrying the Australian Ad Flag Across the World with Ken Landell-Jones', *Advertising News*, 12 May 1972, p. 46.

50 'Award "first" to Major Local Agency', *Advertising & Newspaper News*, 20 February 1970, p. 10.

51 'Australia – the Driving Force in Asian Market', *B&T*, 5 April 1973, p.12.

52 Willi Schalk, interview with Robert Crawford, 9 March 2013.

53 Ian Dawson, interview with Robert Crawford, 14 December 2012.

54 Russell McLay, interview with Robert Crawford, 13 May 2013.

55 'Australian Admen in the East Working Hard', *B&T*, 13 March 1969, p. 44.

56 Graeme Kinsella, interview with Robert Crawford, 9 January 2013.

57 'Masters Limited', *Sydney Morning Herald*, 8 July 1953, p. 22.

58 Kinsella, interview.

59 Alex Hamill, interview with Robert Crawford, 12 April 2013.

60 Ian Alwill, interview with Robert Crawford, 13 September 2012, 6 January 2013.

61 De Brierley Newton, interview with Robert Crawford, 24 April 2013.

62 Faie Davis, interview with Robert Crawford, 27 February 2013.

63   Suzanne Mercier, interview with Robert Crawford, 7 March 2014.
64   M. Holbech, 'Advertising in Southeast Asia – Hong Kong', *B&T*, 7 October 1976, p. 56.
65   B. Smith, 'Spivs are Alive and Well and Working in KL', *B&T*, 8 November 1985, p. 28.
66   Michael Ball, 'Pitching In', *B&T*, 1 July 1982, p. 19.
67   Cousins, interview.
68   Graham Cox, interview with Robert Crawford, 26 April 2013.
69   Geoff Wild, interview with Robert Crawford, 17 May 2013.
70   Hamill, interview.
71   Kinsella, interview.
72   McLay, interview.
73   Dawson, interview.
74   Ken Done, interview with Robert Crawford, 12 February 2013.)
75   Hamill, interview.
76   Ball, 'Pitching In', p. 19.
77   Dawson, interview.
78   D. Hopkins, 'Developing Markets in Asia', *B&T*, 14 August 1969, p. 18.
79   Cousins, interview.
80   Cousins, interview.
81   R. Hawson, 'Comment from Asia on an Article about Asia', *B&T*, 25 September 1969, p. 32.
82   'JWT Asian Staff here for Study', *B&T*, 6 April 1967, p.13.
83   McLay, interview.
84   Luella Copeland-Smith, interview with Robert Crawford, 15 February 2013: Luella Copeland-Smith papers.
85   'Australia – the Driving Force in Asian Market', *B&T*, 5 April 1973, p. 12.
86   B. Gilchrist, 'Understanding the Asian Market', *Advertising News*, 17 October 1980, p. 64.
87   'The Multi-national's Asian Lot', *B&T*, 25 November 1976, p. 28.

Chapter Four: Embracing Creativity

1   'Playing the Game Straight with Paul Jones', *Advertising in Australia*, supplement to *Advertising News*, 21 August 1970, p. 10.
2   'Agencies Must Involve Creative People in All Activities', *Newspaper News*, 27 October 1967, p. 4.
3   Renny Cunnack, interview with Rosemary Francis, 14 May 2013
4   T. Frank, *The Conquest of Cool: Business Culture, Counterculture, and the*

Rise of Hip Consumerism, University of Chicago Press, Chicago, 1997; K. Blackburn, 'In a Sceptical Age the Prize is Greater Credibility: Honest to Badness Advertising in Australia, Britain and the USA', *Journal of Australian Studies*, vol. 20 no. 50–51, 1996, pp. 78–89.

5   R. Crawford, 'Fighting a Lost Campaign: Austac and Australia's Advertising Industry', *Media History*, vol. 12, no. 1, April 2006, pp.61–76; R. Crawford, '"Anyhow … Where d'yer get it?": Ockerdom in Adland Australia', *Journal of Australian Studies*, no. 90, 2007, pp.1–15, 179–80.

6   'Marriage of Figaro', dir. E. Bianchi, *Mad Men*, Episode 3, Series 1, 2007.

7   'An Aussie Views a US Agency', *Printer's Ink*, 30 November 1962, p. 56.

8   M. Meyer, *Madison Avenue USA*, Penguin, Melbourne, 1961 (1958), p. 138.

9   L. R. Samuel 'Thinking Smaller: Bill Bernbach and the Creative Revolution in Advertising of the 1950s', *Advertising & Society Review*, vol. 13, no. 3, 2012.

10 Frank, *The Conquest of Cool*, p. 54.

11 S. Fox, *The Mirror Makers: A History of American Advertising and Its Creators*, University of Chicago Press, Urbana & Chicago, 1997, p. 270.

12 Blackburn, 'In a Sceptical Age', p. 78.

13 Sean Nixon 'Looking Westwards and Worshipping: The New York "Creative Revolution" and British Advertising, 1956–1980', *Journal of Consumer Culture*, doi:10.1177/1469540515571388, 2015, p. 4.

14 Stephan Schwarzkopf, 'From Fordist to Creative Economies: The de-Americanisation of European Advertising Cultures Since the 1960s', *European Review of History*, vol. 20, no. 5, 2013, p. 866.

15 Cited in Nixon, 'Looking Westwards', p.10.

16 Ibid., p.13.

17 'Factors which Sparked the Creative Revolution in USA', *B&T*, 17 August 1967, p. 3.

18 'Financial Review Jan. 5th', Hansen Rubensohn-McCann Erickson Press Cuttings Scrapbook, unpaginated.

19 'Are Creativity and Off-Beatness Only for the New Advertisers?', *B&T*, 13 May 1965, p. 5.

20 'Bill Farnsworth – the Man and His Views', p. 3.

21 'Agencies Billing over $5 Mill.', *Advertising News*, 5 March 1976, p. 5.

22 Ian Alwill, interview with Robert Crawford, 13 September 2012.

23 W. A. Lockley, 'How to Formulate the Campaign', *B&T*, 6 August 1964, p. 13.

24 'Revolutionary Move by Sydney Agency', *Newspaper News*, 24 January 1964, p. 4.

25 M. Tungate, *Adland: A Global History of Advertising*, Kogan Page, London & Philadelphia, 2007, p. 52.

26 D. Ayliffe & J. Ayliffe, *My Brother's Eyes: The True Story of Surviving 16 Years in a Destructive Cult*, John Garatt Publishing, Melbourne, 2009, p. 68.

27 Cited in R. R. Walker, *Communicators: People Practices, Philosophies in Australian Advertising, Media, Marketing,* Lansdowne Press, Melbourne, 1967, pp. 68–9.

28 'Revolutionary Move by Sydney Agency', *Newspaper News*, 24 January 1964, p. 4.

29 Mike Strauss, interview with Rosemary Francis, 4 September 2012.

30 'Singleton to Set Up Own Shop', *Newspaper News*, 13 September 1968, p. 1.

31 B. Parsons & P. Rogers, 'SPASM Exposes Itself', *B&T,* 27 November 1975, p. 18.

32 K. S. Inglis, *This is the ABC: The Australian Broadcasting Commission 1932–1983*, Black Inc, Melbourne, 2006 (1983), p. 226.

33 G. Stone, *Singo: Mates, Wives Triumphs, Disasters*, Harper, Sydney, 2003, p. 30.

34 *Not so Much Hustle as a Way of Life*, dir., Geoffrey Barnes ABC National Television, c.1972.

35 J. Bristow, *How to get Sense out of the Advertising Dollar,* John Bristow, Sydney, 1971, p. 163.

36 Lionel Hunt, interview with Robert Crawford, 22 January 2013.

37 Hunt, interview.

38 Ibid.

39 Ibid.

40 'Is Advertising a Young Man's Game?', *B&T,* 27 June 1968, p. 13.

41 Ibid.

42 'From Grizzly-Man to Advertising Consultant', *Advertising News*, 7 June 1974, p. 6.

43 D. Farrow, 'Why I left McCann', *B&T,* 27 September 1979, p. 32.

44 Robin Stewart, interview with Rosemary Francis, 5 April 2013; Ric Otton, interview with Rosemary Francis, 21 August 2012.

45 'Playing the Game Straight with Paul Jones', *Advertising News* (Advertising in Australia Supplement), 21 August 1970, pp. 10–11.

46 Lionel Hunt, interview with Robert Crawford, 22 January 2013.

47 Mike Strauss, interview with Rosemary Francis, 4 September 2012.

48 Derek Hansen, interview with Robert Crawford, 26 April 2013.

49 Ron Mather, interview with Rosemary Francis, 17 December 2012.

50 J. Singleton, *True Confessions*, Cassell Australia, Stanmore, 1979, p. 35.

51 Ibid.

52 Hunt interview.

53 'Palace Restoration', *Architecture Australia*, October/November, 1979,
    p. 38.

54 Hunt, interview.

55 J. Hawkins, 'How to Kill It, How to Keep It', *B&T*, 12 October 1984,
    p. 39.

56 S. Nixon, 'Looking Westwards and Worshipping: The New York
    "Creative Revolution" and British Advertising, 1956–1980', *Journal of
    Consumer Culture*, doi:10.1177/1469540515571388, 2015, p. 13.:Chris
    Martin Murphy, interview with Robert Crawford, 8 March 2013.

57 Hunt, interview.

58 Doug Watson, interview with Robert Crawford, 19 April 2013.

59 Paul Priday, interview with Robert Crawford, 23 January 2013.

60 'John Sharman: Lion in Winter of Adland's Discontent?', *Advertising
    News*, 23 July 1971, p. 13.

61 Derek Hansen, interview with Robert Crawford, 26 April 2013.

62 Dennis Merchant, interview with Robert Crawford, 15 March 2013.

63 D. Merchant, *Media Man: The Life and Times of Dennis Merchant OAM*,
    Dennis Merchant, Sydney, 2013, p. 70.

64 Ibid., p.71.

65 Harold Mitchell, *Living Large: The World of Harold Mitchell*, Melbourne
    University Press, Carlton, Vic., 2009, pp. 32–3.

66 Harold Mitchell, interview with Rosemary Francis, 20 November 2012.

67 Alan Robertson, interview with Robert Crawford, 23
    November 2012.

68 'Agency's Creative Quality will be Vital in the Future', *Newspaper
    News*, 22 June 1962, p. 2.

69 *JWT: The People*, Sydney, J. Walter Thompson, c.1972, unpaginated.

70 'Reorganisation at JWT', *B&T*, 5 October 1967, p. 6.

71 'Top Creative Man for JWT', *Newspaper News*, 10 May 1968, p.1:
    'Straight to the Point with Denis Everingham', *Advertising and
    Newspaper News*, 18 February 1972, p. 6: See J. Singleton, 'Will
    Rumours kill Denis Everingham', *Advertising and Newspaper News*, 8
    August 1969, p. 6.

72 'John Sharman', p. 13.
73 Geoff Wild, interview with Robert Crawford, 1 May 2013.
74 Ibid.
75 'Agencies Billing over $5 Million', *Advertising & Newspaper News*, 11 June, 1971, p. 7; 'Agencies Billing over $5 Mill.', *Advertising News*, 5 March 1976, p. 6.
76 'Changing Your Agency', *B&T*, 8 May 1975, pp. 14–18.
77 I. Nankervis, 'An Ugly Picture Needs a Thousand Words', *Advertising News*, 26 September 1980, p. 27.
78 Bruce Jarrett, interview with Robert Crawford, 5 April 2013.
79 Mike Ellis, interview with Rosemary Francis, 14 August 2012.
80 John Newton, interview with Robert Crawford, 9 April 2013.
81 Wild, interview.
82 See Crawford, '"Anyhow … Where d'yer get it?"'.

Chapter Five: Taking on the World
1 Greg Daniel, interview with Robert Crawford, 8 February 2013.
2 Ibid.
3 'Sydney's Top 50', *Ad News*, 7 March 1986, p. 36.
4 'JWT's 50th Anniversary', *Advertising News*, 15 February 1980, p. 3.
5 D. Robertson, 'Memo to All JWT-Australia Employees', 17 October 1977, Alun Jones Papers 1930–1984, Box 8, Australia 1978, J Walter Thompson Duke University, USA.
6 D. Robertson, 'Acquisitions Strategy of JWT-Australia', 10 July 1979, Alun Jones Papers 1930–1984, Box 8, Australia 1978, J Walter Thompson Duke University, USA.
7 D. Robertson, 'Acquisitions', 11 July 1979, Alun Jones Papers 1930–1984, Box 8, Australia 1978, J Walter Thompson Duke University, USA.
8 D. Robertson, 'Notes on Melbourne as our No.1 Acquisition Priority', Alun Jones Papers 1930–1984, Box 8, Australia 1978, J Walter Thompson Duke University, USA.
9 Begg Dow Priday, 'A Report on Agency Background & Financial Performance', 30 October 1979, Alun Jones Papers 1930–1984, Box 8, Australia 1978, J Walter Thompson Duke University, USA.
10 G. Reilly, 'Begg Dow Priday Pty Ltd', 6 December 1979, Alun Jones Papers 1930–1984, Box 8, Australia 1978, J Walter Thompson Duke University, USA.
11 G. Reilly, 'Strictly Confidential', 8 January 1980, Alun Jones Papers 1930–1984, Box 8, Australia 1978, J Walter Thompson Duke University, USA.

12 J. Light, 'BDP May be Part New JWT Network', *Ad News*, 1 August 1980, p. 2.

13 Austin Begg, interview with Rosemary Francis, 15 August 2013.

14 See R. Morgan, *J. Walter Takeover: From Divine Right to Common Stock*, Business One Irwin, Homewood, Ill., 1991.

15 T. Levitt, 'The Globalization of Markets', *Harvard Business Review*, vol. 61, May–June 1983, p. 92.

16 Ibid., p.93

17 Ibid., p.102

18 I. Fallon, *The Brothers: The Rise & Rise of Saatchi & Saatchi*, Hutchinson, London, 1988, pp. 202–4.

19 K. Goldman, *Conflicting Accounts: The Creation and Crash of the Saatchi & Saatchi Advertising Empire*, Touchstone, New York, 1998, pp. 37.

20 'Fallon, *The Brothers*', p.200.

21 'Goldman, *Conflicting Accounts*', p. 40.

22 'The Implications of the Patterson Agency's Far Eastern Expansion', *B&T*, 14 February 1963, p. 3.

23 J. Hawkins, 'Compton Pulls Out of Sydney', *B&T*, 8 October 1981, p. 1.

24 Mike Satterthwaite, interview with Robert Crawford, 13 September 2012; Ron Mather, interview with Rosemary Francis, 17 December 2012.

25 Satterthwaite, interview.

26 'Goldman, *Conflicting Accounts*', p. 67.

27 'Fallon, *The Brothers*', p. 216.

28 Satterthwaite interview.

29 L. Wright, 'Saatchi Melbourne Calls in London Creatives', *B&T*, 11 October 1985, p. 3.

30 D. Browne, 'Saatchi Tends to Take it into Accounts', *B&T*, 31 January 1986, p. 15.

31 Satterthwaite, interview.

32 Ibid.

33 M. O'Meara, 'Legal Move by Broadcasting Tribunal after Court Ruling on TV Adverts', *Sydney Morning Herald*, 27 November 1984, p. 17.

34 R. Crawford, *But Wait, There's More… : A History of Australian Advertising, 1900–2000*, Melbourne University Press, Carlton, Vic., pp. 239–41.

35 R. Burbury, 'How Saatchi Views Australia', *B&T*, 15 January 1988, p. 21.

36 Ibid.

37 M. Tungate, *Ad Land: A Global History of Advertising*, Kogan Page, London and Philadelphia, 2007, p.166.

38 L. Wright, 'Saatchi Bites off Bates to Straddle the Globe', *B&T*, 16 May 1986, p. 3.

39 P. Rogers, 'Patterson's Palace Coup', 14 April 1983, p. 1.

40 Geoff Cousins, interview with Robert Crawford, 15 March 2013.

41 Hunt interview.

42 'Monolith or Tea Cosy', *B&T*, 9 November 1984, p. 52.

43 D. Browne, 'Why Geoff Cousins isn't Geoff Saatchi', *B&T*, 11 December 1987, p. 54.

44 Cousins interview; Hunt interview.

45 Cousins interview.

46 'Naked Ambition fuels Saatchi's Rise to the Top', *B&T*, 16 May 1986, p. 8.

47 Bruce Jarrett, interview with Robert Crawford, 5 April 2013.

48 Alex Hamill, interview with Robert Crawford, 12 April 2013.

49 Willi Schalk, interview with Robert Crawford, 9 March 2013.

50 T. Hewat with P. Rankin, *First Fifty Years: Clemenger 1946–1996*, Clemenger BBDO, Melbourne, 1996, p. 57.

51 Peter Clemenger, interview with Rosemary Francis, 22 August 2012.

52 Geoff Wild, interview with Robert Crawford, 1 May 2013.

53 Hewat, *First Fifty Years*, p. 54.

54 'Agencies may Expand into Asian Markets', *Advertising News*, 5 July 1974, p. 5.

55 Wild, interview.

56 Tsang Tsu Yin, 'Giant US Agency Takes State in Batey Ads', *Business Times*, 11 April 1979, p. 1.

57 Schalk, interview.

58 Daniel, interview.

59 Wild, interview.

60 Ibid.

61 Cited in A. Coombes, *Adland: A True Story of Corporate Drama*, William Heinemann, Melbourne, 1990, p. 72.

62 'The Surprising Alchemy of MDA', *B&T*, 14 December 1984, p. 4.

63 Malcolm Spry, interview with Robert Crawford, 24 February 2013.

64 David Mason, 'MDA Milestone', *B&T*, 2 November 1984, p. 1.

65 C. Dwyer, 'Masius backs Breakaways', *B&T*, 9 October 1980, p. 1.

66 Rob Palmer, interview with Robert Crawford, 23 November 2012.

67 'Jo's Fingers are Hurtin' Again', *Ad News: The Legends of Advertising,*

1928–1998, 30 October 1998, pp. 76–7; Coombes, *Adland*, pp. 10, 46.

68 Ian Dawon, interview with Robert Crawford, 10 January 2013.

69 'Coombs, *Adland*.' p.2.

70 John Wright, interview with Robert Crawford, 16 January 2013.

71 Ibid., p.57.

72 Wayne Kingston, interview with Robert Crawford, 6 February 2013.

73 Amanda Moody, personal correspondence to Robert Crawford, 15 June 2013.

74 Julian Martin, interview with Robert Crawford, 23 April 2013.

75 'Coombs, *Adland*,' pp. 65–7.

76 Kingston, interview.

77 D. Housham, 'An Ocker Invasion – A New Look for Advertising', *The Times*, 26 August 1987; 'Bonzer Aussie Woos Poms', *Campaign*, 21 August 1987, p. 18.

78 S. Bannah, 'They're Just Ads: Greville Patterson's Life in Advertising', edited transcripts of interviews with Greville Patterson (20/1198, 27/11/98, 16/3/99), Department of History, University of Queensland, 1999.

79 Kingston, interview.

80 Steve Gray, interview with Robert Crawford, 19 August 2013.

81 R. Kelly, 'Sharp Apple of Chiat's Eye', *B&T*, 15 December 1989, p.18.

Chapter Six: Getting Started

1 Doug Watson, interview with Robert Crawford, 19 April 2013; Alex Hamill describes walking across the Harbour Bridge to save the sixpence, Alex Hamill, interview with Robert Crawford, 12 April 2013; by 1971 the boys were saving 20 cents, John Wright, interview with Robert Crawford, 16 January 2013; this happened in Melbourne, too, Mike Reed, interview with Rosemary Francis, 1 May 2012.

2 John Bevins, interview with Robert Crawford, 10 May 2013; between 1933 and 1946, 190 men and just 15 women passed the Advertising Association exams.

3 Hamill, interview.

4 Advertising Association of Australia, *A Career in an Advertising Agency*, Harbour Press, Sydney, 1955, p. 22; Luella Copeland-Smith, interview with Robert Crawford, 15 February 2013; Tom McFarlane, interview with Robert Crawford, 11 April 2013.

5 Tom McFarlane's sister helped him write letters to 'all the agencies', McFarlane, interview; John Steedman was advised by a friend to write letters to advertising agencies, John Steedman interview with Robert

Crawford, 30 January 2013.

6   *Argus*, 9 January 1957, p. 14; Graham Cox, interview with Robert Crawford, 26 April 2013.

7   Guy Saunders, *Careers in Advertising*, MacMillan, Melbourne, 1968, p. 22, The booklet was produced with the involvement of the Advertising Association of Australia (AAA), pp. 45–9.

8   Derek Hansen, interview with Robert Crawford, 26 April 2013.

9   Dennis Merchant, interview with Robert Crawford, 15 March 2013.

10 John Cowper, interview with Robert Crawford, 24 January 2013.

11 Rod Blakeney, interview with Rosemary Francis, 13 May 2014, 10 June 2014.

12 Reg Bryson, interview with Robert Crawford, 11 February 2013.

13 Hamill, interview.

14 Peter Charlton, interview with Robert Crawford, 11 February 2013.

15 Colin Fraser, interview with Rosemary Francis, 31 May 2013; Greg Graham, interview with Robert Crawford, 30 January 2013.

16 Malcolm Spry, interview with Robert Crawford, 24 February 2013.

17 Keith Aldrich, interview with Rosemary Francis, 15 June 2012.

18 Ron Mather, interview with Rosemary Francis, 17 December 2012.

19 Robin Stewart, interview with Rosemary Francis, 5 April 2013, 26 April 2013.

20 Neil Lawrence, interview with Robert Crawford, 23 October 2013.

21 Rod Bennett, interviews with Rosemary Francis, 21 May 2013, 4 June 2013; Bill Shannon, interviews with Rosemary Francis, 29 October 2012, 14 November 2012.

22 Michael Ball, interviews with Rosemary Francis, 13 March 2013, 3 June 2013; Geoff Cousins, interview with Robert Crawford, 15 March 2013; John Box, interview with Rosemary Francis, 6 July 2012; Spry, interview; Hugh Spencer, interview with Robert Crawford, 3 May 2013.

23 Chris Martin Murphy, interview with Robert Crawford, 8 March 2013.

24 G. Kerr, D. Waller & C. Patti 'Advertising Education in Australia: Looking Back to the Future', *Journal of Marketing Education*, vol. 31, no. 3, 2009, pp. 264–74; R.B. Ellis and D.S. Waller, 'Marketing Education in Australia Before 1965', *Australasian Marketing Journal*, vol. 19, no. 4, 2011, pp. 115–21; 'Personalities', *Sunday Times*, 10 July 1938, p. 9.

25 'University Graduates and Industry', *News*, 8 April 1925, p. 6.

26 'Advertising as a Career', *Cumberland Argus*, 13 October 1930, p. 4.

27 The Association of Australian Advertising Agencies (4As) was formed

in March 1946: 'Saunders, *Careers in Advertising*,' p. 45.

28 'Meeting the Crisis in Agency Manpower', *Advertising*, December 1960, pp. 16–17, 45.

29 'Speaking Frankly: The Growing Need for Advertising Training', *Advertising*, May 1959, p. 4; 'How to Train Young Employees', *Advertising*, April 1959, p. 14.

30 'Speaking Frankly', *Advertising*, p. 4.

31 http://www.unsw.edu.au/about-us/university/history, accessed 11 March 2016.

32 Saunders, *Careers in Advertising*, p. 49.

33 John Wright, interview with Robert Crawford, 16 January 2013; Hamill, interview; Rob Palmer, interview with Robert Crawford, 23 November 2012; Alan Robertson, interview with Robert Crawford, 23 November 2012.

34 Dennis Merchant, interview with Robert Crawford, 15 March 2013; Helen Tudehope, *Sunday Times*, 11 September 1927, p. 20; *Evening News*, 18 August 1930, p. 9.

35 Ian McDonald, interview with Robert Crawford, 18 January 2013. http://www.powmemorialballarat.com.au/world-war-2-s-v.php, accessed 16 December 2016.

36 Renny Cunnack, interview with Rosemary Francis, 14 May 2013.

37 Ian Alwill, interview with Robert Crawford, 13 September 2012.

38 J. Raphaelson (ed.) *The People Book: Ogilvy & Mather Guidelines on How to Attract the Best People and Lead Them to do Their Best*, Ogilvy & Mather Worldwide, New York, 1985, pp. 9–13.

39 Michael Ritchie, interview by Robert Crawford, 14 April 2013.

40 Dickenson, *Australian Women in Advertising in the Twentieth Century*.

41 Marion von Adlerstein, interview with Robert Crawford, 14 December 2012; Suzie Otten, interviews with Rosemary Francis, 28 May 2013, 25 June 2013.

42 Esther Clerehan, interview with Robert Crawford, 4 February 2013.

43 June McCallum, interview with Rosemary Francis, 5 March 2013.

44 Stephanie Borland, interview with Rosemary Francis, 23 April 2013.

45 Marie Jackson, interview with Rosemary Francis, 30 April 2013.

46 Rosem'ry Bertel, interview with Rosemary Francis, 27 April 2012.

47 Faie Davis, interview with Robert Crawford, 27 February 2013.

48 Jane Caro, interview with Robert Crawford, 5 February 2013.

49 Dickenson, *Australian Women in Advertising*, pp. 19–20.

50 Wright, interview.

51 *A Career*, pp. 14–15, 17.

52 John Cowper, interview with Robert Crawford, 24 January 2013.

53 Cowper, interview; Hamill, interview.

54 Otto Kleppner, *Advertising Procedure*, Prentice-Hall, New York, 1925.

55 Andrew Killey, interview with Robert Crawford, 13 December 2013.

56 John Newton, interview with Robert Crawford, 9 April 2013.

57 For example, Reg Bryson, interview with Robert Crawford, 11 February 2013.

58 C. B. Higginson, 'The Status of Advertising Men', *Ink*, December 1926, pp. 21–6.

59 'Teach Advertising', *Cairns Post*, 5 April 1924, p.11; 'Federal Education Board', *Ink*, February 1925, pp. 18–21.

60 'Advertising Association: Education Board, Annual Examinations', *Mercury*, 21 May 1936, p. 11; 'Advertising Education Board', *Sydney Morning Herald*, 10 March 1939, p. 10; 'Advertising Education Board Examinations', *Advertiser*, 6 July 1940, p. 8; 'Benefits of Advertising', *Western Star and Roma Advertiser*, 5 July 1933, p. 1; 'Advertising Education', *West Australian*, 14 March 1935, p. 14.

61 'Teach Advertising', *Cairns Post*, 5 April 1924, p. 11.

62 'Book Reviews: Psychology and Business', *West Australian*, 26 September 1931, p. 4.

63 Michael Anderson, interview with Rosemary Francis, 26 October 2012; Von Adlerstein, interview; Rod Blakeney, interviews with Rosemary Francis, 13 May 2014, 10 June 2014.

64 'Commercial Art: Importance in Advertising', *Argus*, 12 December 1928, p. 16; 'Versatile Artist: Mr Harry Julius', *Mercury*, 2 December 1929, p. 5; 'Commercial Art', *Argus*, 26 March 1930, p. 15; 'Metropolitan Advertising Agencies', *Cootamundra Herald*, 23 March 1949, p. 3; John Brennan, 'Australia's Artists Owed this Man a Debt', *Sunday Herald*, 21 May 1950, p.10; Peter Spearitt, 'Northfield, Isaac James (1887–1973), *Australian Dictionary of Biography*, National Centre of Biography, Australian National University, adb.anu.edu.au/biography/northfield-isaac-james-11259/text20083, accessed online 18 September 2014; Art Training Institute, *Prospectus*, The Art Training Institute, Melbourne, 1950.

65 *Fox Art Academy: Fine and Commercial*, 8pp booklet, circa late 1930s? [Fox Art Academy: Australian Gallery File] State Library of Victoria; 'Melrose Theatre', *The Daily News*, 30 December 1914, p. 3; 'New Turns at the National', *Evening News*, 30 April 1915, p. 8; 'Advertise All Times: American Business Slogan', *Cairns Post*, 6 May 1935, p. 10;

'Work of Students', *Argus*, 24 May 1938, p. 13; 'Art in Advertising', *Argus*, 29 July 1938, p.15.

66   Graham Cox, interview with Robert Crawford, 26 April 2013; Greg Daniel, interview with Robert Crawford, 8 February 2013; Leigh McLaughlin, 'Political Ads: A Capitalistic Evil or a Basic Freedom?', *Ad News*, vol. 2, December 1988, p. 2.

67   Sue Johnson, 'Advertising's Reluctant Woman of Firsts', *Sydney Morning Herald*, 17 September 1986, p. 15; 'King Moves Up-market to Vuitton', *Sydney Morning Herald*, 23 November 1989, p. 32.

68   Jackson, interview.

69   Esther Clerehan, interview with Robert Crawford, 4 February 2013.

Chapter Seven: Keeping Clients Happy

1   E. Nussbaum, 'Joan's Decision', *New Yorker*, 29 May 2010, http://www.newyorker.com/culture/culture-desk/joans-decision.

2   Luella Copeland-Smith, interview with Robert Crawford, 11 December 2013.

3   Graeme Kinsella, interview with Robert Crawford, 9 January 2013.

4   Eugene Catanzariti, interview with Rosemary Francis, 18 January 2013.

5   Wayne Kingston, interview with Robert Crawford, 30 January 2013.

6   Michael Anderson, interview with Rosemary Francis, 26 October 2012.

7   Graham Nunn, interview with Robert Crawford, 21 May 2013.

8   Catanzariti, interview.

9   Ric Otton, interview with Rosemary Francis, 21 August 2012.

10   Kevin Luscombe, 'Strategy is King', undated, Supplementary Material, Box 25, Barry Banks Blakeney Archive.

11   Kingston, interview.

12   Renny Cunnack, interview with Rosemary Francis, 14 May 2013.

13   Alex Hamill, interview with Robert Crawford, 12 April 2013.

14   Graham Cox, interview with Robert Crawford, 26 April 2013.

15   Colin Fraser, interview with Rosemary Francis, 31 May 2013.

16   John Cowper, interview with Robert Crawford, 24 January 2013.

17   Fraser, interview.

18   Mike Strauss, interviews with Rosemary Francis, 4 September 2012, 13 November 2012.

19   Suzie Otten, interview with Rosemary Francis, 28 May 2013.

20   Peter Clemenger, interview with Rosemary Francis, 22 August 2012.

21   John Wright, interview with Robert Crawford, 16 January 2013.

22 Kinsella, interview.
23 Hamill, interview.
24 Otton, interview.
25 Marie Jackson, interview with Rosemary Francis, 30 April 2013.
26 Ogilvy & Mather 'Performance Appraisal and Development Plan: Account Director', 2 September 1988, Supplement, Box 25, BBB Archive.
27 Wright, interview.
28 Cowper, interview.
29 Tania Farrelly, interview with Rosemary Francis, 23 July 2013; Jane Mara, interview with Robert Crawford, 7 March 2013.
30 Ian Strachan, interview with Rosemary Francis, 9 April 2013.
31 K. Roman and J. Raphaelson, *How to Write Better: The Ogilvy & Mather Guide to Writing Effective Memos, Letters, Reports, Plans and Strategies*, Ogilvy & Mather Incorporated, New York, 1978; J. Raphaelson (ed.), *The People Book: Ogilvy & Mather Guidelines on How to Attract the Best People and Lead Them to do Their Best*, Ogilvy & Mather Worldwide, New York, 1985.
32 Otten, interview.
33 Wright, interview.
34 Cox, interview.
35 Otton, interview.
36 Fraser, interview.
37 Toni Lawler, interview with Rosemary Francis, 25 May 2013.
38 Otten, interview.
39 Strachan, interview.
40 Ogilvy & Mather 'Performance Appraisal', Supplementary Material, Box 25, BBB Archive.
41 Marie Jackson, interview with Rosemary Francis, 30 April 2013.
42 Kinsella, interview.
43 Peter Clemenger, interview with Rosemary Francis, 22 August 2012.
44 Toni Lawler, interview with Rosemary Francis, 25 March 2013.
45 Anderson, interview.
46 Cowper, interview.
47 Fraser, interview; Lawler, interview.
48 Cox, interview; Anderson interview.
49 'What Makes a Top-class Ad Manager?', *Advertising in Australia* (supplement to *Newspaper News*), 13 May 1966, pp. 6–7.
50 Cox, interview.
51 'The New Professor of Marketing at the University of New South

Wales, Roger Layton', *Advertising in Australia* (supplement to *Newspaper News*), 12 May 1967, pp.19–21.

52 Kinsella, interview; Alwill, interview.

53 Otten, interview.

54 Clemenger, interview.

55 Mo Fox, interview with Robert Crawford, 11 September 2012.

56 Ibid.

57 Michael Anderson, interview with Rosemary Francis, 26 October 2012.

58 Julian Martin, interview with Robert Crawford, 23 April 2013.

59 Kingston, interview; Cunnack, interview.

60 'We Need the Creative Freedom that Comes from Tightly-defined Strategies', Ogilvy & Mather Australia, internal document, c. 1986. p. 1.

61 Cunnack, interview; 'What is Values Segmentation', Ogilvy & Mather/Roy Morgan document, undated, Supplementary Material, Box 25 BBB Archive.

62 Jackson, interview.

63 Wright, interview.

64 Reg Bryson, interview with Robert Crawford, 11 February 2013.

65 R. Langtry, 'Strategic Planning: It's the Discipline of the Year', *B&T Weekly,* 13 December 1985, p. 12; 'Account Planning's not Just a Clever Ruse', *B&T Weekly*, 17 January 1986, p. 25; L. Wright, 'All Aboard the Planning Wagon!', *B&T Weekly*, 24 January 1986, pp. 14, 39; 'USP Pushing Planning for Clients that Need It', *B&T Weekly*, 28 March 1986, p. 4; D. Browne, 'How Planners Can Back Ideas with Personality', *B&T Weekly*, 25 July 1986, p. 14.

66 Kevin Luscombe, 'Strategy is King'.

67 Kevin Luscombe, interview with Rosemary Francis, 28 November 2012.

68 Eugene Catanzariti, interview with Rosemary Francis, 18 January 2013.

69 Cunnack, interview.

70 Laura Henschke, interview with Robert Crawford, 1 February 2013

71 Laura Henschke, interview with Robert Crawford, 1 February 2013.

72 Kinsella, interview.

73 Tania Farrelly, interview with Rosemary Francis, 23 July 2013.

74 www.youtube.com/watch?v=vHJxL8h1PSA, accessed 18 September 2014.

75 Ogilvy & Mather Australia, internal document, c. 1986, p. 1, Box 25,

BBB Archive.

76 Otton, interview.

77 Lawler, interview.

78 Cunnack, interview.

79 Kinsella, interview; Strachan, interview.

Chapter Eight: Ruling the Roost

1 Tania Farrelly, interview with Rosemary Francis, 23 July 2013.

2 Andrew Killey, interview with Robert Crawford, 13 December 2013; Marie Jackson, interview with Rosemary Francis, 30 April 2013.

3 'The Penalty of Leadership', *Saturday Evening Post*, 2 January 1915.

4 Claude C. Hopkins, *Scientific Advertising*, 1923: http://www.warc.com/Blogs/Advertising_Science_or_art.blog?ID=1603, accessed 19 December 2015.

5 L. T. Phillips, *Ink*, December 1926, p. 30.

6 'Advertising: its Function and its History', 'Advertising is Printed Salesmanship', *Ink*, September 1928, p. 13.

7 Guy Saunders, *Careers in Advertising*, Melbourne, Macmillan, 1968, p. 2.

8 Rosem'ry Bertel, interview with Rosemary Francis, 27 April 2012.

9 Hugh Spencer, interview with Robert Crawford, 3 May 2013; Rod Bennett, interviews with Rosemary Francis, 21 May 2013, 4 June 2013.

10 Spencer, interview.

11 John Newton, interview with Robert Crawford, 9 April 2013.

12 Rod Bennett, interview; Spencer, interview.

13 Carl Andrew, interview with Jackie Dickenson, 27 September 2013.

14 Ray Black, interview with Robert Crawford, 15 February 2013.

15 'Youthful Confidence and Faith in the Future Led to Success', *Advertising: The Magazine of Marketing*, June 1960, p. 8.

16 Robin Stewart, interviews with Rosemary Francis, 5 April 2013, 26 April 2013.

17 Killey, interview.

18 Black, interview.

19 Peter Carey, interview with Jackie Dickenson, 13 June 2013.

20 Bertel, interview.

21 Graham Nunn, interview with Robert Crawford, 21 April 2013.

22 William Bernbach, *Bill Bernbach's Book: A History of Advertising That Changed the History of Advertising*, 1987.

23 William Bernbach, 'Facts are Not Enough', paper from 1980 Annual

Meeting of American Association of Advertising Agencies, 14–17
May 1980, p. 2, Other Advertising Agencies and Personnel, Box 25,
Supplement No. 2, Barry Banks Blakeney (BBB) Archive.

24 Bernbach, 'Facts', pp. 2, 4, 12, 13.
25 Ken Done, interview with Robert Crawford, 12 February 2013.
26 Jackson, interview; Farrelly, interview; Bennett, interview: Bennett
    calls advertising 'the make up department of business'.
27 'The Ad-writer's Frustrations: How Does the Writer View His
    Relationships with Other Associates on an Advertising Agency's
    Staff?', *Advertising in Australia*, Supplement to *Newspaper News*, 19
    February 1965, p. 28.
28 Terry Blake, 'What Makes a Top-class Copywriter?', *Advertising in
    Australia*, Supplement to *Newspaper News*, 27 November 1964, p. 23.
29 'The Ad-writer's Frustrations', p. 29.
30 Fysh Rutherford, interview with Rosemary Francis, 11
    December 2012.
31 Stephanie Borland, interview with Rosemary Francis, 23 April 2013.
32 Keith Aldrich, interview with Rosemary Francis, 15 June 2012; David
    Mattingly, the principal of the agency that handled the Don account,
    is also proud of the 'Is Don. Is Good' campaign, interview with
    Rosemary Francis, 17 September 2013.
33 Carey, interview; Stewart, interview.
34 'Newsmakers', *B&T*, 18 August 1969, p. 8; 'Newsmakers', *B&T*, 14
    December 1972, p. 14; 'Newsmakers', *B&T*, 5 April 1973, p. 33.
35 Bertel, interview.
36 'Newsmakers', *B&T*, 7 May 1970, p. 8.
37 Graeme Kinsella, interview with Robert Crawford, 10 January 2013.
38 Rutherford, interview.
39 Ibid.
40 Neil Lawrence, interview with Robert Crawford, 23 October 2013;
    Mike Reed, interview with Rosemary Francis, 1 May 2012.
41 Ric Otton, interview with Rosemary Francis, 21 August 2012.
42 Ron Mather, interview with Rosemary Francis, 17 December 2012.
43 Aldrich, interview.
44 Mike Strauss, interviews with Rosemary Francis, 4 September 2012,
    13 November 2012.
45 Rutherford, interview.
46 Doug Watson, interview with Robert Crawford, 24 September 2014.
47 Rutherford, interview.
48 Kinsella, interview; Mike Ellis interview with Rosemary Francis, 14

August 2012; Lawrence, interview.

49 Lawrence, interview.

50 Michael Anderson, interview with Rosemary Francis, 26 October 2012.

51 Ian Strachan, interview with Rosemary Francis, 9 April 2013.

52 Marie Jackson, interview with Rosemary Francis, 30 April 2013.

53 O&M Account Director Appraisal 1988 form, Supplementary Box 25, BBB Archive.

54 Borland, interview.

55 Jackson, interview.

56 Newton, interview.

57 Paddy Stitt, interviews with Rosemary Francis, 15 June 2012, 17 July 2012.

58 John Steedman, interview with Robert Crawford, 30 January 2013.

59 Watson, interview.

60 *Advertising; the Magazine of Marketing*, June 1959, p. 16; Blake, 'What Makes a Top-class Copywriter', p. 23.

61 Bennett, interview.

62 Allan Hartley, interview with Robert Crawford, 26 November 2013

63 'The Plan's the Thing', *Ink*, April 1926, p. 20; 'The Perfect Table for Copywriters', *Ink*, April 1926, p. 22; 'A Two Minute Lesson in Copywriting', *Ink*, December 1926, p. 13.

64 Lloyd Bassett, interview with Robert Crawford, 5 March 2013.

65 Valwyn Wishart, interview with Jackie Dickenson, 27 November 2014.

66 Bill Shannon, interview with Rosemary Francis, 31 October 2012.

67 Faie Davis, interview with Robert Crawford, 27 February 2013.

68 Watson, interview.

69 Two 'art directors' arrived in Australia in 1966 and 11 in 1967: 'Newsmakers', *B&T*.

70 Black, interview.

71 Done, interview,

72 Killey, interview.

73 Jack Room, interview with Rosemary Francis, 27 May 2013.

74 Newton, interview

75 Bertel, interview.

76 Newton, interview

77 Bertel, interview.

78 Aldrich, interview.

79 Newton, interview.

80 Rutherford, interview.

81 Done, interview.

82 Aldrich, interview.

Chapter Nine: Supporting the 'Stars'

1 Mike Reed, interview with Rosemary Francis, 1 May 2012.

2 Ibid.

3 Peter Rankin, interview with Rosemary Francis, 19 August 2014;
   Greg McIntyre, interview with Rosemary Francis, 9 September
   2014; '"Too Old at 35", Agencies Tell Job Seekers', *B&T*, 1 October
   1970, p. 6; D. Light, 'The Headhunters', *Advertising News*, 13 May
   1977, p. 14; 'Short of Talent Getting Worse', *B&T*, 15 February 1979,
   pp. 34, 39.

4 Neil Lawrence, interview with Robert Crawford, 23 October 2013.

5 Esther Clerehan, interview with Robert Crawford, 4 February 2013.

6 R. R. Walker, *Communicators: People, Practices, Philosophies in Australian
   Advertising, Media and Marketing*, Melbourne: Lansdowne Press, 1967,
   p. 132; Crawford, *But Wait There's More*, pp. 73–4.

7 Robert Crawford, 'More than Froth and Bubble: Marketing in
   Australia, 1788–1969' in Brian Jones & Mark Tadjewski (eds.), The
   Routledge Companion to Marketing History, Abingdon, Routledge,
   2016, pp.297–314.

8 Walker, *Communicators*, p. 144; Rankin, interview.

9 Stollznow, interview.

10 Greg Graham, interview with Robert Crawford, 30 January 2013.

11 Margaret Boston (Lady Boston of Faversham), interview with
   Rosemary Francis, 22 September 2014.

12 Malcolm Spry, interview with Robert Crawford, 24 February 2013.

13 Paul Gaskin, interview with Rosemary Francis, 10 September 2014.

14 Ian Alwill, interview with Robert Crawford, 13 September 2012.

15 'Newsmakers', *B&T*, 29 April 1971, p. 10.

16 Gaskin, interview; 'Planner for JWT', *B&T*, 26 May 1983, p. 4;
   'Strategic Planning: It's the Discipline of the Year', *B&T Weekly*, 13
   December 1985, p. 12.

17 Walker, *Communicators*, p. 183.

18 Ian McDonald, interview with Robert Crawford, 18 January 2013;
   David Mattingly still considers media the 'most boring' department,
   interview with Rosemary Francis, 17 September 2013.

19 Dennis Merchant, interview with Robert Crawford, 15 March 2013;
   John Steedman, interview with Robert Crawford, 30 January 2013.

20 Gaskin, interview.

21 Ric Otton, interview with Rosemary Francis, 21 August 2012.

22 McDonald, interview.

23 Harold Mitchell, *Living Large: The World of Harold Mitchell*, Melbourne University Press, Carlton, Vic., 2009, p. 32.

24 Walker, *Communicators*, pp. 255–9.

25 McDonald, interview.

26 McDonald, interview

27 Dennis Merchant, interview with Robert Crawford, 15 March 2013; The future CEO of George Patterson Michael Anderson also got his start in the checking department, at Sydney's Fergus Canny Advertising in 1956, Michael Anderson, interview with Rosemary Francis, 26 October 2012.

28 Merchant, interview.

29 Renny Cunnack, interview with Rosemary Francis, 14 May 2013; Rankin, interview.

30 Gaskin, interview.

31 John Steedman, interview with Robert Crawford, 30 January 2013.

32 Mike Satterthwaite, interview with Robert Crawford, 13 September 2012; Rankin, interview.

33 Alan Robertson, interview with Robert Crawford, 23 November 2012.

34 Cunnack, interview.

35 Alwill, interview.

36 Graham, interview.

37 'Ball Outlines New Ambitious Strategies', *Sydney Morning Herald*, 16 July 1987, p. 27.

38 Cunnack, interview.

39 'TPC Inquire: Advertising Rates Could Increase', *Canberra Times*, 11 December 1975, p. 31.

40 'Media Council to Continue Rules', *Canberra Times*, 25 May 1976, p. 7. 'Agency Accreditation System Approved', *Canberra Times*, 11 February 1978, p. 9. 'Ad Industry Shocked by Accreditation Axe', *Canberra Times*, 6 October 1995, p. 15.

41 According to Mitchell, John Singleton called media buyers 'wombats', Mitchell, *Living Large*, p. 32.

42 'Ad Industry Shocked by Accreditation Axe', *Canberra Times*, 6 October 1995, p. 15.

43 Cunnack, interview.

44 'Media Legend Don Fox Retires', *Ad News*, 22 June 2001, http://www.adnews.com.au/4EE2A536–6CB4–4200–8CB4F811C8F6022C,

accessed 17 December 2015.

45 Cunnack, interview; Satterthwaite, interview.

46 'Ad Industry Shocked by Accreditation Axe', *Canberra Times*, 6
    October 1995, p. 15; Mitchell, *Living Large*, p. 39.

47 Cunnack, interview.

48 Peter Clemenger, interview with Rosemary Francis, 22 August
    2012; 'Ad Industry Shocked by Accreditation Axe', *Canberra Times*, 6
    October 1995, p.15.

49 Steedman, interview; Fysh Rutherford, interview with Rosemary
    Francis, 11 December 2012.

50 Geoff Cousins, interview with Robert Crawford, 15 March 2013.

51 Colin Fraser, interview with Rosemary Francis, 31 May 2013.

52 Mitchell, *Living Large*, p. 32.

53 Rob Palmer, interview with Robert Crawford, 23 February 2012.

54 Russell McLay, the future Chairman and CEO of George Patterson,
    started at the agency as an accountant in 1969, Russell McLay
    interview with Robert Crawford, 9 May 2013.

55 Satterthwaite, interview.

56 Gay Merchant, interview with Robert Crawford, 14 June 2013; Marin
    von Adlerstein, 14 December 2012.

57 Roger Rigby, interview with Robert Crawford, interview with
    Rosemary Francis, 2 May 2015.

58 Rob Palmer, interview with Robert Crawford, 23 February 2012.

59 Doug Watson, interview with Robert Crawford, 19 April 2013.

60 Paul Priday, interview with Robert Crawford, 23 January 2013.

61 Lee Harrington, interview with Rosemary Francis, 16 August 2012.

62 Reg Bryson, interview with Robert Crawford, 11 February 2013.

63 Harrington, interview.

64 John Wright, interview with Robert Crawford, 16 January 2013.

65 Palmer, interview.

66 Bryson also spent time as a press production manager at Sydney's
    Compton agency in the late 1960s; Michael Anderson moved from
    checking to press production before being allowed to write copy.

67 Watson, interview

68 Rigby, interview.

69 McIntyre, interview.

70 Mike Ellis, interview with Rosemary Francis, 14 August 2012.

71 Rigby, interview. Patterson was the first Australian agency to
    purchase a computer for data processing by the media department:
    'Top Agency's Two Major Statements', *Newspaper News*, 9 August

1963, p. 1; 'Australia's First Advertising Agency Computer Working',
Newspaper News, 2 April 1965, p. 6. Other agencies gradually
followed Patterson's lead: 'Bristow sees Major Ad Changes in Aust.',
Newspaper News, 16 September 1966, p. 1; 'Agency's Computer Plan',
Newspaper News, 21 June 1968 p. 20; 'JWT's Chief Aims for Better
Communications', *B&T Weekly*, 13 June 1969, p. 20; 'The Computer in
Advertising – The Right Perspective', *B&T Weekly*, 30 June 1966, p. 3;
'Computer Ordered for Big Agency', *B&T Weekly*, 3 May 1971, p. 4.

72   Ellis, interview.
73   Rigby, interview.
74   Ellis, interview.
75   Rigby, interview; McIntyre, interview.
76   Rigby, interview.
77   Valwyn Wishart, interview with Jackie Dickenson, 25
     November 2014.
78   Harrington, interview.
79   Ken Done, interview with Robert Crawford, 12 February 2013.
80   Alex Stitt, interview with Rosemary Francis, 15 June 2012.
81   *Creative Source Australia,* Armadillo Publishing, Melbourne, 1982–1990.
82   Lauchlan, interview.
83   Hansen, interview.
84   Newton, interview.
85   Keith Aldrich, interview with Rosemary Francis, 15 June 2012.
86   Reed, interview.
87   Walker, *Communicators,* p. 307.
88   Reed, interview.

Chapter Ten: Running the Show
1   Ric Otton, interview with Rosemary Francis, 21 August 2012; See
    also *Ad News: The Legends of Advertising, 1928–1998*, 30 October 1998,
    p. 91; N. Delbridge, 'A Man for All Reasons', *Ad News*, 13 August
    1983, p. 21; *Age*, 1 September 2003, Business Section, p.5; *Age*, 2
    September 2003, Business Section, p.5; *Age*, 3 September 2003, p.17;
    J. Dickenson, 'Nowhere Else to Work: The Left in Advertising',
    Labour History, no. 108, June 2015, pp. 17–36.
2   Rod Blakeney, interview with Rosemary Francis, 13 May 2014, 10
    June 2014.
3   Ian Alwill, interviews with Robert Crawford, 13 September 2012, 6
    January 2013.
4   David Mattingly, interview with Rosemary Francis, 17 September

2013.

5 Renny Cunnack, interview with Rosemary Francis, 14 May 2013.

6 Chris Martin Murphy, interview with Robert Crawford, 8 March 2013.

7 Heather Leembrugen was promoted to Deputy MD at Advertising Partners in mid-1983, *B&T Weekly*, 5 May 1983, p. 53; Julia King became MD at SSC&B: in Sydney three years later, *B&T Weekly*, 8 August 1986, p. 5; *B&T*'s 'Newsmakers' column recorded ten women as creative directors between 1960 and 1990 (including Rosem'ry Bertel and Jacqueline Huie), as well as a number of women media and finance directors; for more on women's leadership, see Chapter 9 in J. Dickenson, *Australian Women in Advertising in the Twentieth Century* Palgrave Macmillan, London, 2016.

8 Michael Ball, interviews with Rosemary Francis, 13 March 2013, 3 June 2013.

9 Ian Strachan, interview with Rosemary Francis, 9 April 2013.

10 Peter Clemenger, interview with Rosemary Francis, 22 August 2012.

11 Tom McFarlane, interview with Robert Crawford, 11 April 2013.

12 Geoff Wild, interview with Robert Crawford, 1 May 2013.

13 Geoff Cousins, interview with Robert Crawford, 15 March 2013.

14 Cousins, interview.

15 P. Rogers, 'Inside George Patterson', *B&T Weekly,* 17 November 1977, p. 18.

16 R. Burbury, 'Booze and Breakfast Laid On', *Ad News*, 16 January 1989, p. 10.

17 Ian Dawson, interview with Robert Crawford, 14 December 2012; Geoff Cousins, interview with Robert Crawford, 15 March 2013; Wild, interview.

18 Bruce Harris, interview with Robert Crawford, 23 November 2013.

19 Mike Strauss, interview with Rosemary Francis, 4 September 2012; Ian Alwill, interview with Robert Crawford, 13 September 2012; Ray Black, interview with Robert Crawford, 15 February 2013; Warren Fahey, interview with Robert Crawford, 14 March 2013.

20 Peter Hamilton, interview with Robert Crawford 19 November 2012.

21 John Bevins, '1963 BC – John Bevins on Bryce Courtenay', *Ad News*, 30 November 2012, http://www.adnews.com.au/adnews/1963-bc-john-bevins-on-bryce-courtenay, accessed 15 November 2015; John Bevins, interview with Robert Crawford, 10 May 2013.

22 Max Gosling, interview with Robert Crawford, 28 February 2013.

23 Bryson, interview.

24 Peter Rankin, interview with Rosemary Francis, 19 August 2014.

25 Peter Charlton, interview with Robert Crawford, 11 February 2013.

26 'McCann's New Boy at the Top', *B&T Weekly*, 27 September 1979, pp. 24–6.

27 Cunnack, interview.

28 Rankin, interview.

29 Mattingly, interview; Ian Alwill, interview.

30 Wayne Kingston, interview with Robert Crawford, 30 January, 6 February 2013; Charlton, interview; Martin Murphy, interview; Rodney Blakeney, interviews with Rosemary Francis, 13 May 2014, 10 June 2014.

31 Willi Schalk, interview with Robert Crawford, 9 March 2013.

32 Alex Hamill interview with Robert Crawford, 12 April 2013; Cunnack, interview; Kingston, interview.

33 Rankin, interview.

34 Cunnack, interview.

35 Hamill, interview.

36 Clemenger, interview.

37 Ball, interview; Kingston, interview.

38 Bryson, interview.

39 Ian Dawson, interview with Robert Crawford, 14 December 2012.

40 Trevor Fearnley, interview with Robert Crawford, 8 February 2013.

41 Alwill, interview.

42 Ric Otton, interview with Rosemary Francis, 21 August 2012.

43 Rochelle Burbury, 'Booze and Breakfast Laid on', *Ad News*, 16 January 1989, p. 10.

44 Kaye Schirmann, interview with Robert Crawford, 10 May 2013.

45 Marilyn Georgeff, 'Spasms Follow FCB Merger', *B&T Weekly*, 31 July 1980, pp. 1, 8; Pat Rogers, 'Through a Minefield to a Merger', *B&T Weekly*, 18 January 1981, pp. 17, 20.

46 Kingston, interview.

47 Greg Daniel, interview with Robert Crawford, 8 February 2013.

48 Malcolm Spry, interview with Robert Crawford, 24 February 2013.

49 Clemenger, interview.

50 Rankin, interview.

51 Martin Murphy, interview.

52 Kingston, interview.

53 Alwill, interview; Cunnack, interview.

54 Bill Shannon, interviews with Rosemary Francis, 29 October 2012, 14 November 2012.

55 Tom McFarlane, interview with Robert Crawford, 11 April 2013.

56 Rankin, interview; Charlton, interview; Michael Anderson, interview with Rosemary Francis, 26 October 2012.

57 Between 1960 and mid-1966, 'Newsmakers' recorded twenty-eight overseas tours by agency principals, most of which were at least six weeks in length.

58 See, for example, 'Newsmakers', *B&T*, 12 October 1967, p. 23; *B&T*, 21 August 1969, p. 8; *B&T*, 2 October 1969, p. 8; *B&T*, 28 May 1970, p. 8; *B&T*, 6 August 1970, p. 8; *B&T*, 6 May 1976, p. 51; *B&T*, 30 March 1978, p. 24; *B&T*, 13 July 1978, p. 1; *B&T*, 30 April 1980, p. 26.

Conclusion

1 Geoff Cousins, interview with Robert Crawford, 15 March 2013.

2 Lionel Hunt, interview with Robert Crawford, 22 January 2013.

3 *A Career in an Advertising Agency*, Australian Association of Advertising Agencies, Sydney c1960, p. 4.

4 Andrew Killey, interview with Robert Crawford, 13 December 2013.

5 Ric Otton, interview with Rosemary Francis, 21 August 2012.

INDEX

Index

Index

www.ingramcontent.com/pod-product-compliance
Lightning Source LLC
Chambersburg PA
CBHW021459210326
41599CB00012B/1054